Golf Club Maker

Thomas Carruthers 1840–1924

Golf Club Maker

Thomas Carruthers
1840-1924

Tom Carruthers

Cualann Press

ISBN 0 9544416 4 8

First Edition November 2004

British Library Cataloguing in Publication Data. A catalogue record of this book is available at the British Library.

Printed by Bell & Bain, Glasgow

Published by Cualann Press Limited, 6 Corpach Drive, Dunfermline, KY12 7XG Scotland
Tel/Fax 01383 733724
Email: cualann@btinternet.com
Website: www.cualann-scottish-books.co.uk

Dedication

To Elaine: golfer, researcher, computer wizard –
I couldn't have written it without her patience and
support.

Contents

Illustrations

Acknowledgements

The author gratefully acknowledges the assistance received from the following libraries and archives in bringing the book to publication: The National Library of Scotland; The Edinburgh Room of the City of Edinburgh Central Library (A. Bethune); The Mitchell Library, Glasgow; Scottish Borders Archive and Local History Centre; Midlothian County Libraries (S. M. Millar); Aberdeen Central Library (M. Allan); Motherwell Heritage Centre (M. McGarry); Renfrewshire Libraries (J. Ritchie); Dumbarton Library (G. Hopner); Sheffield Central Library; Derby City Library; Birmingham Central Library – Patents (E. Hunt); British Library – Newspaper Library; British Library – Patents (M. Lampert and S. Van Dulken).

The services provided by the following are also much appreciated: General Register Office for Scotland; Sasine Register for the County of Midlothian; The Kelvingrove Art Gallery and Museum (S. K. Hunter); Southampton Archives Centre; Chartered Institute of Patent Agents (M. Ralph); J. Y. & G. W. Johnson (S. G. Hayle).

Permission to reproduce illustrations from other publications was given by the following: J. M. Cooper; J. B. Ellis; J. S. Forson; P. Georgiady; P. H. Knowles; A. R. Mullock; G. J. Rowley; D. I. Stirk; Edinburgh Thistle Golf Club; Eyemouth Golf Club; Scotsman Publications Ltd; The British Museum; City of Edinburgh Central Library and C. Furjanic.

R. A. Durran and J. F. Moreton provided assistance with structure and editing; Derrick Elliss gave me his encouragement throughout the project.

Finally, I would like to thank my family and relations: my wife Elaine; Iain and Linda Douglas; Wallace and John Fyfe and Bob Reith.

Tom Carruthers
August 2004

Introduction

Thomas Carruthers, club maker, is well known to golf collectors on both sides of the Atlantic as the inventor of the short socket for metal playing clubs, also referred to as the through-bore or drilled-through hosel, but no full account of his life has hitherto been written.

When I was growing up in Edinburgh I remember my father telling stories about my great grandfather, Thomas Carruthers, but being a typical youngster, I paid little attention at the time. However, my interest in his life began in earnest about ten years ago when I had bundled a number of old family golf items, including patent papers, newspaper cuttings, a golf club head, a club maker's stamp and golf balls into a large briefcase for a visit to Sotheby's. I was taken aback to learn from David Neech, Sotheby's golf consultant, that he knew all about the Carruthers' patent and that it was well known within the golf-collecting fraternity.

About four years ago I decided to begin my research and to seek what information might be available apart from the family's own records, and so began countless visits to libraries, archives and auction houses.

The amount of published information available about the achievements of Thomas Carruthers from the late 1850s to about 1910, a time when he was active in two major sports, was staggering.

Much of this period coincided with the reign of Queen Victoria, an age of *laissez-faire* in Britain that gave birth to great advances in technology and manufacturing processes, huge movement of country people into the cities and often much hardship for those employed in the drudgery of factory life and for those living in poor housing.

The innovations of his day were undoubtedly a major influence in his life and a catalyst for all that he achieved. He certainly packed a lot into an eventful working life. From journeyman tailor he became Scotland's champion professional sprinter, a sports promoter, a dairy keeper, a golf shop retailer, a golf club maker, a golf course designer and golf clubhouse proprietor. Above all, he was a resourceful and inventive golf club maker whose 1892 price list offered twenty-eight different types of golf club, including many wooden clubs. In 1899 it was reported that he had sold 35,000 of his most famous club – the driving cleek! All the early United States' golf club manufacturers of the 1890s sold his short socket design clubs.

The golf collector is enriched when he learns about the life and times of a club maker. Now, following four years of research, when I pick up one of Thomas Carruthers' clubs, I feel I know the man who was my great-grandfather.

I hope that this book will help to fill at least one gap in the history of the game: the period that was arguably the most inventive in its history.

Tom Carruthers
August 2004

Chapter 1

The Professional Runner

The industrial revolution of Victorian times brought about many changes in the lives of ordinary people. Tom Carruthers was profoundly influenced by a new world developing around him, a world which enabled him to become one of the country's most celebrated athletes, and more importantly, a golf club maker whose through-bore short socket for metal playing clubs patent was one of the most influential and long lasting developments in golf club design.

The Early Years

Tom was born on 27 April 1840 at Caverton Mill in the Scottish Borders in a farm worker's cottage situated on a large farm owned by the Duke of

Tom Carruthers at the Arniston & Vogrie Games in 1869

Roxburghe. The Roxburghe family had, and still have, large agricultural and property interests in the Borders of Scotland and their ancestral home is at Floors Castle, the largest inhabited castle in Scotland, near Kelso, Roxburghshire, some seven miles from Caverton Mill.

It was a time of great social change. Agricultural labouring and domestic jobs were the main source of work in the neighbourhood. The period 1846–1873 was one of general prosperity for Scottish agriculture but the mechanisation of farming methods took its toll on the numbers of agricultural labourers employed in the industry. Handloom weaving of textiles was in rapid decline as factory production took over in major industrial centres. There was a relentless and substantial movement of country folk to the cities as the industrial revolution took a firm hold.

Tom's father, Peter Carruthers, was an agricultural labourer who died when Tom was thirteen years' old. At that time the average life expectancy in Kelso was thirty-four years. His death was devastating for the family and young Tom was left the elder male of the family.

The family's immediate need was to protect the tenancy of their small cottage, comprising a kitchen-living room and bedroom, and young Tom left school to become apprenticed as a journeyman tailor. The rolling hills of the Border countryside were rich in farmland and the journeyman tailor would travel by foot to isolated farms to make clothes for farming families and their workers instead of their having to travel to neighbouring towns. Although ready-made mill-produced clothing was available in towns such as Kelso and Melrose and road networks in the Borders had improved greatly, access to remote farms could only be gained by unmade tracks.

Many lonely hours walking long and weary miles in all weather conditions to farming customers was an arduous job for someone so young, but the experience toughened Tom both mentally and physically and reinforced his resolve to see the family escape from their straightened circumstances. Visiting tradesmen were always made welcome and well looked after in the domestics' quarters when staying overnight at farms. This enabled him to supplement the family's provisions.

Tall for his age with a strong frame, Tom grew to display a natural aptitude for athletic pursuits, picking up prizes in local Fair Day celebrations that included events such as wrestling, running and leaping. As he grew into a young man his income from tailoring was increasingly supplemented by his winnings on the track. His determination to see the family recover from its impoverished circumstances gradually bore fruit. The death certificate of his mother, Euphemia, (née Burns) who was born in 1814, shows that she died on the 16 December 1897, aged eighty-three years, still living at Caverton Mill where Tom was born. His younger brother completed his education, qualified as a public school teacher and subsequently became an inspector of the poor and registrar.

Border Games

Early accounts of Tom's athletic abilities in the Border towns' hugely popular annual Gymnastic Games, when spectators amounted to around 10,000, were widely recorded in local press reports. At the age of eighteen, at the Kelso Gymnastic Games held in July 1858 he ran second in a Foot Hurdle Race of 300 yards, open to all, over a flight of five three-foot-high hurdles to win his first cash prize as a professional runner. The following year, at the long established Jedburgh Border Games, he came first in the 100 yards, 400 yards and 800 yards foot races, the last of which earned him a prize designated as a 'Purse of Gold'. He then added another four sprint and hurdle 'firsts' at the Wooler Gymnastic Games, where he was proclaimed as the Border Champion by his Northumbrian friends, and at the Kelso Gymnastic Games, all run within the space of one week.

His precocious talent soon attracted the attention of a sponsor, most likely a bookmaker acting as the lead party of other wealthy lovers of the sport who were then known as 'the fancy'. He joined the ranks of professional runners who had been recruited initially from estate workers and farm labourers. It was vital to the young runner, and to his backers, that their expert advice and guidance were available to ensure that his professional career was successfully developed.

The Sport and its Gambling Culture

Professional running, or pedestrianism as it was known at the time, was a popular sport in Victorian Britain, and was at the height of its popularity in the 1860s and 1870s. One report states that 'Few nobler sports exist in Britain than foot racing. It is a healthy exercise, good in principle and justly popular.' (*Illustrated Sporting News and Theatrical and Musical Review 1865*)

Working class athletes called 'peds' ran for stake money and received a share of the gambling winnings of the syndicates that were involved for financial gain and which often sponsored the runners.

Promoters made money from staging races, and large scale gambling accompanied the events. Professional foot racing events featured a handicap system whereby faster runners gave starts to slower runners, thus ensuring that all competitors had a fair chance of winning. Handicap races were renowned for producing nail-biting finishes and were ideally suited for betting.

The industrial revolution brought about a huge investment and rapid expansion in the railway infrastructure, leading to a significant reduction in the cost of transport and the ability to travel throughout the country. In 1850 there were already more than ten thousand miles of railroad track criss-crossing Great Britain and this opened up the possibility for athletes from all over to compete in towns and cities across the whole country.

At stadiums in cities, such as London, Sheffield, Birmingham, Manchester, Newcastle, Edinburgh and Glasgow, promoters organised professional running events, which carried substantial money prizes, for the sporting public. Promotions were also held in smaller towns across the country.

For a young athlete with potential from a poor background the events provided an opportunity to share in the spoils that went with the sport – the cash prizes for winning races and a share of the financial gains from his backers. According to Emma Lile in her book *Professional Pedestrianism in South Wales in the Nineteenth Century,* 'The prestige bestowed on talented athletes was so great that pedestrianism success could elevate local men to celebrated heroes.'

In the flourishing days of Sheffield Handicaps, the 'headquarters' of the sport during the 1860s and 1870s, there were very large sums of money lost and won over those races. This period was notable for some extraordinary bouts of gambling fever on the Turf and on the running track, with some competitors involved in dubious practices in order to influence the betting and the financial return for their sponsors.

John Calvert, pastor of Sheffield's Zion Congregational Chapel, was reported in the *Sheffield Post* in 1873 as saying:

> ... a craving for amusements and a general rush for them has become a prominent feature of our times ... Handicapping (professional running) and horse racing are the visible manifestations of a ramification of poisonous influence and pernicious arrangement constantly at work in thousands of workshops and homes.

Gambling was widespread amongst all social classes and organised bodies actively sought to suppress what they regarded as a malign influence, in much the same way as the nonconformists aligned themselves with the temperance movements. Pedestrianism's gambling culture was tied to pubs known as 'sporting houses' by its followers. The warm and welcoming atmosphere of the pubs contrasted starkly with the poor living conditions of the workingman's family home. In the 1850s, first the railways and then the development of the electric telegraph, brought about the fast transmission of results of prize fights, horse racing and foot running events. The speed and availability of current news and sporting results inevitably drew more people into gambling. Many now felt that their gambling judgment was more solidly based.

After a successful summer in 1861, which saw Tom Carruthers extend the Gymnastic Games and Handicaps in which he competed beyond his native Border country, his backers decided that he was ready to tackle one of the major Handicap sprints at Sheffield. This race would be a 330 yards Handicap to take place at Sheffield's Hyde Park Stadium on the first Winter's Fair Day, promoted for the holiday crowd by Mr James Darley, proprietor of the Green Dragon in Sheffield.

Hyde Park Stadium, Sheffield, 1862

Often the race promoters, who provided the prize money, owned the ground over which the event would be run. Sometimes they also owned nearby licensed-premises from which their bookmaking businesses could be conducted. The licensed-premises or 'sporting houses' would be crowded with the lovers of pedestrianism – all anxious to get the latest 'tips'. These were the centres of intelligence for the lovers of the sport, their smoke-filled rooms echoing with the babble of conversation about the latest inside information received and the up-to-date betting odds of their favoured runners.

The 'peds' backers chose the events where money was to be made and their runners and trainers would up sticks and travel from their training quarters to install themselves at hotels not too far from the stadiums. In the days prior to the race the names of the entrants were published for a fee of 2/6d. This was followed later by the names of those accepting their fiat or handicap with a payment of 5/- at which point the serious betting started and the cards with the draw for the first day's heats appeared. Meanwhile the experienced race officials, guardians of the rulebook, fine-tuned their antennae and prayed that the money men and their 'peds' had not indulged in any plots or malpractices, the merest whiff or hint of which could turn the excited crowd into a raging frenzy.

When the sport was at its height the promoters and the management at Sheffield had converted pedestrianism into a highly organised public spectacle. The city boasted a number of famous venues for their promotions, including the Queen's and Newhall Grounds, but the most famous was Hyde Park.

The racing of the 300 yards Handicap, which took place at Sheffield's Hyde Park Stadium, was spread over two days to accommodate the large number of contestants. Carruthers battled his way to the final and took first place, beating John Nuttall, the English half-mile record holder into second place. The betting for the final had him at 5 to 4 on, which meant his party would have made a good financial return on money placed earlier at favourable odds.

This win immediately marked Tom Carruthers as a sprinter of championship class and the news of the success of the twenty-one year old was heralded throughout his native Scotland and in the north of England. He realised that if he were to capitalise on his great achievement he had to be available to run in the towns and villages where he was admired. This meant that he would need to move his quarters away from his home near Yetholm at the foot of the Cheviot Hills. It was a big wrench for him but his success at Sheffield would ensure the financial security that he had been seeking for his family. Married in 1860, he now also had his own family to provide for. His affection for his hometown of Yetholm endured right through his running career, for he regularly used Yetholm instead of using the actual name of his base when entering race details.

His decision to move to Edinburgh coincided with news of a new railway development. Although the railway infrastructure had spread widely throughout the country, journey times could be very lengthy and uncomfortable, especially if the trip involved non-mainline routes. It was timely therefore when the Midland Railway announced in July 1862 the opening of a new route to and from Scotland, between London, Edinburgh and Glasgow, using the Midland Railway System. An express train would leave Edinburgh's Caledonian Station at 10.00 a.m., arriving at Sheffield at 6.00 p.m. and at London King's Cross Station, at 10.00 p.m. The announcement was coupled with the acceleration of speeds throughout the railway system and improved connections to Yorkshire and the North of England. This significant improvement now made travelling to the main towns and cities that staged important handicap promotions quicker and less stressful.

During 1862 Tom competed in many events that he would not have previously considered feasible, including events in the West of Scotland and Newcastle in the North of England.

Scottish Rivals

In Scotland, his greatest native rivals over the shorter foot race and hurdle distances were Gavin Tait from Douglas Castle in Lanarkshire and Anthony Hall from Edinburgh. The crack Sheffield flyer T. 'Cobbler' Wood was the most frequent visitor amongst a hot school of English sprinters, which included W. Johnson of Stockton and J. Clowrey of Birmingham, to compete on Scottish soil. To a lesser extent, Tom also competed against the renowned Robert McInstray from Maybole and Donald Dinnie from Aboyne in Aberdeenshire. The former was a specialist distance runner, while the latter was a man of immense strength who primarily concentrated on the leaping, hop step and jump events and the traditional Highland Games heavy throwing events with the hammer and stone.

During the early 1860s, Carruthers and Tait regularly competed in summer games held throughout Scotland with considerable success but it was obvious that they did their utmost not to clash with each other. However, an enterprising promoter brought the two great rivals together to compete in a match for the Championship of Scotland at the Stonefield Running Grounds on 2 January 1863. *The Sporting Life* newspaper included the following fascinating insight in its edition on Monday 5 January 1863:

STONEFIELD RUNNING GROUNDS, GLASGOW

Tait and Carruthers – it will be remembered that these men were matched some time since to run a hurdle race of 200 yards, over five hurdles, 3ft. 6 ins. high, and a flat race of 200 yards, for the Championship of Scotland and £30 a side. From the fact of both having contended together with varied success in the different games throughout Scotland during the last three years, a good deal of interest was taken in the match. It will also be recollected that Carruthers won a handicap at Sheffield some eighteen months ago. Agreeably to articles, the men met at the above grounds on Friday, January 8, to run their hurdle race, in presence of a goodly number of spectators, including a strong muster of the Edinburgh fancy, where Carruthers hails from. Both men were in first-rate trim. The betting was 6 to 4 on Tait, at which odds a good sum was invested. Tait's backers also sported a pretty fair amount at 3 to 1 against Carruthers winning both events. After a long delay, caused by Carruthers and his party not coming to the ground in time, the men toed the scratch. At the first report of the pistol, Tait bounded away, but not being followed by Carruthers, (who did not leave the mark), went over the course alone. A wrangle followed; Tait claimed the race, saying that the articles stated, that they were to start by *first report* of pistol. Carruthers' party alleging, on the other hand, that they only said *report* of pistol. The referee appointed a meeting at the Globe – a well-known sporting house in the city, when the starter stated that the pistol went off accidentally, and the referee ordered the men to run the following day. On Saturday the competitors again met at the appointed time, and at the *first* report of pistol both went away, Tait getting the best of the start. They went over the first hurdle together, when Carruthers took the lead, and at the last hurdle was two yards in advance, but taking a stagger, and Tait at the same time putting on a tremendous spurt, caught Carruthers in the last two or three strides, and won, after a splendid race, by a yard. About an hour after the above event was decided, they again came to the mark to run the flat race. The betting opened at evens, but veered round to 6 to 4 on Carruthers. But little money was invested, the backers of Tait holding out for 2 to 1. When the signal was given, a capital start was effected. Carruthers at once took the lead, and won very easily by seven yards. The backers of Carruthers were in ecstasies at the manner in which their 'ped' performed. He has a lengthy stride – equal if not superior to Mower*; and from his style altogether, it will be no surprise to see him hailed this coming season as Champion of England at 200 yards.

*(Charlie Mower, English champion mile runner, was a famous distance runner from Norwich beaten by McInstray for the two-mile championship and £50 at Stonefield Running Grounds in March 1864.)

A correspondent for *The Sporting Life*, writing about the average stride of foot-racers, made the following observations on Tom Carruthers' stride:

In the early seventies I repeatedly measured, at the Powderhall Grounds, Edinburgh, the stride of Tom Carruthers, a working tailor, belonging to Yetholm, while he was training for sprint races. At his top Carruthers averaged a nine-foot stride; sometimes he was an inch over or under. He was a magnificently proportioned man. I may say that Carruthers was the most extraordinary hurdle racer I ever looked at. He did not leap his jumps; he simply walked over them. At all the Border games in the district he was invariably successful as a runner, etc., while his mode of taking his hurdles is seldom seen nowadays as he seemed to fly over them.

The Scottish Champion

An extract from an article in the Edinburgh newspaper, *The Evening Dispatch,* of 21 April 1910, entitled 'Golden Wedding in Edinburgh' contained the following synopsis of Carruthers' running career:

In his early days Mr. Carruthers had a predilection for foot racing, both on the flat and over hurdles, and he devoted himself to a thorough training, with the result that forty years ago he had the honour of being Scotland's greatest 'ped.' and some of his best performances have rarely been eclipsed. When at the height of his career as an athlete there was no one who could give him serious trouble at the hurdles.

Between the years 1860 and 1872 Mr. Carruthers was the Champion all-round runner of Scotland. During this period he travelled round nearly all the games in Scotland, and as at that time all the runners were of a mark, Carruthers, being so exceptionally fleet of foot, had a pull over the other competitors. He more than held his own in England against the fliers there, frequently taking part in the Sheffield meetings.

His wife whom he married on the 20th day of April 1860, at Town Yetholm, a village not far from his birthplace, when she was seventeen and he nineteen years of age, accompanied him on these great occasions and witnessed his triumphs.

What singled out Tom Carruthers from so many of his contemporaries was the consistency of his performances over more than a decade as evidenced by the low handicaps awarded to him by the handicappers, based on timed performances conducted by official timekeepers, at stadiums hosting the big events. An examination of his performances at Sheffield over the three-year period from 1869 to 1871 shows that, in every sprint race in which he competed against the top fliers in the country, he was consistently rated in the top three. In Scotland he stood out amongst his native peers as the runner with the lowest handicap in all sprint and middle distance races in which he competed. He was a phenomenon because his long raking stride of nine feet put him at a disadvantage in the final stages of sprint races at a time when most of the running tracks for these races finished on a curve, making the low handicap runners run wide to overtake the slower runners. It wasn't until 1870 that the problem of the finishing curve in sprint races was eliminated.

The organisers of the major sprint handicaps of these hugely popular events, which could attract crowds of up to 20,000, would typically receive about 120 entries. Once the handicapper had announced his decision on the handicaps of the entrants, the number of runners accepting their fiat or handicap would typically be reduced to sixty-four. The handicap competition lasted two days. The winners of the first day's round of sixteen heats, of four runners each, qualified for the second day. The sixteen survivors from the first day went on to contest the next round of four heats, of four runners each. This left the four winners to compete in the final. When the number of runners exceeded sixty-four, the concluding day's running would involve an extra heat, making a total of four races until the winner of the handicap competition emerged.

Carruthers remained in the top flight with the best of the professional runners of the period. The sport's popularity had never been, nor was ever to be, as great again as it was in the 1860s and 1870s. Without doubt his achievements were due to his natural ability and his devotion to thorough training as the preceding article points out. A good measure of just how much the punters regarded the big Scotman's ability was the low odds quoted by the on-site bookmakers in many of his races, and recorded in newspaper articles of the time.

Annual Highland and Gymnastic Games

In the summer months Tom Carruthers and other celebrated professionals would compete in Annual Highland and Gymnastic Games, including the Border Games, which were organised by districts throughout Scotland, until there was scarcely a village that did not boast of its annual games. They had, however, a more festive ambience, unlike the fiery cauldrons of the promotions held in the industrialised cities. Many annual games were established during the 1860s, taking their place alongside those with a more ancient pedigree. They were highly popular events, attracting many thousands of spectators to each meeting, but were occasionally frowned upon by some of the local gentry. There was usually the chance to celebrate in the drinks' tent or to make a wager with the local bookie. The meetings were held on Fair Days or on a day declared as a general holiday in the district for the occasion.

Competitors at the Grand Highland Gathering held under the auspices of the London Club of True Highlanders, at Beaufort House, Waltham Heath, near London, in July 1862

Traditional Highland Games of agility and strength had been practised in the North within the Celtic communities from time immemorial but after

Bonnie Prince Charlie's defeat at the battle of Culloden, traditional culture was all but destroyed by the Act of Proscription. Following its repeal, annual gatherings in a formalised form were established, encouraged by Sir Walter Scott, and during the three decades from 1850 there was a surge in their formation by local communities, parallel to that of the annual Gymnastic Games in the South.

Some press reports at the time adopted a very moralistic tone in writing about these occasions, signalling to their readers the attendant dangers of the great social upheaval, which had resulted from Victorian industrialisation. A strong body of opinion was concerned that workers in industries situated in crowded cities, such as the great cotton factories of Glasgow and Manchester, would be unable, unlike previous generations of young men whose stamina and physical power were sustained by outdoor labours, to protect the country if assailed by an armed foe. They therefore supported all forms of outdoor activities while at the same time warning against the evils of gambling and drinking often associated with these competitive events. It should be borne in mind, however, that the Crimean War, 1853–1856, was still a vivid memory in people's minds.

Across the length and breadth of Scotland nearly every village held its annual games festival in the summer months. These popular events were supported by the local inhabitants, the nobility, and sometimes by royalty. There was, naturally, heightened interest in viewing the touring pedestrian celebrities, even though these visitors would carry off nearly all the prizes in races which were 'open to all' and not restricted to competitors living in the district. Their presence was always welcome to games' secretaries. Many of the organisers of these local games measured the success of events by their ability to attract the pedestrian 'cracks'.

Some measure of the extent to which the professional athletes valued their participation in these games, where money prizes could amount to a significant sum for a two or three months' tour of the Scottish Annual Games, can be given by detailing Carruthers' summer itinerary in 1869. The total mileage travelled by him, including to English events, was well in excess of 3,000 miles. His earnings in a typical summer amounted to £150, representing approximately 1½ times the annual earnings of a teacher, double the annual earnings of a skilled worker in the printing, textile or shipbuilding industries, or four times the annual earnings of an agricultural worker in the 1860s. In addition he would receive appearance money, sometimes gambling returns should the local bookmaker be in attendance, and his expenses were paid.

Carruthers' Scottish Annual Games Race Itinerary in Summer 1869 was as follows:

26 June 1869:	Muiravonside Annual Games, Linlithgow, Fife
15 July 1869:	Kirkcaldy Gymnastic Games, Kirkcaldy, Fife
17 July 1869:	Dunkeld Highland Games, Perth & Kinross
28 July 1869:	West Calder Gymnastic Games, Barony Estate, West Calder, Lothian
31 July 1869:	St Ronan's Border Games, Innerleithen, Borders.
6 August 1869:	Dunblane Games, Dunblane, Stirling
7 August 1869:	Strathallan Meeting, Bridge of Allan, Stirling
11 August 1869:	Alloa Scottish Games, Hawkhill, Alloa, Clackmannanshire
12 August 1869:	Alva Gymnastic Games, Alva, Clackmannanshire
13 August 1869:	Tillicoultry Games, Tillicoultry, Clackmannanshire
14 August 1869:	Arniston & Vogrie Gymnastic Games, Greenhall, Midlothian
21 August 1869:	Jedburgh and Border Games, Dunion Moor, Jedburgh, Borders
27 August 1869:	Birnam Highland Games, Birnam, Perth and Kinross
28 August 1869:	Huntly Athletic Games, Castle Park, Huntly, Aberdeenshire
29 August 1869:	Denny Scottish Games, East Boorland, Stirling
31 August 1869:	Aboyne Annual Gathering, Aboyne, Aberdeenshire
10 September 1869:	Wishaw National Games, Wishaw Public Green, Glasgow
11 September 1869:	Dalkeith Gymnastic Games, Thorniebank, Dalkeith, Midlothian
18 September 1869:	Lasswade, Bonnyrigg & Loanhead Gymnastic Games, Lasswade, Midlothian
20 September 1869:	Kinghorn Gymnastic Games, Kinghorn, Fife
21 September 1869:	Kirkcaldy Gymnastic Games, Kirkcaldy, Fife
23 September 1869:	Northern Meeting, Inverness, Highland

In the above twenty-two Highland and Gymnastic Games, Carruthers won a total of fifty-three first prizes, sixteen second prizes and three third prizes. These wins were all made in 'open to all' category races against other professional runners, not just against the district inhabitants. This astounding performance is due in no small measure to the fact that the competitors in most of the races started from the same mark as in today's athletics. An athlete's schedule was very demanding and Carruthers must have had enormous resources of stamina. The services of a very efficient railway system and postal service (in those days many districts had two mails and two deliveries per day and a letter posted in the morning could expect a reply the same day in many areas of the country) were essential for his success. Above all, however, he had the unswerving support of his wife who accompanied him on these great occasions and witnessed his triumphs.

Peak Performance

Apart from Tom Carruthers' regular annual tour of the Scottish summer games, records show that he ran in London, Birmingham, Sheffield, Manchester, Newcastle, Glasgow and Edinburgh.

Running was a full-time occupation for successful professional runners or 'peds' of the latter half of the nineteenth century. To be sponsored, the runner had to demonstrate consistently to his backers, 'under the watch', that he was worth their bet. If a backer was not confident that he could win, there could be no betting returns and therefore no share for their runner. Consequently, the athlete had to devote himself to a strict training schedule just like the top athletes of today. Training schedules and methods were planned and were practised on stadium tracks under the watchful eye of the trainer.

Champion class athletes had to be supremely fit and dedicated. This perhaps can be shown by the series of events for Tom that began with Sheffield's massively popular Winter Fair Handicaps in 1871. At this point he was approaching the end of his career as a sprinter. Sheffield's Winter Fair Handicaps were renowned for the huge amounts of betting money that passed through the hands of the bookmakers as described by the press reporters for the following day's editions:

> We are indulging in no infigurative language in affirming that £10,000 can be won ... and that upwards of a dozen men have already been supported for half that amount ... The termination of the (horse) racing season has caused many levanthium bookmakers to transfer their patronage from the turf to the running track.

After competing in the first of the Winter Fair Handicaps at the end of November, he ran in four 200 yard sprint heats, including the final, of the Great All-England Handicap at Sheffield, in which eighty-four runners competed, held on 26 and 27 December 1871. During the following two days, 28 and 29 December, he ran in two heats, including the final of a 300 yards Handicap, also at Sheffield. The following day he travelled by train to compete at Edinburgh's famous Powderhall Stadium, soon to take over from Sheffield as the Headquarters of the sport after a series of betting related malpractices. On 1 and 2 January 1872 he ran a further three 150 yards sprint heats, again including the final, of the New Year Gala. This extraordinary performance involved a total of three sprint handicap competitions, nine sprint heats, of which three were finals, against a clutch of the country's top performers, within the space of eight days.

Below is the advertisement that appeared in *The Scotsman* newspaper on the day of the climax to the New Year Gala:

NOTICE TO PEDESTRIANS.
PRACTICE will be allowed on all parts of the Path except the
SPRINT COURSE TO-DAY (TUESDAY) up till Eleven o'clock.
BY ORDER
Powderhall Grounds, 2 January 1872.

POWDERHALL GROUNDS
All the WINNING CELEBRITIES will contend in the Final Heats to day at
one o'clock.
CLOSE and EXCITING RACING will be seen.
Amongst those left are CARRUTHERS, SKELTON (Sheffield), WIGHT
(Jedburgh),
WALSH (Royton), BENNETT (Alva), and HINDLE (Paisley).

GREAT NEW YEAR HANDICAPS
Mr. Gray, Victoria Hotel, Broughton Street, will supply the refreshments at
Powderhall Grounds.
Sandwiches, Pies, Ale, Porter, etc., all of the best description and at
moderate prices.

This was Tom Carruthers' last appearance in a major Handicap as later in the year he suffered a broken leg at Dumbarton that finished his running exploits. At this point he was still regarded as one of the greatest athletes in the country and had the honour of being the Scottish Champion.

Records

Authenticated records of runners' performances were rarely divulged but the following reports provide an indication of Carruthers' merit as a sprinter:

Powderhall Grounds in 1894 showing the old grandstand

To show his exceptional qualities, his times for the 120 yards was 1 yard inside evens; 300 yards, 31 ¼ seconds; and the quarter-mile, 50 seconds. It is well known that owing to the perfect state of the tracks now, these distances are faster by 2, 6 and 8 yards, respectively. These performances speak for themselves. (*Golfing* 16 March 1899)

In a letter to the *Melbourne Sportsman* of November 10, 1886, Donald Dinnie, Tom's old rival, gives ample proof of the prowess of the subject … when he says: 'On page 51 of the *Athletic Times Annual* for 1877 you can see a record of 23 feet 4 inches at long jump done on Leven Links, Fifeshire, Scotland, by Thomas Carruthers of Edinburgh, on level ground, in 1871.' If we mistake not, this feat of his still stands as the Scottish record. (*Golfing* 16 March 1899)

His best sprinting effort – although this has not been authenticated – was said to be 14 3/5th seconds for 150 yards. (D. A. Jamieson, *Powderhall and Pedestrianism*)

Chapter 2

Sixty Years at Bruntsfield Links

Tom had moved to Edinburgh in 1862 to further his running career. Early records of Carruthers' home address show that the family moved in 1868, when Tom was still at the height of his career, from Edinburgh's Pleasance to Home Street adjacent to Bruntsfield Links. Following the accident at the Dumbarton Athletics Meeting in 1872 which finished his professional running career, he continued his involvement in professional running as a promoter at the Royal Hippodrome Grounds before starting a dairy business in rented premises at 5 Gillespie Place next to Bruntsfield Links, where golf had been played for some four hundred years. The *Edinburgh Evening Dispatch* of 15 April 1910 records that he became a dairy keeper in the early 1870s. This is confirmed by an entry in the *Edinburgh and Leith Post Office Directory* of 1874, which gives the dairy's address as 5 Gillespie Place, Bruntsfield. Bruntsfield was at the time an expanding suburb of Edinburgh. It was in this area beside the Links that Tom Carruthers was to live at various addresses, raise a family of six daughters and five sons, and work as a golf club maker, golf shop and clubhouse owner, golf course designer, and dairy keeper for the next sixty years.

Bruntsfield Links

Becoming involved in the game of golf was inevitable for Tom considering he had had a sports' career as an athlete stretching back to the 1850s and was now living beside the famous Bruntsfield Links. Bruntsfield Links and its golfers supported a sophisticated golfing infrastructure in the 1870s. Here they had their golf course, clubs and clubhouses, golf club and ball makers, caddies and keepers of the green, but even at this time the Links was starting to come under pressure from a huge influx of migrants into the city of Edinburgh because of the industrial revolution. The Victorian Age was to bring about great change and development in all aspects of the game – its own revolution. Tom Carruthers' working life as a golf club maker straddled the exciting transitional years in golf's development in which he himself was to make a lasting contribution.

James Grant in his three volume works on *Old and New Edinburgh* states the following about the Links at Bruntsfield circa 1860:

> No part of Edinburgh has a more agreeable southern exposure than those large open spaces around the Meadows and Bruntsfield Links … the latter have long been famous as a playground for the ancient and national game of golf, and strangers who may be desirous of enjoying it, are usually supplied with clubs and assistants at the old Golf Tavern (Hotel), that overlooks the breezy and grassy scene of operations, which affords space for the members of no less than six golf clubs.

He names the clubs as the 'Burghers, instituted 1735 (better known as the Burgess); the Honourable Company of Edinburgh, instituted prior to 1744; the Bruntsfield, instituted 1761; the Allied Golfing Club, instituted 1856; the Warrender, instituted 1858; and the St. Leonards, instituted 1857.' When Grant's book was published in 1882 the Burgess and the Honourable Company had both moved to Musselburgh, the latter's 'Home Green' having been at Leith Links rather than Bruntsfield Links.

The Links at Bruntsfield was not strictly a links course in the true sense of the word as it was situated a few miles inland from the sea. The reason for it being named 'a links' is given by Charles Blair Macdonald, born of Scottish descent at Niagara Falls, New York and winner of the first amateur championship of the United States Golf Association (formed 1894) at the Newport Golf Club, in an article written in 1895 for *Outing* magazine entitled 'The Why and Wherefore of Golf Rules':

> Turning to the old Scottish dictionaries, we learn from Jamieson's *Scottish Dictionary* (Edinburgh, 1803) that links were originally the windings of a river. The word also meant the rich ground lying among the windings of a river. Later it also meant the sandy flat ground on the seashore covered with bent-grass, furze, etc. It was on such ground the ancient game was first played, so far as history harks back, that is, on links at the mouths of the Eden, the Tay, and the Forth. Jamieson says: 'In time the name was transferred, but improperly, to ground not contiguous to the sea.' 'The most probable reason of the designation is, that it having been customary to play golf on the links of Leith, when the ground in the vicinity

of Bruntsfield came to be used in the same way, it was in like manner called links.'

'View of Bruntsfield Links looking towards Edinburgh Castle' by Paul Sandby RA, dated 1746 (*Courtesy of the British Museum*) also shows the village of Wright's Houses, with the old Golf Tavern (Hotel) on the right of the cluster of buildings. Barely discernible, above the roof of a long barn-like building, is the ancient mansion of Wrychtis-housis (Wright's Houses) on the extreme left of the picture.

In 1827 the Edinburgh City Improvement Act that contained the following clause protecting the Meadows and Bruntsfield Links from building encroachment was passed:

> That it shall not be competent to or in the power of the Lord Provost, Magistrates, and Council of Edinburgh, or any other person or persons, without the sanction of Parliament, obtained for the express purpose, at any time hereafter to erect buildings of any kind upon any part of the ground called the Meadows and Bruntsfield Links, so far as the same belong in property to the said Lord Provost, Magistrates, and Council.

But in 1863 George Robb, a member of the Bruntsfield Allied Golf Club, gave a rather downbeat view of recent happenings in his historical account of Bruntsfield Links (Appendix I), which was surely a worrying portent of future events:

> Little remains to be said about the Links except to notice the change that has taken place for the worst, so far as golfing is concerned, in consequence of Greenhill having been feued for villas. The inhabitants of Greenhill have managed to get an opening in the wall that leads by a footpath across the green and seriously interrupts the play. Not content, however, with getting leave to open this gap in the wall, they memorialised the Town Council in 1860 to get golf abolished from the green altogether; but after sundry procedures the Magistrates, wisely as we think, declined to interfere.

Although Bruntsfield Links and the Meadows were protected from building under the 1827 Act, the surrounding land comprising the Bruntsfield district of the city of Edinburgh and its neighbouring districts of Tollcross and Lauriston, which ran north of the Wright's House Toll, had been under attrition for many years and it underwent a massive, unprecedented and sustained period of primarily new housing development in the period 1860–1890. Between the years 1851 to 1861 three quarters of the total increase in population in Great Britain had taken place in the towns. According to Charles J. Smith in *South Edinburgh in Pictures,* 'Nowhere did Edinburgh's "other new town" develop so steadily and with such density'. The population of Edinburgh more than doubled between the years 1837 and 1891, from 120,000 to 261,261.

The tenement building housing the Carruthers' dairy 'over the road' at 5 Gillespie Place was built in 1871 and it was well sited to serve the surrounding occupiers of the newly built tenements and for its business to prosper. Deliveries were made by handcart to the 'big houses' of a fine residential district to the south of Bruntsfield Links in Greenhill Gardens where distinguished people in many fields were attracted by the secluded surroundings.

The district plan of 1872 on page 35 illustrates the immense scale of the developments when compared to the 1864 plan on page 34. From the Meadows in the east and moving westwards and southwards, rose robust new tall stone-built, mainly four-storey, tenement buildings. The list is truly impressive: Londsdale Terrace, Panmure Place, Glen Street, Lauriston Place, Leven Terrace, Drumdryan Street, Tarvit Street, Valleyfield Street, Glengyle Terrace, Gillespie Place, Gillespie Crescent, Leamington Terrace, Bruntsfield Terrace and Bruntsfield Crescent, not forgetting the new Royal Infirmary situated opposite George Heriot's School.

Lord Cockburn, the distinguished statesman and lawyer, makes the following reference to the changes that had taken place around Bruntsfield's open spaces:

> There has never in my life been any single place in or near Edinburgh which has so distinctly been the resort at once of our philosophy and our fashion. Under these poor trees walked, and talked, and meditated, all our literary and scientific, and many of our legal, worthies of the last and beginning of the present century. Now the once sequestered Meadows, save on the southern quarter, which is open to Bruntsfield Links, are well nigh completely encircled by new lines of streets and terraces, and are further intersected by the fine modern drive named after Sir John Melville, who was Lord Provost in 1854–59.

This then was the new order, the great expansion of residential property development brought about by the advance of centres of industrial expansion in the great cities of the Victorian era. But by 1872 the building works had not yet run their course, for over the next two decades Sir George Warrender, in his great feuing and building plan of 1876, gave rise to quite a unique network of streets and terraces of varied architecture. James Grant gives the following succinct comment:

> Within the last few years the parks around the old Bruntsfield House (see 1872 plan) have – save for a small space in its immediate vicinity – been intersected, east, west, north and south, by stately streets and lines of villas, among the chief of which are Warrender Park Crescent, with its noble line of ancient trees, and Warrender Park Road, running from the Links …

Wright's Houses

The family occupied many addresses in the Bruntsfield area over a period of fifty-six years (see Appendix 2) but perhaps one family address, recorded in the *Edinburgh and Leith Post Office Directory* for 1877, carried special significance:

Thomas Carruthers   House 32 Wright's Houses   Dairy   5 Gillespie Place

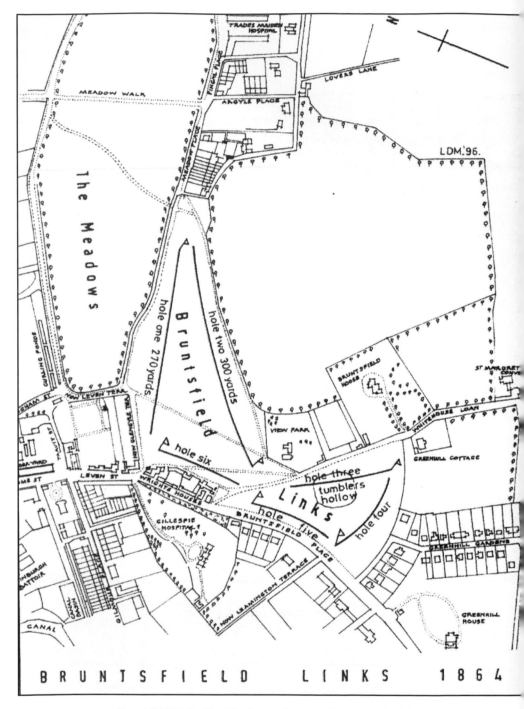

Bruntsfield Links, The Meadows and surrounding streets in 1864

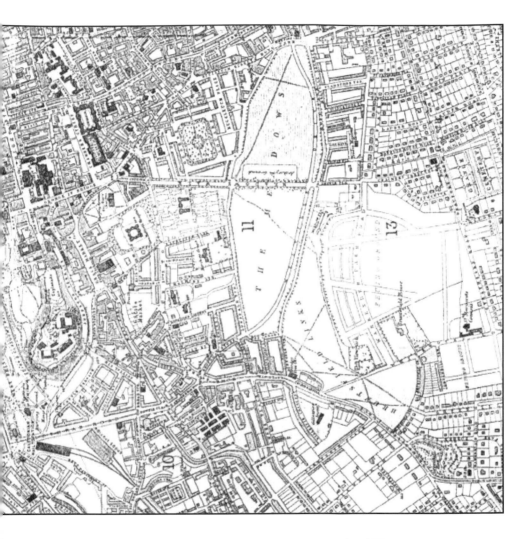

Bruntsfield Links, The Meadows and adjacent districts 1872

'Wright's Houses was at one time a village outside the city of Edinburgh on the Burgh Muir', a tract of land which, according to Maitland, extended from 'St. Leonards Loning in the Pleasants', north of Bruntsfield Links and the Meadows, to the 'grounds of Neulands belonging to the Laird of Braid' (Braid Hills), a few miles to the south; and from the Powburn on the east to the 'Caithouse belonging to the Laird of Wryte's Houses' on the west. In 1508 the Edinburgh Magistrates applied to James IV and obtained a Charter, under the Great Seal, called the Golden Charter, empowering them to let the Burgh Muir in feu. Under Scots Law feu is a right to the use of land in return for a fixed annual payment (feu duty). The Burgh Muir after this date was gradually feued and built upon, until all that remained were the Meadows and Bruntsfield Links. James Grant in *Old and New Edinburgh* provides the origin of the name Wright's Houses:

> The name Wright's Houses was derived from a nearby picturesque mansion of very great antiquity, quadrangled in form, striking in outline, with its peel-tower, turrets, crowstepped gables and gablets, encrusted with legends, dates and coats of arms, for ages formed one of the most important features of the Boroughmuir. It was undoubtedly one of the oldest, and by far the most picturesque, baronial dwelling in the neighbourhood of the city; and blending as it did the grim old feudal tower of the twelfth or thirteenth century with more ornate additions of the Scoto-French style of later years, it must have formed – even in the tasteless age that witnessed its destruction – a pleasing and striking feature from every part of the landscape around it, especially when viewed from Bruntsfield Links against a sunset sky.

Wright's Houses in the nineteenth century comprised a conglomeration of about fifty ancient buildings, mainly of eighteenth century origin that formed the Links western boundary. Apart from the demolition of an old villa with a carriage entrance to the north to make way for the construction of the Barclay Free Church in 1863 from the bequest of £10,000 from a lady of like name, the eastern part of the 'wedge' of Wright's Houses survived without major change until about 1885. A progressive period of re-building then commenced. Between the Barclay Free Church and The Auld Toll Bar on the other side of the highway, now Bruntsfield Place, had stood tollgates from 1706 until their removal in 1852.

The houses were mainly of two or three-storey stone construction clustered close together, some with stuccoed coatings, divided into several habitations, each accessed by either an internal or external stone staircase. Here was a thriving and bustling community. A study of the censuses of population of its inhabitants at that time records the great influx of people from far and wide to Edinburgh. Between the years 1877 and 1887 the population of Edinburgh grew by 20%.

The diversity of the trades and crafts of the occupants of Wright's Houses was great. Among those listed as Tom's near neighbours towards the end of the 1870s were a number of golf ball makers, club makers and golf clubs:

The old Golf Tavern (Hotel)	27–28 Wright's Houses: Golf Clubhouse & Tavern
Edinburgh Thistle, Warrender, Viewforth, Bruntsfield Allied, Merchiston, St Leonards, Edinburgh St Andrew	27 Wright's Houses: Golf Clubs
Bruntsfield Links Golf Club	30–31 Wright's Houses: Golf Club
Thomas Carruthers	32 Wright's Houses: Dairy Keeper & Golf Shop Owner
(Later: Workshop at 26A Wright's Houses from 1895–1899)	
William Frier	34 Wright's Houses: Golf Club & Ball Maker
(Later at 29 Wright's Houses)	
William Thomson	36 Wright's Houses: Golf Club Maker
D. McEwan & Son	36 Wright's Houses: Golf Club & Ball Makers
Ronald and John Ross	44 Wright's Houses: Golf Club & Ball Makers

The picture overleaf (left) of Wright's Houses shows the Golf Hotel (No. 28), the first home of the Edinburgh Burgess Golfing Society, as it stood in the mid 1890s. The painted board bears the two words 'Golf Hotel', with two crossed golf clubs and three golf balls, above a 'For Sale' board. To the left of the Golf Hotel stands the single storey structure of Carruthers' workshop (No. 26A), which he occupied from 1895–1899. At the side of the workshop a small passageway leads to No. 27, the original Golf Tavern. Nos. 27 and 28 were listed together in the 1894 edition of the *Edinburgh and Leith Post Office Directory* as the 'Golf House Tavern' (the term 'old Golf Tavern (Hotel)' is used to describe the two buildings in this book). William Frier, golf club maker, was listed as the occupant of No. 29 in 1894. This striking picture shows the towering tenements whose encroachment eventually forced the removal of the golf clubs and societies from the Links.

Above: Wright's Houses Nos. 26A – 29. *Next two pages:* Wright's Houses Nos. 28–36
(Courtesy of Edinburgh City Libraries)

The pictures on the previous pages of Wright's Houses circa 1895 show No. 28 (formerly the clubhouse of the Edinburgh Burgess Golfing Society), No. 29 (William Frier) and Nos. 30 and 31, formerly the home of the Bruntsfield Links Golfing Society, with the Links in the foreground. Next door at No. 32 is the family home of Tom Carruthers from 1877–1879. William Frier, golf club maker, occupied No. 34 from 1886 until 1894. There are two painted boards at No. 36 on the extreme right of the picture. The top board bears the name 'F. Doleman, Manager' followed by 'D. McEwan & Son, Golf Club and Ball Maker'. The bottom board bears the name 'Peter McLaughlan, Joiner and Cabinet Maker'. William Thomson, golf club maker, was also listed at No. 36 at the end of the 1870s. The tenements dominating the skyline were built in 1885.

The Carruthers' family home at No. 32 Wright's Houses looked straight over the Green, the term used for the golf links at Bruntsfield. The view was striking; first, there was a great sward of grassed land with undulating low grassy mounds, clumps of gorse and handsome trees which marked its boundaries. Beyond the trees to the east were the broad pastures of the Meadows, and then rising dramatically, the vertical cliffs of the Salisbury Craigs and Arthur's Seat. To the north, Edinburgh Castle sat majestically, high atop old volcanic rocks and at a lower level new stone-built blocks of tenements swept south close by the Green to Bruntsfield House and its parklands – already designated for future grand building works.

Golf on the Links

John Kay, the well-known engraver and caricaturist whose collection of portraits of old Edinburgh characters and anecdotal biographies is renowned for its uniqueness, describes the extraordinary golfing feats of some intrepid Bruntsfield golfers on the summit of Arthur's Seat. Towering to a height of 822 feet above the river Forth, Arthur's Seat, with the Craigs of Salisbury, occupied the greater portion of the ancient Sanctuary of Holyrood, which included the Royal Park:

> Bets of a novel nature, which set the ordinary routine of the game entirely aside, are occasionally undertaken by the more athletic. An amusing and difficult feat, sometimes attempted from Bruntsfield Links, is that of driving the ball to the top of Arthur's Seat! In this fatiguing undertaking, being a species of steeplechase over hedges and ditches, the parties are usually followed by bottle-holders and other attendants, denoting the excessive exertion required.

Holyrood and Arthur's Seat: driving the ball to the top of Arthur's Seat in the fewest strokes was the bet!

This does not appear to have been attempted prior to the period when Hugo Arnot wrote his *History of Edinburgh*. In a critical note on the Letters of Topham, who wrote in 1775, Arnot remarks that the author:

> ... has been pleased to make the top of Arthur's Seat, and those of the other hills in the neighbourhood of Edinburgh, fields for the game of the golf. This observation is still more unfortunate than the general train of his remarks. Were a person to play a ball from the top of Arthur's Seat he would probably have to walk half a mile before he could touch it again; and we will venture to say that the *whole art of man could not play the ball back again*.

This, states Arnot, has been done.

A few doors away, up the slope from the Carruthers' family home at No. 32, stood the old Golf Tavern (Hotel), Nos. 27 and 28 Wright's Houses. The Edinburgh Burgess Golfing Society, which claimed to have been formed in 1735 (although there is no evidence available until 1770) and the earliest golf club to have existed, entered into a tenancy agreement with Thomas Comb, club maker, for the old Golf Tavern (Hotel) in 1792 for the next eighty-five years, renewable annually.

The elegy of Maggie Johnston, a famous Bruntsfield hostess, who kept a howff at Bruntsfield and who died in 1711 is reproduced below and an interesting article (overleaf) which appeared in *Golfing*, 2 January 1908, contains other snatches of ballads from old golf hosteries at Bruntsfield, St Andrews and Musselburgh.

> When in our pouch we fand some clinks,
> An' took a turn o'er Bruntsfield Links,
> Aften in Maggy's, at high jinks,
> We guzzled scuds,
> Till we could scarce wi' hale-out drinks
> Cast aff our duds.

The practice of the Burgess was to sub-let such parts of the property that it did not require. The golf clubs listed previously at No. 27 rented rooms at the old Golf Tavern (Hotel) in the 1870s and 1880s. The Bruntsfield Allied and Edinburgh Thistle Clubs continued to rent premises at the old Golf Tavern (Hotel) until 1900 when they transferred their occupation to the former clubhouse of the Bruntsfield Links Golfing Society. Meantime, the Edinburgh Thistle Club, now playing at the new Braid Hills Golf Course which was opened in 1889 some two miles to the south, had also celebrated the opening of an additional clubroom in William Frier's clubhouse at the Braid Hills in November 1894. Mr James Smith, Honorary President, stated that the new clubroom would be a means of uniting members and adding more bloom to the Thistle.

James Braid was a playing member of the Edinburgh Thistle Club from 1891 to 1893. Bernard Darwin in his biography, *James Braid,* states that 'James Braid joined the Edinburgh Thistle Club which had its club room at an hotel on Bruntsfield Links but played on the Braids.'

The Burgess moved their headquarters from Bruntsfield Links in 1874 to a nine-hole course at Musselburgh owned by Musselburgh Town Council, from which they were also subsequently to move, also because of overcrowding, to their own privately owned property at Barnton in Edinburgh. However, many Burgess members continued to socialise at the old Golf Tavern (Hotel) and play golf for several years on the Links at Bruntsfield. When the Burgess vacated their premises at Nos. 27 and 28 Wright's Houses, in due course to be followed by the Bruntsfield Links Golfing Society at Nos. 30 and 31, the other private golf clubs listed at No 27 were able to continue to rent rooms at the old Golf Tavern (Hotel).

Old Golf Hostelries.

IN these days of handsome club houses and splendid hotel-hydros, the little house of call has been forgotten. Yet a hundred years ago it had a real part in the golfer's life. Some snatches of ballad have come down to us in praise of these snug havens.

There is still in existence the ancient Golf Hotel at Bruntsfield Links, Edinburgh. Its most famous hostess was Maggie Johnston, who died in 1711, and whose elegy reads :—

> " When in our pouch we fand some clinks,
> An' took a turn o'er Bruntsfield Links,

She ne'er ran sour jute, because
    It gi'es the batts."

And at St. Andrews, long before the Royal and Ancient Club house was built, when round the links were only plain stone and slated dwellings, there was a small house with a licensed kitchen.

> " Sacred to hope and promise is the spot—
> To Philp's and to the Union Parlour near,
> To every golfer, every caddie dear—
> Where we strike off."

The Union Club was well known in St. Andrews sixty or seventy years ago. And an-

"YE OLDE GOLF TAVERN."
For over four and a half centuries at Bruntsfield Links, Edinburgh.

> Aften in Maggy's, at high jinks,
>   We guzzled scuds,
> Till we could scarce wi' hale-out drinks
>   Cast aff our duds."

The Golf Hotel is still there, and has been entertaining golfers ever since the year 1456. Nowadays players over Bruntsfield links are restricted to the short-hole game.

There was a Canongate rival, Lucky Wood, who :—

> " Ne'er ga'e in a lawin' fause
>   Nor stoups a-froth aboon the hause,
>   Nor kept dowd tip within her waws,
>   But reamin' swats ;

other haunt, the old Cross Keys Hotel, had a golfing landlord in Mr. Hastie.

At Musselburgh, there is still the corner house known at Forman's ; it was for many years in charge of Mrs. Forman. It was in its glory in the days of Gourlay, the famous ball-maker, who got four and even five shillings a-piece for his " featheries." This was in 1820. An Innerleven poet of the middle of last century described the feather balls in terse language :—

> " And though our best wi' them we tried,
> And nicely every club applied,
> They whirred and fuffed and dooked and
>   shied,
> And sklentit into bunkers."

**Snatches of ballads from old golf hostelries at Bruntsfield, St Andrews and Musselburgh,
Golfing, 2 January 1908**

Next door to Tom Carruthers' house at No. 32 Wright's Houses were premises numbered 30–31 containing several dwellings including Gilchrist's Tavern. This housed the private clubhouse of the Bruntsfield Links Golfing Society which is claimed to have originated in 1761 (although there is no evidence until 1784 in support of this claim), the third oldest golf club in existence. A number of their members had been travelling to Musselburgh for some years, where the seaside links were open for play all the year round. Not all members went along with this trend which gathered pace in the 1870s. The Club's headquarters remained at 30–31 Wright's Houses, although rooms were also rented at Musselburgh, and continued to be the Club's home for those members who remained at Bruntsfield Links. The premises eventually changed hands on 15 December 1887, when the entire Bruntsfield Links Golfing Society moved to Musselburgh. The property was subsequently converted and renamed firstly as the 'Golf House Tavern' in 1900, then as the 'Golf Hotel, Ye Olde Golf Tavern' and finally as the 'Ye Olde Golf Tavern' as it is known today. It is the only building of the original Wright's Houses village to survive into the 21st century.

According to Ian T. Henderson and David I. Stirk in their book, *Royal Blackheath,* it is believed that the lack of evidence of the exact dates for the formation of these earliest Golf Clubs may be because golf was not the original primary objective of these societies. Groups of Scottish freemasons had adopted golf as a healthy form of exercise prior to feasting. Over time, as the number of freemasons playing golf declined, the later traditional form of member-based golf clubs emerged.

Thomas S. Aitchison and George Lorimer's *Reminiscences of the old Bruntsfield golf club* provide this account of the life of the Bruntsfield Links Golfing Society during the period 1866–1874:

> In those days, the club met in a house facing the Links, close to the old Golf Tavern, which formed the headquarters of the Burgess Golf Club. It consisted of ground floor and sunk flat, the latter being occupied by Mrs. Stewart, who took charge of the premises, and attended to our comforts on the occasion of our dinners. For our own use we had one long, low-roofed room. Originally there were two, with an intervening passage, but the partitions had been cleared away. That one room was all we had. In one corner was an arrangement of basins behind a screen, which served the purpose of a lavatory; in another stood a cupboard, in which, along with a plentiful supply of plates and glasses, were to be found the various kinds of liquid refreshment most in demand, together with bread and cheese and biscuits, in addition to which there was usually a cask of draught ale on tap, which stood beside one of the windows.

To these good things we helped ourselves, dropping the equivalent into a box, which stood on the mantelpiece; but it was a most unsatisfactory mode of procedure, for the box could not give change, and so payment had often to be postponed to the occasion of the next visit, when it was perhaps forgotten. There was an ever-recurring deficit in regard to which every treasurer in turn made his protest.

Leith Links

The Burgess and Bruntsfield Links Golfing Societies had not been the first clubs to move to Musselburgh. The Honourable Company of Edinburgh Golfers, founded in 1744, the second oldest Golf Club in existence, had played at Leith Links and moved to Musselburgh in 1836, for reasons explained by the Reverend John Kerr in *The Golf Book of East Lothian*:

Golf on Leith Links in the early 1800s with horse-drawn coaches and encroaching buildings in the background

The history of the Honourable Company of Edinburgh Golfers is rather an awkward commentary on the Great Chamber of the Edinburgh Corporation by which the Company was assured of perpetual endurance and succession. What with buildings and encroachments, the Links of Leith, never very commodious, became unattractive and unsuitable for play.

Whether this move to Musselburgh also had some connection with the change in the administration of Leith is not known but in 1833 Edinburgh's seaport town was made an independent parliamentary borough. From this point onwards a provost, four bailies, a treasurer, and ten councillors now managed its civic affairs.

James Grant provides this historical note about golf on the Links:

> During the seventeenth and eighteen centuries, the Links of Leith were the chief resort of the aristocracy resident in Edinburgh as the best place for playing golf; nobles of the highest rank and the most eminent legal and political officials taking part with the humblest players – if skilful – in the game.

Although the Honourable Company of Edinburgh Golfers moved from Leith in 1836 golf continued to be played on the Links beside the shore of the Firth of Forth. One such famous occasion, in which Old Tom Morris and his son, Young Tom Morris, both competed, took place on Saturday 18 May 1867. The event was described in the following Monday's edition of *The Scotsman*:

> The National Golf Tournament on Leith Links, which was opened on Friday, was brought to a close on Saturday afternoon. The weather in the morning was fair, with a gentle wind from the east. Towards mid-day, a dense fog from the sea set in, and being accompanied by drizzly showers of rain, rendered the turf exceedingly heavy. The rain, however, did not either damp the enthusiasm of the players or the large number of spectators who had assembled to witness the sport. The first match – a Consolation Stakes, – commenced at one o'clock, the course being two rounds of the Links. After a keen competition, the prizes were gained as under: – 1st (£4), Willie Dow, Musselburgh – score 63; 2nd (£3) Rob Kirk, St Andrews – score 64; 3rd (£2), Davie Park, Musselburgh – score 65; the 4th and 5th prizes (£1 10s and £1 respectively) were divided between Tom Morris Jun., St. Andrews, A. Strath, Prestwick, and G. Morris, Leith, each of whom scored 66. In the foursome match for £5, between Willie Dunn, of Leith, and Willie Park, of Musselburgh, against Tom Morris, of St. Andrews, and Willie Dow, of Musselburgh, the former won by two holes. The play in this match was very fine, one of the rounds being holed by Dunn and Park in 28 strokes – two strokes less than any competitor during the meeting. So marked has been the success attending the tournament now closed that the members of the Thistle Golf Club, under whose auspices the gathering took place have, we understand, resolved to continue it annually.

In the eighteenth century Leith was the sporting capital of Scotland, with a cock pit, a bowling green, tennis courts, annual athletic games, golf on the links and the regular attendance of the Company of Archers. The Honourable Company of Edinburgh Golfers had from time to time applied to the Town Council of Edinburgh for a Silver Club to be played for annually. This was finally granted in 1744 upon condition that proper regulations be observed. Before the first tournament thirteen rules were drawn up that were adopted by the Society of St Andrews Golfers and were later to become the basis for the rules by which golf was played all over the world. The idea for petitioning The Town Council is said to have come from the Royal Company of Archers who were given a Silver Arrow in 1709 to be competed for annually on Leith Links. Burgh patronage of sport also extended to the Silver Jack for bowlers in 1771 and the City Purse at Leith races.

The most important horse races in Scotland took place on the long stretch of bare sands at Leith. In 1816 the races were transferred to a newly constructed race-course at Musselburgh, when, just as the golfers were to experience some years later, conditions became so difficult. The loss of such a vibrant and colourful annual event, described in the following résumé from James Grant's book, must have been very unpopular:

> They took place on the east side of the harbour of Leith, where now the great new docks are formed. The Leith race week was a species of carnival to the citizens of Edinburgh, and in many instances caused the partial suspension of work and business. They were under the direct patronage of the magistrates of the City, and it was usual for one of the town officers, in his livery, to walk in procession every morning from the Council Chambers to Leith, bearing aloft on a pole or halberd, profusely decorated with ribbons and streamers, the 'City Purse', accompanied by a file of the capital city guard with their bayonets fixed and in full uniform, accompanied by a drummer, beating that peculiar cadence on his drum which is believed to have been the old 'Scottish March'.
>
> This procession gathered in strength and interest as it moved along Leith Walk, as hundreds were on the lookout for the appearance of this accredited civic body. The crowds preferred 'gaun doon wi' the Purse', as the phrase was, to any other mode of proceeding thither. 'Such a dense mass of boys and girls finally surrounded the town officers, the drummer, and the old veterans' wrote one who must have seen it many times, 'that long before the procession could reach Leith the functionaries had disappeared and nothing was visible amid the moving myriads but the purse on the top of the pole.'

The scene at Leith races, as described by those who had been present, was very striking. Vast lines of tents and booths, covered with canvas or blankets, stretched along the level shore; recruiting-sergeants with their drummers beating, sailors ashore for a holiday, mechanics accompanied by their wives or sweethearts, servant girls, and motley groups, were constantly passing in and out of the drinking places; the whole varied by shows, roley-poleys, hobby-horses, wheels-of-fortune, and many of those strange characters which were once familiar in the streets of Edinburgh.

Saturday, which was the last day of the races, was the most joyous and outrageous of the seashore carnival. On that day the 'subscription' for the horses beaten during the week was held, and these unfortunate nags contended for the negative honour of not being the worst on the course. Then, when night closed in, there was invariably a general brawl, a promiscuous free fight being maintained by the returning crowds along the entire length of Leith Walk.

There were interruptions to the golfers' play at Bruntsfield just as had been the case at Leith when its open spaces were used in years past for popular public occasions such as Fair Days.

Interruptions to Golf on Bruntsfield Links

Up until about 1850 the Links at Bruntsfield were quiet and peaceful unless an occasional garrison review or game of football was taking place. The rights of the golfers and members of the public to go peaceably about their lawful business were clearly set out in the conditions of a public roup or auction held at Bruntsfield Links in November 1738. An extract from Stewart Cruden's *Bruntsfield Links Golfing Society* outlines these rights:

The Magistrates and Council reserve to themselves and their successors and the whole inhabitants of the City of Edinburgh and Libertys thereof full powers to use the exercise of Golf and Walking upon the said Links at any time of the year, also clothes drying, the use of natural spring water, the making of holes and burying the dead in case of plague, and the mustering of the city Train bands, Guards, Militia and fencible men of His Majesty's regular Forces.

Until the Royal Park at Holyrood was opened up, levelled, and improved, at the suggestion of the Prince Consort, Prince Albert, husband of Queen Victoria, in the 1850s, Bruntsfield Links was invariably the place for garrison reviews and field days for the troops. According to Grant, 'Neither they nor anyone else were able to interfere with the vested right of the golfers to play over any part of the open ground at all times'. The following description, contained in James Grant's book, of a garrison review held at the Royal Park in 1860 gives some measure of the massive disruption that these events would have caused on the Links at Bruntsfield in earlier years:

> A public event of great importance in this locality was the Royal Scottish Volunteer Review before the Queen on the 7th of August 1860, when Edinburgh, usually so empty and dull in the dog days, presented a strange and wonderful scene. For a few days before this event regiments from all parts of Scotland came pouring into the city, and were cantoned in schoolhouses, hospitals, granaries, and wherever accommodation could be procured for them. The Breadalbane Highlanders, led by the white-bearded old marquis, attracted especial attention, and, on the whole, the populace seemed most in favour of kilted corps, all such being greeted with especial approbation.
>
> Along the north wall of the park there was erected a grand stand capable of containing 3,000 persons. The royal standard of Scotland – a splendid banner, twenty-five yards square – floated from the summit of Arthur's Seat, while a multitude of other standards and snow-white bell-tents covered all the inner slopes of the Craigs. By one o'clock all the regiments were in Edinburgh, and defiled into the park by four separate entrances at once, and were massed in contiguous close columns, formed into divisions and brigades of artillery, engineers, and infantry, the whole under the command of Lieutenant-General Sir G. A. Wetherall, K.C.B.
>
> The scene which burst upon the view of these volunteers as they entered the park, and the vast slopes of Arthur's Seat came in sight, will never be forgotten by those who were there, and made many a strong man's heart beat high and his eyes glisten. The vast hilly amphitheatre was crowded by more than 100,000 spectators, who made the welkin ring with their reiterated cheers, as the deep and solid columns, with all their arms glittering in the sun, were steadily forming on the grassy plain below. Every foot of ground upon the northern slopes not too steep for standing on was occupied, even to the summit, where the mighty yellow standard with the red lion floated out over all.

Two other early anecdotes, the first a bloodthirsty tale of seventeenth century origin relating to golf played by a public executioner, the second, of nineteenth century origin, a threatened incursion by thousands of cattle, are worthy of recording as events which could affect a peaceable round of golf on Bruntsfield Links:

About the reign of Charles II, the office of public executioner was taken by a reduced gentleman, the last member of an old family that had long possessed an estate near Melrose. His earlier years had been passed in profligacy; his patrimony was gone and at length, for the sake of food, he was compelled to accept this degrading office, 'which, in those days,' says Chambers, 'must have been unusually obnoxious to popular odium, on account of the frequent executions of innocent and religious men. Notwithstanding his extreme degradation, this unhappy reprobate could not altogether forget his former tastes and habits. He would occasionally resume the garb of a gentleman and mingle in the parties of citizens who played at golf in the evenings on Bruntsfield Links. Being at length recognised, he was chased from the ground with shouts of execration and loathing, which affected him so much that he retired to the solitude of the King's Park and was next day found dead at the bottom of a precipice, over which he is supposed to have thrown himself in despair. The rock was afterwards called the Hangman's Craig.'

In 1843 the Bruntsfield Golfing Societies took alarm when they learned that the magistrates had permitted the holding of the annual 'All Hallow Fair', a cattle market for the sale of as many as 3,000 cattle, preventing golf for several days at a time. After a public meeting, a petition signed by over 400 people was drawn up and permission to hold the fair was withdrawn by the magistrates. By 1860 the cattle markets had found a permanent home at nearby Lauriston Place.

Naturally, the early rules of golf allowed for every eventuality that a golfer could face. Among the rules were:

... neither trench, ditch or dyke made for the preservation of the links, nor the Scholar's holes, or the Soldiers lines, shall be accounted a hazard, but the ball is to be taken out, teed, and played with any iron club.

In 1851 the R&A ruled that 'when a ball is on clothes or within a club-length of a washing-tub the clothes may be drawn from under the ball and the tub may be removed.'

A quiet stroll down the Avenue, one of several pathways which crossed Bruntsfield Links, shaded from the summer sun by an avenue of trees, the branches of which formed a cover of green foliage, had been from ancient times a popular and tranquil custom. Small groups of golfers in scarlet red coats and pale breeches, with long-nosed wooden clubs and feathery balls, added a colourful and interesting distraction for the walkers.

The Avenue, Bruntsfield Links, with the Barclay Church in the background

After 1850, these tranquil scenes on the Links were to change – the industrial revolution had brought a new realism to Scotland. The ceremony and ritual practised by the two Burgess and Bruntsfield private clubs were no longer considered appropriate. The cheaper gutta-percha ball and iron clubs of stronger construction were now to open the door to a much wider population and golf, not socialising, became the most important consideration. By 1860 there was only a total of thirty-seven golf clubs and societies in existence in Great Britain and Ireland. Six of those played golf at Bruntsfield Links, four of which had been instituted in the previous five years. This obviously led to an increase in usage of the green for golfing and, being common land open to the public, golfers who did not belong to a club swelled the numbers. The few clubs which had headquarters at the Links paid for its entire upkeep.

A summer stroll down the Avenue across Bruntsfield Links would now expose the public to some danger, although for those spectators seated on the benches of the tree-lined boundaries, the spectacle would hold a certain fascination. Assembled on the tee of the first hole, near the Barclay Free Church, and running parallel to the Meadows, might cluster about two dozen early morning golfers. Dressed in a sea of red jackets, their attire would have been used as a warning to non-golfers using the Links, and would have been unrelated to the old tradition of wearing a uniform of red coats and pale breeches practised by the Burgess and Bruntsfield Links Golfing Societies in times past. Bunnets (a soft flat cap) was the popular golfers' headwear with the Glengarry (a brimless cap with a crease down the crown) and Tam o'Shanter (a brimless wool or cloth cap with a bobble in the centre) would also have been worn by a few. The order of the day would have been collar and tie, waistcoat, trousers or sometimes knickerbockers, and tackety boots or shoes. Nearby groups of young lads, caddies for the players, would stand waiting, a bundle of clubs loosely tucked under one arm, ready for their hirers to set off with their first swing of the day.

When the gutta-percha ball was first introduced it was dark, even black. It could not be painted and was frequently lost. As a result caddies had to carry at least half a dozen spares to add to their load of wet sand for tees. Interestingly, the term 'caddie' is derived from the word for a messenger used in Edinburgh in the seventeenth century. Here is how James Grant describes the caddies:

> Close by St Giles' Church in the High Street, the cross, the font or basin of which ran with wine on festive occasions, was the peculiar rallying point of those now extinct lazzaroni – the street messengers or caddies. A ragged half-blackguard looking set they were, but allowed to be amazingly acute, intelligent, and also faithful to any duty entrusted to them. A stranger coming temporarily to reside in Edinburgh got a caddie attached to his service, to conduct him from one part of the town to another, and to run errands for him; in short, to be wholly at his bidding. A caddie did literally know everything of Edinburgh, even to that kind of knowledge that we now expect only in a street directory; and it was equally true that he could hardly be asked to go anywhere, or upon any mission, that he would not go. On the other hand, the stranger would probably be astonished to find that, in a few hours, his caddie was acquainted with every particular concerning himself, where he was from, what was his purpose in Edinburgh, his family connections, tastes, and dispositions. Of course for every particle of scandal floating about Edinburgh the caddie was a ready book of reference. We sometimes wonder how our ancestors did without newspapers. We do not reflect on the living vehicle of news which then existed; the privileged beggar for country people; for towns-folk the caddies.

With about three hundred Links golfers, members of the eight private clubs who used the clubhouses at Nos. 27–28 and 30–31 Wright's Houses in the 1870s, Match Days must have involved early starts and late finishes and a crowded course. On these occasions club golfers played for the club trophies and prizes. Two rounds of the six-hole golf course entailed a continuous stream of golfers on the course for most of the day.

The growing band of golfers who were not members of private clubs also had the right to use the Links, and, although they would defer to the traditional rights of the established golf clubs, they would fill the course on other days, work commitments, daylight and weather permitting.

As the Links was common land it was inevitable that incidents would lead to confrontation with the public who used the Green for such daily tasks as drying washing, carpet beating, strolling or spectating. In addition, the nearby residents and business people were also in the firing line from the occasional stray shot out of the many thousands of shots played on an average Match Day.

Since the formation of the early golfing societies in the eighteenth century, post golf dining and conviviality had become a tradition that endured into the next century. The private rooms of the old Golf Tavern (Hotel) and what was to become the new Golf Tavern, after the Bruntsfield Links Golf Club had decamped to Musselburgh, would echo with the sound of toasts and responses, song and recitation, well into the evening. This extract from Thomas H. Aitchison and George Lorimer's *Reminiscences of the old Bruntsfield golf club 1866-1874* brings to life such occasions:

> By the time we had got thus far the atmosphere was usually so thick with tobacco smoke that the captain and croupier could just see each other and no more. After dinner we mostly drank whisky toddy, the effect, after an ample allowance of champagne in such an atmosphere may be imagined.

Golfers not attached to the private clubs took their refreshment at 'the nineteenth hole' – the nearby howffs or hostelries. As night closed in the golfers spilled out onto the streets around Wright's Houses, the echoes of continuing good humoured merriment ringing round its ancient stone buildings, until they finally dispersed towards home.

It was inevitable that in due time this increased mass of golfers, partly because of the new affordability of the game and the ever encroaching property developments around the Links, would bring about a cry from the public and the Edinburgh Town Council to rein-in the golfers.

Chapter 3

Golf Club Maker

Tom Carruthers' exposure to the golfing community at Bruntsfield Links was considerable. Not only was he operating a dairy business around the corner from the Links, but he and his family, then comprising one son, Peter, (born 1860) and six daughters (Jane, born 1863; Euphemia, born 1865; Agnes, born 1868; Jessie, born 1870; Lizzie, born 1872; and Maggie, born 1875) were living right on the Links at No. 32 Wright's Houses. The lively ambience of his environment soon led to active involvement in the golfing community. First of all he took up golf. Soon he was selling golf clubs from the basement of the property which housed his dairy business. Not long afterwards he went on to learn the skills and craft of golf club making.

Golf in 1875

The following extract from the *Manual of British Rural Sports* by John Henry Walsh under the pseudonym 'Stonehenge' provides a useful overview of the game in 1875 when Tom Carruthers was first drawn to the sport:

GOLF: SECTION 1 – GENERAL REMARKS
Golf is daily becoming more popular amongst all classes of the Scottish community, and is making rapid progress in other parts of the United Kingdom and also in the Colonies. Boys and old men enjoy its fascinations with equal zest, and both gain health and strength by the exercise and easy muscular exertion brought into play. Ladies' golf clubs are now becoming established on various links. They play at a set of short holes, from twenty to fifty yards apart, and have their medals and other competitions. The principal ladies' club is at St. Andrews, the headquarters of golf in Scotland. The following are the chief golfing centres in Scotland: Aberdeen; St. Andrews, Fife; Bruntsfield, Edinburgh; Burntisland, Cupar,

Elie, Leven, Fife; Glasgow; Greenock; Monifieth, Carnoustie, Montrose, Forfar; Musselburgh, Mid-Lothian; North Berwick, Gullane, Aberlady, Dirleton, and Dunbar, East Lothian; Perth; Prestwick, Ayrshire; and Lanark. The game has likewise its votaries in England at Blackheath and Wimbledon; at Bideford, North Devon; Crookham, Berks; Manchester; Alnmouth, Northumberland; and Hoylake, Cheshire; and in Ireland at the Curragh Camp; in several provinces of India; and the Cape of Good Hope, Australia, &c.

SECTION 2 – THE LINKS

The ground over which golf is played is called 'links', and is usually a sandy soil in the neighbourhood of the seashore, its surface covered with short grass, here and there interrupted by breaks, pits, and inequalities, and a mile or more in extent. These interruptions are necessary to impart interest to the game, for where the ground is completely smooth the sport becomes insipid, there being then little opportunity of exhibiting dexterity of play. The track along which the players proceed is denominated 'the course', and may be either rectilinear, or a figure of any number of sides. A series of small round holes, about four inches in diameter, and several inches in depth, are cut in the turf, at distances of from 100 to 400 or 500 yards from each other, according to the nature of the ground. If the links happen to be broad and expansive, the holes are placed so as to make the golfing course a somewhat circular one; if they are long and narrow, the holes are placed from end to end. But, whether the direction taken be from the starting-hole once round a course somewhat circular, or from the starting-hole to the end and back again on a straight course, the term invariably applied to each series of holes played is a round.

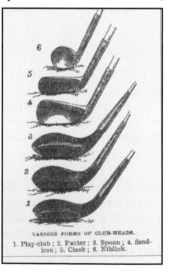

VARIOUS FORMS OF CLUB-HEADS.

1. Play-club; 2. Putter; 3. Spoon; 4. Sand-iron; 5. Cleek; 6. Niblick.

Golf clubs in use circa 1875

SECTION 3 – THE CLUBS AND BALLS

The materials employed consist of small hard balls of gutta-percha, and clubs of forms suited to the nature of the ground. The latter are named as follows: The play-club, putter, driving-putter, long-spoon, mid-spoon, short-spoon, baffing-spoon, sand-iron, cleek and niblick:

the last three have iron heads, the others are of wood. In some links, several of these clubs may be, and usually are, dispensed with, and the number reduced to six or seven; but on greens such as St. Andrews, Musselburgh, Prestwick, and some others, they all come into requisition more or less.

The PLAY-CLUB, or DRIVER, is for swiping off the tee, and is further used throughout the green if the ball is lying fair, and the distance more than a full drive between the ball and the hole you are approaching.

The LONG-SPOON comes into play when the ball lies in a hollow, or a declivity, or on slightly rough grassy ground; it derives its name from having the face scooped, so as to allow of its getting under the ball, and driving it forth a longish distance, if well struck. This club is useful, too, for elevating a ball, and driving it over hazards, such as bunkers, whins, &c.

The SHORT-SPOON is a very useful club, and is frequently in the golfer's hands during the course of the day. It is used for playing either good-lying or bad-lying balls when within a hundred yards or so from the hole; this is termed playing the 'short game.' Much depends on this short game; and many a far, and even sure driver through the green has been beaten by the indifferent swiper but deadly short-game player.

The PUTTER (u sounded as in 'but') is a short-shafted stiff club, with a flattish head and square face; it is used when the ball arrives within close proximity to the hole, generally within thirty yards, and is usually considered the best club for 'holing out' the ball. To be 'a good putter,' is what all golfers aim at, and comparatively few ever attain. Long and showy driving is of much commoner occurrence than 'deadly' putting, and one who can gain a full stroke on his opponent between two far-distant holes frequently loses his advantage by missing a 'put' within a yard of the hole!

The SAND-IRON comes into play when the ball lies in a 'bunker,' or sandpit. It is a short, thick-shafted, stiff weapon with an iron head, hollowed out in the centre, and somewhat sloped backward. On its lower edge, it is straight and sharp, which allows of its digging under the ball, and pitching it out of 'grief' on to grass. When a ball lies in whins or other hazards of a similar nature, in roads amongst 'metal,' or over the head in long deer grass or bents, the iron is the best club for freeing it from such impediments, and is, therefore, the one generally used. It is well adapted for 'lofting' balls over hazards; or for lofting or pitching 'steimies' – that is, when the opponent's ball lies so directly between the player's ball and the hole as to render it impossible for the player to use his putter. He then takes his iron and attempts to loft his own ball over his adversary's and into the hole – a feat which, when accomplished, invariably calls forth admiration.

The CLEEK is not so thick in the shaft, and is rather longer than the sand-iron; it is used chiefly for driving balls out, or lofting them over, certain hazards that happen to lie between the ball and hole near the putting green; it is also useful for putting where the ground is rough. The iron head of the cleek is straight in the face, and slopes backward.

The NIBLICK is of very important service when the ball lies in a cart-rut, horse-shoe print in sand, or any round or deep hollow not altogether beyond the player's reach, and not well suited for the iron. The head is very small and heavy, about one-half the size of that of the sand-iron, and is shaped into a hollow about the size of a crown-piece, with the iron sloping slightly backward. This peculiarity of shape enables the player to raise his ball out of difficulties from which no other club could extricate it, and ought invariably, where there are bunkers and roads, to form one of every golfer's set.

The manufacture of balls used to be a distinct trade by itself, and that of clubs another, but now most club-makers also make balls. The price of a ball is 1s., and of a club 4s.6d: irons are rather dearer.

Blacksmiths made early iron golf clubs. (See article on James Anderson in chapter 6) They were mostly much heavier than their modern counterparts with longer sockets, cruder 'nicking' where the joint grasps the shaft and the shafts themselves were thicker. Later, as the number of iron clubs in use increased, most of the blacksmiths became ironmasters specialising in making the metal heads only and were termed 'cleekmakers'. They forged the heads of the clubs for the club makers who fitted the shaft and grip. Many club makers were innovators whose designs were often protected by patent law.

The Golf Shop at 5 Gillespie Place

The explosion in popularity of golf in Edinburgh in the 1870s and 1880s led to severe congestion on the Links at Bruntsfield, and as its popularity continued to rise and the number of players increased, so did the demand for clubs and balls. Tom Carruthers saw the neighbouring club-making firm of D. McEwan & Son at No. 36 Wright's Houses struggling to keep up with rising demand. They had remained wedded to their wooden club production methods and when mechanisation took off they refused to follow the trend.

He recognised the potential to expand his own business interests, especially at a time when more attention was being turned to the manufacture and use of iron clubs. When the opportunity arose he purchased the property at 5 Gillespie Place from Thomas Nisbet on 15 May 1878, the location of his dairy business, and began to sell golf clubs about this time. The beginnings of Tom Carruthers' golfing interests were rooted in these premises, which remained in family ownership until 11 May 1945.

The Deed of Sale describes the new premises as:

5 Gillespie Place , Bruntsfield, as it stands today

Shop at 5 Gillespie Place, Edinburgh, with cellar under the same, being part of centre tenement of the three new tenements of shops and dwelling houses recently erected by W. & D. McGregor at the corner of Gillespie Place and Gillespie Crescent, Edinburgh, on the eastern portion of piece of ground part of the Mansion House of Wright's Houses sometime belonging to the Governors of James Gillespie Hospital in the Parish of St. Cuthberts.

It is interesting to note the mention of W. & D. McGregor because it was the same Edinburgh firm of builders which was associated with a transaction in 1869 which led to the construction of the famous Powderhall Athletics Stadium in Edinburgh where Tom Carruthers had trained and competed during the later stages of his professional running career. David A. Jamieson in his book, *Powderhall and Pedestrianism,* published in 1943 states the following:

It was in the summer of 1869 that a small syndicate was formed to acquire … a portion of ground forming that part of the estate of Powderhall which had been purchased by an Edinburgh firm of builders – W. & D. McGregor – with a view to feuing at a future date. It was proposed by the syndicate to lay-out upon this piece of land an up-to-date athletics enclosure, and to engage upon a series of sports promotions for which, it was submitted by the promoters, there was a public demand.

While Tom had come into the sport of golf comparatively later than his contemporaries, for his professional athletic career had lasted until the age of thirty-two, it was natural that his sporting background, as a sprinter and later as a sports' promoter, would lead him in this direction. He had retained the skills of a working tailor, which he had combined with his track exploits, especially during the early years of his athletic career, to supplement his income. Incidentally, one of his Edinburgh customers was Mr George Harrison, later to become Lord Provost of Edinburgh and Member of Parliament for Edinburgh South. Tom's skill and dexterity working with his eyes and hands naturally also leant itself to the skilled trade of golf club making.

Golf club manufacture had hitherto been the domain of a few golfing families whose club-making skills had been handed down through the generations. The old order was now changing as ambitious new men, such as William Frier, William Thomson and Tom Carruthers at Bruntsfield, saw the opportunities presented by the throngs of new players who were taking to the links.

Tom learned the trade and craft of golf club making at the hands of his close neighbour and friend, Frank Doleman, a ball and club maker, who was the manager of D. McEwan & Son's interests at 36 Wright's Houses and 6 Braid Road, 'the oldest business in the trade' which had been established in 1770. *Golf* of 20 January 1891 considered that:

> There is no-one who can turn out a better article than Frank Doleman, the respected and intelligent manager of the branches at Bruntsfield Links and Braid Road.

Frank Doleman was one of four brothers who were associated with golf for over seventy years.

> He was born at Musselburgh and learned his golf trade there. He went to London and was Professional to the London Scottish Club in 1869. Next year he shifted his quarters away up to Bruntsfield and 1871 saw him again at Musselburgh when he was with McEwan until 1880. On New Year's day of the following year he came over to Bruntsfield and took charge of McEwan's business until 1896, when he took the whole business over himself.'
> (*Golfing*, 23 February 1899)

During the year 1879 the Carruthers family moved from the old 32 Wright's Houses property to a tenement in 18 Valleyfield Street, only a couple of streets away. Two years later, in 1881, the family, together with their newly-

Thomas Carruthers (right) with Frank Doleman who took over the Bruntsfield business of D. McEwan & Son at 36 Wright's Houses in 1896

born second son named Thomas, again moved to another larger tenement property at 34 Leven Street, once again only a couple of streets away and almost opposite the shop at 5 Gillespie Place which he had acquired in 1878. This home was the birthplace of John Scott Carruthers, the grandfather of the author. Both sons were later to become skilled joiners and golf club makers, employed in their youth in their father's golf club-making business' workshop at 26A Wright's Houses, Bruntsfield Links.

In 1884 the family was soon on the move again but this time to a newly-built tenement property, a short distance to the south, and now even closer to the Links. The address was Marchmont Street, part of the great expansion created by Sir George Warrender that removed the last swathe of green land on the south side of the Links.

Over a sixty-year period the family was to reside in a total of fourteen different rented homes in Edinburgh. All, with the exception of one at the Pleasance when Tom first moved to the City from the Borders, were located adjacent to Bruntsfield Links. Tom owned 5 Gillespie Place, housing the dairy and the golf shop, and he acquired the Golfers Tryst in 1899, a purpose-built golf clubhouse at the Braid Hills. In the latter half of the nineteenth century the proportion of people owning property was about one in twelve. (See Appendix 2)

Naturally, the steady growth of his family and his increasing prosperity were particular reasons for the extraordinary number of family addresses but there was another reason: nowhere did Edinburgh's 'Other New Town' develop so steadily or with such density as in the Bruntsfield area. The family had had to tolerate the constant disruption and encroachment of one construction project after another until they were eventually housed in the recently completed residential development in Warrender, beside the Links.

He now played golf to a good standard and had mastered the craft of golf club making. He had purchased the property at 5 Gillespie Place, comprising a shop and basement, and had begun club making, repairing and selling golf clubs and balls.

The demand from the golfing community playing over Bruntsfield Links was such that on 17 May 1884, he raised £130 (a considerable sum of money in those days) by way of a bond secured over 5 Gillespie Place and used the money to finance the expansion of his golf business.

Golf Clubs Made and Sold

The following extracts from *Golf* 6 and 13 March and 29 May 1891, provide some description of the range of clubs and irons made and sold by Tom Carruthers at 5 Gillespie Place in the 1880s and early 1890s when there was a veritable explosion in the game of golf.

The first is a letter from D. G. Robertson, Captain of the Brunswick Golf Club, in reply to an article entitled 'Another New Cleek' which appeared in

Golf, 6 March 1891. This article concerned a new design by Tom Morris of a cleek specially adapted to play cupped balls:

> The army of inventors promises soon to rob golf of its manifold terrors, and recently the veteran Tom Morris has been applying his genius in designing a cleek specially adapted to play cupped balls. The result is a very serviceable-looking implement, and those who have been playing with it speak in high terms of Tom's idea. The straight sole of the ordinary cleek is somewhat rounded, whilst the greatest breadth of the blade is nearest the front. In general appearance it is egg-shaped, but a little elongated, the length from heel to toe being three inches. It is admirably balanced, and the rounded sole permits of the cleek being used at an angle. Besides being useful for cupped balls, it will also prove very serviceable for hanging balls. Altogether the cleek is likely to meet a felt want, and Tom is to be congratulated upon having evolved out of his own thought and experience what will prove a friend to many a golfer. The cleek has been patented.

D. G. Robertson's letter of reply appeared in *Golf,* 13 March 1891:

The Cleek for Cupped Balls
To the Editor of *Golf*

> Sir,
> It was with not a little surprise that I read the notice of 'Another New (?) Cleek' in your last issue. There is really nothing new at all about the round sole. In Edinburgh it is quite common. I am a member of three Clubs, in each of which there are several in use. I have played with one for three years, made by Mr. Carrick, Musselburgh, and I have seen others made by Mr. White of St. Andrews. I also know that Mr. Anderson, of Anstruther, is at present making round soled lofting irons for Mr. T Carruthers, Edinburgh, who has regularly sold them to golfers for some years past.'
>
> I am, Sir, your &c.,
> D. G. ROBERTSON,
> Capt. Brunswick Golf Club
> 4, Mureston Terrace, Edinburgh,
> March 7th 1891.

The second extract referred to above is contained in a letter from a correspondent using the initials 'R. J. B. T.' dated 22 May 1891, published in *Golf*, 29 May 1891, entitled 'Carruthers' Patent Cleek', describing a visit made to Carruthers' golf shop to discuss his new patent:

> ... There are all kinds of clubs, driving cleeks, putting cleeks, lofting irons, heavy irons, and niblicks; and his latest is a neat little cleek ...

The word 'club' is used in 'R. J. B. T.'s letter for wooden-headed clubs. The word 'cleek' is used to describe a club with a straight and narrow face used for playing long shots to the green or for putting. The lofting iron was used to give the ball a more elevated flight, either from the fairway or out of reasonable lies in the rough. Heavy irons were used to play from the rough or 'heavy' lies and the niblick, with a small heavy round head, was used to extricate the ball from very difficult lies or positions from which no other club could move it.

Until a comprehensive price list of clubs, the cover of which is reproduced below, was unearthed from the archives of the Eyemouth Golf Club in Berwickshire, no definitive documentation of the range of golf clubs manufactured by the Carruthers' golf business had come to light. It has been possible to date this price list to autumn 1892.

It is made up of two sections. The first section, reproduced on page 65, headed 'List of Ordinary Clubs', includes wooden and iron clubs of all types, golf bags, balls and repairs to golf clubs. These clubs would have been pretty much the same clubs as those that Tom Carruthers made and sold to Bruntsfield golfers from his golf shop at 5 Gillespie Place throughout the 1880s.

The second section of the price list, headed 'List of Patent Clubs' is reproduced in chapter 6 and lists a further range of clubs. The range of clubs is indeed impressive and marks Carruthers out as a club maker of some importance.

Carruthers' Patent.

Patent,
Perfect Balance.

The Longest Driving Cleek in the World.

T. CARRUTHERS,

(PATENTEE),

5 GILLESPIE PLACE, EDINBURGH.

PRICE LIST

Cover of Carruthers' 1892 Price List

A comparison of the list of clubs used in 1875, as described earlier, and Carruthers' 'List of Ordinary Clubs' highlights the greater variety of clubs that became available during this period. The use of the gutta-percha ball and improvements in iron forging technology as well as the need to adapt the long narrow wooden club heads to the grassy characteristics of the new inland courses led to this development.

LIST OF ORDINARY CLUBS

Drivers,	4/6
Spoons,	4/6
Putters,	4/6
Brasseys,	5/6
Driving Cleeks,	5/-
Putting Cleeks,	5/-
Driving Irons,	5/-
Sand Irons,	5/-
Lofting Irons,	5/-
Iron Putters,	5/-
Mashies,	5/-
Niblicks,	5/-
Left-handed Cleeks, &c.	

GOLF BAGS

7/6, 9/6, 10/6, and 14/-

············

Repairs.

Driver, Spoon, and Putter Heads,	2/6
Brassey Heads,	3/6
Iron Club Heads,	3/-
Shafts of all kinds,	2/-

············

BALLS.

All kinds of Balls Sold or Re-made.

Boys' Clubs 1/- less in all cases.

LEFT-HANDED CLUBS, CLEEKS, &c.

LADIES' CLUBS OF ALL KINDS.

All Clubs are carefully selected and highly finished, without any extra charge.

⊹ TRADE SUPPLIED ⊹

Agents Wanted.

T. CARRUTHERS,

5 GILLESPIE PLACE, EDINBURGH.

Page 1 of Carruthers' Price List: List of Ordinary Clubs

The heads of the wooden clubs, except the putter, had become shorter and thicker, the modern cleek with its narrower face and shorter head had replaced the long spoon, the lofting iron or mashie had superseded the baffing spoon and a new wooden club called a brassie had been introduced. This club had a brass sole to give it protection when the ball was played off hard surfaces.

But the most noticeable change was the increased variety of iron clubs available to the golfer. Eight different irons are listed in Carruthers' 'List of Ordinary Clubs' and the 'List of Patent Clubs' includes another thirteen different types, mainly Carruthers' patent short socket irons.

When the gutta-percha ball was invented, it cost half as much as its forerunner, the feathery. It did not become damaged as easily and it had a much longer life. Because it could withstand the downward hit by an iron club, golfers began using more iron clubs with the result that by the end of the century a golfer's bag held more iron clubs than wooden clubs. These were, typically, the driving cleek, driving iron, mid-iron, mashie, putting cleek and niblick. Golf, which had hitherto been very expensive due to the high cost, in terms of damage, breakage and repair of wooden clubs and feathery balls, now became more affordable. The explosion in the numbers of golfers playing the game was largely attributed to these developments.

Carruthers' golf business appears to have recognised early the new developments in the game – in this instance the growing importance of iron clubs to the golfer. A range of iron golf clubs, enthusiastically received by the waves of new golfers, was soon provided.

The mention of Anderson of Anstruther in D. G. Robertson's letter refers to the renowned cleekmaker whose trading relationship with Carruthers began in the early 1880s and continued into the 1920s, latterly through his son Thomas Jun. who was to carry on the business from new premises at the family-owned Golfers Tryst, Braid Hills Golf Course, Edinburgh.

In addition to the foregoing, another important document, which authenticates Tom Carruthers presence in the golfing community in the early 1880s, appeared in *Edinburgh Evening Dispatch* of Saturday, 19 September 1908, under the heading 'Famous Golfers – The Irish Open Champion's Career'. The following is an extract from the article by Mr J. F. Mitchell (Midlothian Champion, 1900; member of Alliance – twice winners of Insurance Trophy; scratch player of Stewart's College, Edinburgh, St Andrews, Plewlands, Blackford, and Gillespie Clubs, Edinburgh) who won the Irish Golf Championship in 1908:

Like many golfers around Edinburgh, I first handled a club on the historic Bruntsfield Links about sixteen years ago (1892), when many of Bruntsfield's old worthies were still about, such as Mr Thomas Aitken, Mr. Smith (for many years closely associated with the Thistle Club), Mr. Ronald Ross, the late Mr. Martin McCall, Mr Alexander Stevens, and Mr. Tom Carruthers. My first club was a cleek purchased from Mr. Frank Doleman, and with it I practised at the short holes, and won there my first prize – one of Mr Carruthers' patent irons. If it be the case that I have any aptitude in the short game, I would attribute the fact to the experience I gained at these short holes in Bruntsfield.

It is quite a coincidence and a recognition of Tom Carruthers' achievements in the fields of golf and athletics that on the same page in the same edition of *Edinburgh Evening Dispatch* of Saturday, 19 September 1908, an adjacent leading article by John James Miller, author of *Scottish Sports,* entitled 'Highland Games Athletes Past and Present Champions' refers to 'Carruthers' creditable places in old time records.' These records refer to the traditional Highland Games events such as leaping, jumping and throwing rather than to sprinting events in which Carruthers specialised.

The expression 'when many of Bruntsfield's old worthies were still about … ' refers to the year 1892. It establishes that these old golfing worthies had been active in the sport of golf for many years before this date, as shown by the following additional information about the people mentioned in the article:

Mr. Thomas Aitken: Aged 51, founder member of Bruntsfield Allied Golf Club in 1856. Member of Committee representing the interests of Bruntsfield golfers when Edinburgh Town Council sought to control play on the Links in 1886. This led to the opening of the Braid Hills Golf Course in 1889.

Mr Smith: James Smith, Captain of the Edinburgh Thistle Golf Club when the Club won the Dispatch Trophy in 1890 and the *Glasgow Evening Times* Trophy in 1893.

Mr Ronald Ross: Founder member of Bruntsfield Allied Golf Club in 1856. Brother of John Ross, golf ball and club maker.

Mr Martin McCall: Partner in the firm of solicitors, Martin McCall and James Kidd Andrews. (Thomas Carruthers purchased the Golfers Tryst Clubhouse at Braid Hills Golf Course, from Martin McCall (who died in 1901) in 1899 following the sequestration of

William Frier, golf club maker). Member of Committee representing the interests of Bruntsfield golfers when Edinburgh Town Council sought to control play on the Links in 1886. This led to the opening of the Braid Hills Golf Course in 1889. Member of Bruntsfield Allied and a past Captain of Warrender Golf Club.

Mr Alexander Stevens: Founder member of Bruntsfield Allied Golf Club in 1856.

Mr Thomas Carruthers: Aged 52, member of Bruntsfield Allied, Edinburgh Thistle and Warrender Golf Clubs. After his successful athletics career, when he had the honour of being Scottish Champion, he lived adjacent to Bruntsfield Links from 1868 until his death in 1924. Built up a successful golf club-making business and patented the through-bore short socket club. Owner of the Golfers Tryst, Braid Hills Golf Course.

Tom Carruthers was invited to join the Bruntsfield Allied Golf Club in 1887 and remained a member until 1904, winning the Silver Medal in 1894. The Club was instituted in 1856 and its founder members had in common, beyond an obvious love of golf and the fact that they lived close to the Links, the manual skills of craftsmen and tradesmen. At that time it was quite common for golfers to be members of more than one club and he was also a member of the Edinburgh Thistle and Warrender Golf Clubs that were founded in 1850 and 1858 respectively. He competed in club competitions and inter-club golf matches. He also played in other amateur championships, such as the Braids' Tournament, where newspaper articles record him competing in the tournaments of 1889 and 1891. (See Chapter 9)

Overleaf: **Record of Tom Carruthers' golf match between Bruntsfield Allied and St. Andrews (Edinr.), 18 May 1889**

Golf Match

Brunstfield Allied versus St Andrews (Colms)

Edinburgh 18th May 1889.

No	Name	1st Round	2nd Round	3rd Round	Total Rounds	Result	No	Name	1st Round	2nd Round	3rd Round	Total Round	Result
1	Thos Hogg	0	1	4	5	5	1	J. Stevens	0	0	0	0	-
2	Wm North	2	5	2	9	9	2	J. Weston	0	0	0	0	-
3	Hy. Hunter	1	0	0	1	1	3	J. Pearson	0	0	0	0	-
4	Jas. Swan	1	0	3	4	2	4	J. Glass	0	2	0	2	-
5	Jas. Riddell	0	0	2	2	-	5	J. Knowles	3	0	0	3	1
6	Alex. Stevens	2	1	0	2	-	6	A. G. White	0	2	3	5	3
7	John McLeod	4	1	3	8	8	7	W. Stirling	0	0	0	0	-
8	D. Robertson	3	0	4	7	6	8	W. Artoom	0	0	1	0	-
9	Jas Addison	3	0	0	3	-	9	R. Jeffrey	0	1	2	6	3
10	J. R. Andrews	2	0	2	2	2	10	J. M Witchcham	0	4	0	0	-
11	J. Carruthers	0	0	0	0	-	11	D. Lowe	2	0	0	3	3
12	J. S. Sharpe	0	0	0	0	-	12	D. Paterson	3	2	2	7	7
		18	7	18	43	33			8	12	7	27	17
	St Andrews					17							
	Majority for Allied					16							

69

Chapter 4

A New or Improved Socket for Metal Playing Clubs

Perhaps an early suggestion of Carruthers' inventiveness was contained in Mr. D. G. Robertson's letter, dated 7 March 1891, previously quoted, when he said:

> There is nothing new at all about the round sole ... Mr. T. Carruthers, Edinburgh, has regularly sold them to golfers for some years past.

Tom Carruthers produced transitional wooden-headed clubs in the late 1880s. These clubs, sold under his Sylviac brand name, marked the transition from the long-headed wooden club to the more compact shorter wooden-headed club. No doubt this was an important influence in the development of his successful invention which is described in the Carruthers' patent specification:

> ... a metal club head which transfers the weight from the part of the club where it is not required so as to make the centre of gravity or balance not at the heel as is the case with irons at present in use but at the place where the most effective driving power can be obtained, that is to say immediately behind the ball.

Changes in the Shape of Golf Clubs

The change in design of wooden clubs from narrow, long-nosed heads with concave faces, to the shorter, deeper-faced transitional club and then to the modern bulger design was probably influenced by: (1) the use of hickory, instead of the more whippy ash, for shafts; (2) the need to limit the damage caused by the hard gutta-percha ball; (3) the more grassy fairways of the many new golf courses, where the ball really sat up.

Bruntsfield Links was an inland course, situated about three miles from the sea, and in certain summer conditions its grassy fairways could make play almost impossible when using the old narrow-headed wooden clubs. The manufacture of the transitional and then the bulger by the Carruthers' golf business for the Bruntsfield golfers in the late 1880s must have been a welcome development but more importantly it provided the catalyst for his patented design for metal clubs in 1890.

The following article, which appeared in *Golf*, 30 December 1898, under the heading 'Things Old and New, Golf Clubs', sums up succinctly the path along which Carruthers' thinking was developing in the late 1880s and which was to result in his patent number 19684, dated 3 December 1890, for 'a new or improved socket for metal playing clubs':

> The great radical change that has taken place in the shape of all golf clubs, be they wood or iron, namely the shortening of the head, is the immediate outcome of the difficulty of playing on grassy courses with long heads. The golfer himself was long headed enough to recognise that a concentration of power by shortening and thickening of the head was necessary ... The true merit of the bulger lies not in the convex face imparting straightness, but rather in the thickness and compactness of the head. The head, moreover, when 'filed up' after play becomes of greater solidity than the thinner shaped weapon of the past, and greater driving power is the result. It has been this line of compactness and solidity that all modern developments of the golf club have worked out ...

Garden G. Smith, well known in the golfing world as the editor of *Golf Illustrated*, commented along similar lines in that magazine's edition of Friday, 10 September 1909:

> The old clubs had usually very narrow faces. Those of drivers and putters, including the horn, seldom exceeded an inch in depth, and the faces of spoons were almost invariably a little less. The rubber-cored ball is more resilient than the gutty, and flattens more on the clubface. It therefore requires a deeper–faced club, but the deepening of clubfaces began before the advent of the American ball. This was probably due to the great alteration in the fairway of courses. In the old days it was the rarest exception to get a ball really sitting up, as it usually does nowadays anywhere on the fairway of the course. Usually, it was lying cupped, or, if not cupped, lying very close to the ground. The narrow-faced spoons were very much more efficacious for getting down to these close lying balls than the deeper-faced weapons that superseded

them. With them if a ball was lying very close on firm turf it is not easy to get down far enough to hit it quite cleanly with the centre of the face.

N° 19,684   A.D. 1890

Date of Application, 3rd Dec., 1890
Complete Specification Left, 6th Aug., 1891—Accepted, 12th Sept., 1891

PROVISIONAL SPECIFICATION.

A New or Improved Socket for Metal Golf Playing Clubs.

I, THOMAS CARRUTHERS of Number Five Gillespie Place Edinburgh Dairyman do hereby declare the nature of this invention to be as follows :—

To shorten the length of socket of metal golf playing clubs and by running socket down through and out at heel of metal golf playing clubs so having socket open at both ends.

Dated, at Edinburgh, the First day of December 1890.

THOMAS CARRUTHERS,
5, Gillespie Place, Edinburgh, Dairyman.

Provisional Specification submitted to the Patent Office on 1 December 1890 for a New or Improved Socket for Metal Golf Playing Clubs

Patent Application and Acceptance of Provisional Specification

On 1 December 1890 Thomas Carruthers submitted a patent application, along with a provisional specification for '*A New or Improved Socket for Metal Golf Playing Clubs*' to the Patent Office, 25 Southampton Buildings, Chancery Lane, London WC2.

The origins of patents for inventions are obscure and no one country can claim to have been the first in the field with a patent system. However, Britain does have the longest continuous patent tradition in the world.

The Government grants a patent for an invention to the inventor, giving the inventor the right for a limited period to stop others from making, using or selling the invention without the permission of the inventor. When a patent is granted the invention becomes the property of the inventor which, like any other form of property or business asset, can be bought, sold, rented or hired. A patent brings the right to take legal action against others who might be infringing the invention and to claim damages. The mere existence of a patent may be enough to deter a potential infringer.

The Patent Office, on receipt of the Carruthers' application, sent a letter of acceptance of the provisional specification, dated 3 December 1890:

> In conformity with the provisions of the Patents, &c., Act, 1883, I hereby give you notice of the acceptance of your Application for 'A New or Improved Socket for Metal Golf Playing Clubs.'

This letter set out the procedure to be followed if the inventor wished to secure letters patent:

> A Complete Specification must be left at the Patent Office within 9 months of the date of application, if a patent is desired.
> This Complete Specification must be prepared upon Form C, stamped £3, must bear the number and date of the application, and must end with a distinct statement of the invention claimed.
> If the Complete Specification is not left at the Patent Office within the prescribed 9 months, an extension of time for 1 month more may be applied for upon Form U, stamped £2.
> At the end of 10 months, if no Complete Specification has been filed, the application will be regarded as abandoned.
> Forms C and U may be purchased in London at the Inland Revenue Office, Royal Courts of Justice (Room No. 6), or may be obtained at a few days' notice through any Money Order Office in the United Kingdom, upon prepayment of the value of the stamp.

During the time from Patent Office notification of acceptance of the provisional application to the submission of the complete specification, should it be accepted by the Patent Office, or abandoned by the applicant, the applicant was free to produce, advertise and sell his product in the knowledge that his invention was protected from infringement under patent law.

Indeed, Carruthers quickly proceeded with a great deal of confidence and upon receiving acceptance of the provisional specification from the Patent Office, he placed a production order with his supplier of metal club heads, the respected cleekmaker, James Anderson of Anstruther, whose advertisements proclaimed himself as 'the first and best maker of hand-forged golf cleeks … ' Anderson had been Carruthers' iron club head supplier since he had begun selling golf clubs from about 1878.

James Anderson despatched the first production batch of the new design to Tom Carruthers at 5 Gillespie Place, in early February 1891, i.e., within three months of the receipt of the Patent Office's letter of acceptance of the provisional application. On receiving the club heads he took immediate steps to make the shafts and grips and fix them to the new club heads and then to place the new iron club with respected and well-known golf critics to test their reaction to what was to become one of the most successful, best selling and widely advertised golf club inventions of its age. His first advertisement appeared in *Golf*, 13 March 1891:

CARRUTHERS' PATENT SOCKET IRONS.
Perfect Balance, 7s. each. Only to be had from the
Patentee, T. CARRUTHERS, 5 Gillespie Place, Edinburgh.
For description of this Cleek, see GOLF, Feb. 27th.

Acceptance of Complete Specification by the Patent Office

The complete specification was submitted to the Patent Office on his behalf by Johnsons, patent agents, 115 St Vincent Street, Glasgow, on 5 August 1891 and was accepted by the Patent Office on 12 September 1891. The Royal Letters Patent headed 'VICTORIA, BY THE GRACE OF GOD, OF the United Kingdom of Great Britain and Ireland, Queen, Defender of the Faith:' along with the Royal Coat of Arms and bearing the seal of the Patent Office (see Appendix 3) was issued bearing the sentence 'IN WITNESS whereof we have caused these our letters to be made patent this *third day of December one thousand eight hundred and ninety* and to be sealed as of the third day of December one thousand eight hundred and ninety.'

The origins of Johnsons of 115 St Vincent Street, Glasgow, Tom Carruthers' patent agent, date back to 1846 when William Johnson, a civil engineer and mechanical engineer, established a practice in Scotland. By 1850 he practised in both Glasgow and Edinburgh. He was also the proprietor and editor of *The Practical Mechanics Journal* which started publication in 1848. Before that he edited *Practical Mechanic and Engineers Magazine*. In 1850 John Henry Johnson, a brother of William Johnson, who was then a solicitor, went into partnership with William Johnson and had offices in London, Glasgow and Edinburgh. John Henry Johnson ran the London office. He was author of the *Patentees Manual* and was engaged as a solicitor in some of the most important patent cases during the period 1860–1900.

N° 19,684   A.D. 1890

Date of Application, 3rd Dec., 1890
Complete Specification Left, 6th Aug., 1891—Accepted, 12th Sept., 1891

PROVISIONAL SPECIFICATION.

A New or Improved Socket for Metal Golf Playing Clubs.

I, THOMAS CARRUTHERS of Number Five Gillespie Place Edinburgh Dairyman do hereby declare the nature of this invention to be as follows :—

To shorten the length of socket of metal golf playing clubs and by running socket down through and out at heel of metal golf playing clubs so having socket
5 open at both ends.

Dated, at Edinburgh, the First day of December 1890.

THOMAS CARRUTHERS,
5, Gillespie Place, Edinburgh, Dairyman.

COMPLETE SPECIFICATION.

10   ### A New or Improved Socket for Metal Golf Playing Clubs.

I, THOMAS CARRUTHERS of 5 Gillespie Place, Edinburgh, in the County of Midlothian, North Britain, Merchant, do hereby declare the nature of this invention and in what manner the same is to be performed, to be particularly described and ascertained in and by the following statement :—

15   This invention which relates to a new or improved socket for metal golf playing clubs consists in shortening the length of the iron socket or neck and running the end of the wooden shaft right through the socket and out at the heel of the socket so that the socket is open at both ends, the object of the said arrangement being that the weight is taken from the part of the club where it is not required so as to make
20   the centre of gravity or balance not at the heel as is the case with irons at present in use, but where the most effective driving power can be obtained, that is to say immediately behind the ball.

In the accompanying drawings
Figure 1 shews the general appearance of the shortened iron socket.
25   Figure 2 is a section of the socket and
Figure 3 shews the end of the shaft appearing out through the heel of the socket.

In ordinary cases the socket or neck may be about 2 inches shorter than that of the ordinary iron and thus the shaft may be two inches longer. Owing to the
30   socket being open at both ends a better fitting shaft is obtained. The shaft has also a better grasp of the head which gives the player a greater command of the implement. Also the increased length of the shaft gives it greater leverage, and brings the "spring" into the proper place.

Having now particularly described and ascertained the nature of my said inven-
35   tion and in what manner the same is to be performed I declare that what I claim is.—

In golf playing clubs shortening the length of the iron socket or neck and making the socket open at both ends substantially as and for the purposes hereinbefore described.

40   Dated this 5th day of August 1891.

JOHNSONS,
115, St. Vincent Street, Glasgow, Applicant's Agents.

London : Printed for Her Majesty's Stationery Office, by Darling & Son, Ltd.—1891.

[Price 6d.]

Complete Specification submitted to the Patent Office, 5 August 1891, for a New or Improved Socket for Metal Golf Playing Clubs

J. H. Johnson became a patent agent as well as a solicitor, and was a founding member of the Institute of Patent Agents, and its first president. His memoir describes him as having 'great business ability, especially in the direction of organisation'.

Johnsons, who had extremely well-qualified and able practitioners at its helm, may have provided Tom Carruthers with sound practical mechanical engineering advice in the development period of his short socket invention and may also have had discussions with James Anderson in the development of the tools needed to turn out the short socket metal heads from his forges. The short through socket was new and required a departure from the normal production method used in connection with the forging of the traditional socket.

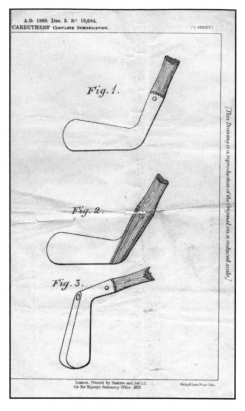

Drawings submitted to the Patent Office with Complete Specification on 5 August 1891

Published Reviews of the Patent Socket Iron Club

Two early reviews of Carruthers' patent socket cleek appeared in *Golf*. The first was written by the Reverend Dr J. G. McPherson, born in St Andrews in 1843. He was a golf historian and frequent contributor to *Golf*. A formidable golfer, one of the most talented amateurs, he had at one time held the amateur record. He retired early from playing the game to return to his ministerial vocation but continued to contribute to golf through his literary talents, proclaiming Allan Robertson as the greatest of all golfers. He wrote *Golf and Golfers – Past and Present* in 1891 and numerous golf articles. Amongst his writings was an article in 1902 for *Golf Illustrated* recounting the life story of the Rev Dr Paterson in which he declared him the inventor of the gutta-percha ball. McPherson had a long association with the Alyth

Golf Club in Perthshire and was elected its first Captain in 1894. The following appeared on 27 February 1891:

ANOTHER NEW CLEEK

Mr. Thomas Carruthers, 5, Gillespie Place, Edinburgh, has sent me a specimen of his Patent Socket Cleek. I have tried it for driving, wrist shots, and putting, and I am very favourably impressed with its superior merits. I am going to play at Blairgowrie soon, and shall tell the readers of this Journal what I think of it after a day's play.

Meanwhile let me describe it. The socket, which is the patent part, is two inches shorter than that of the ordinary cleek, and the shaft is a little longer than my regular driving cleek. That the shaft may be firmly attached, it is made to pass right down to the heel, where the socket has an opening. After being well driven in, the projecting part is cut off and filed flush with the iron. One of the defects in the old style is the uncertainty that the shaft exactly fits the socket, for the shaft-maker did not know the cleekmaker's work. Here, however, the shaft-maker drives the shaft right through, making all perfectly tight.

Besides, when the socket is short and thin and tubular, the weight of the cleek-head is less in the heel and more in the blade. If an unshafted cleek of the old make be balanced, you will find that it will rest when leaning over a stick which passes through between the socket and the blade. But in this case the metal is so adjusted that the cleek-head balances on a stick, right under where the ball should be struck, in the centre of the blade. In striking the ball with the patent cleek, therefore, the greatest certainty is available, the centre of gravity of the head being on the same spot as in the case of a wooden driver by the adjusting of the lead. In the old cleek the centre of gravity of the head – on the line of balancing – is at the heel, whereas here it is just behind the best striking-place of the ball. In this way greater driving power and more certain direction are secured. For there need be no heeling – a capital exception in the game.

I am not so sure about the advantage of a longer shaft. In the specimen sent to me there seems to be too much spring – certainly for my play; but many may prefer this for long cleek driving. A brassie would not be required, for this weapon will drive as far from any position. The straightness of the driving, especially in windy weather, is a great boon, which seems to be counted on with this cleek.

Mr. Anderson of Anstruther makes a very neat cleek, and I am glad to see that Mr. Carruthers sticks to the time-honoured leather grip. Irons are made in the same style; but I have not seen one.

Golf
27th February, 1891
J. G. McPherson

Gregor Macgregor, a well-known scratch golfer of distinction, wrote the second early commentary. He was a member, former captain and secretary, of the Edinburgh Burgess Golfing Society and its gold medallist in five separate years. He was also a member of other East Lothian golf clubs and distinguished himself in them all. He reached the last eight of the British Amateur Championship in 1887 at Hoylake when he lost to Horace Hutchinson, who went on to defeat Mr John Ball in the final to win the championship. He was also a talented craftsman who made all his own clubs.

Still another tribute to the popularity of the Royal Game is announced in the invention of the patent socket for iron clubs by Mr. T. Carruthers, Edinburgh, another amateur who has entered the lists with the professionals in the contest for the improvement of the implements of the noble game. Without in any way derogating from the credit due to previous inventors, I am free to say that I have not come across any invention so meritorious in my own judgment as this one. It would not be desirable that all golfers should be of the same taste with respect to the clubs they use, and I have no doubt many will prefer one or other of the cleeks now in use to Carruthers' cleek, but in the language of the great Golf magician, 'commend me' to the latter. The patent socket from which the various advantages flow is equally applicable to all iron clubs; but I shall treat only of the cleek, as it is in that club that the merits of the invention are most apparent, and I think also real.

For years back I have been in the habit of selecting my cleek-heads, and altering them myself to suit my fancy. There is great pleasure to be derived from operations of this sort by golfers. My first point was to secure superabundance of metal to stand reduction. My second was to select the shortest neck, and I preferred also a short blade, and this involved thickness of blade, which I regarded as of first-rate importance. Having laid aside after careful weighing a few heads that fulfilled these conditions, I then introduced my pencil into the socket and selected the one which had the tube reaching down furthest towards the sole, or in other words that had the longest hollow in the neck.

If the 'set' was not to my taste, I put the head into the fire, and when red hot placed it in a vice with cheeks adjusted, gave it a twist with an iron bar, fitted into the socket, which made it flat or upright, straight faced or spooned, according to the character I wished to give it for driving, pitching or putting. This is a matter of no difficulty to one having a mechanical turn. The cleek being now firmly shafted, I filed down the shell of the socket till it was little more than sufficient to hold the wooden shaft, in order to concentrate the weight as near as possible at the point of contact between the blade and ball. Every golfer knows that for effective driving this is of the greatest importance. It constitutes the chief merit of Park and Forrester's patents. I was in the habit of treating my cleeks thus before these patents were obtained, and was satisfied of the advantages gained.

The points desired were:

1. To get the greatest length of wood in a cleek-shaft of given length, thus securing the maximum of elasticity and power.

2. To get the requisite weight immediately behind, or as near as possible to, the ball which secured the most effective energy at the proper point.

3. To get a shorter blade so as to minimise the danger of 'wobbling' when the stroke is being delivered, and to present less surface to the resisting atmosphere, grass, or sand.

4. To get a broader sole, less liable to cut the turf.

Each of these advantages in itself was trifling, but the cumulative effect was considerable. So much, however, did I reduce the iron in the socket that I had to use the sand-paper sparingly; and in the event of the shaft being broken it was a delicate operation to fit in another, from the danger of splitting the socket. The life of my cleek was thus necessarily short.

Now all the advantages I was seeking and obtaining on a modest scale are secured by Mr. Carruthers most happily and in abundance.

In the patent two inches are taken off the socket. The tube is carried down the neck and out at the sole. The metal thus taken from the socket is transferred to the blade, and the result is two inches longer of the wooden shaft, and the weight being equal, the centre of gravity is transferred from the angle in the old to near the centre of the blade in the new. The sole is a good deal broader, and minimises the agricultural proclivities of this most effective weapon, and the strength is fully kept up, there being as much wood in the new as in the old socket.

I may mention that I have no interest in the patent or patentee, but having quickly recognised the merits of the invention from my own experience, I willingly give my brother golfers my views on them.

Gregor Macgregor.
Golf
27th February 1891

Although the newly-patented club had clearly impressed the first reviewers a cautionary letter was sent by 'An Old Golfer' to the Editor of *Golf*, dated 14 March 1891, and published on 20 March. He was clearly an advocate of the George Forrester school, one of the most innovative club makers of the 1890s, but the flow of approval for the new invention continued and a further favourable review appeared in the magazine a couple of months later in the form of a letter from R. J. B. T. dated 22 May 1891, and published on 29 May 1891. This clear expression of support for 'Carruthers' New Patent Cleek' caught the mood of the golfing public which was to establish it as 'one of the soundest and most serviceable of permanent improvements in the game'. (*Golf* 1892) Both letters are reproduced below:

THE CARRUTHERS' CLEEK

To the Editor of *Golf*
Sir,
I have read with interest the letters of Mr. M'Pherson and Mr. Gregor Macgregor on the 'patent golf cleeks.' While not possessing the mechanical ingenuity of my friend, Mr. Macgregor, I have, like him, seen the evil of the unnecessary weight of iron in the hose, and have tried to effect a remedy. I have made suggestions to makers, as to ways of altering this, without infringing on Mr. Carruthers' patent, and so do away with an objection to that gentleman's cleek, viz., exposing the end of the shaft to the weather.

I think the shortening of the hose to the extent of Mr. Carruthers' cleek takes away its graceful appearance, giving it much the appearance of a garden hoe. Were Mr. Forrester, the inventor of the mashie, and the centre balance-cleek and iron, to reduce the length of the hose of his patent cleek by an inch or less, and make it thin in the style described by Mr. Macgregor, adding the metal thus saved to the blade of his cleek, he would produce a 'driving cleek' which could not be excelled, and would keep him in first place in the rank of inventors. As it is, a player, armed with one of Forrester's driving cleeks, an iron and a concentrated mashie, for bunkers and approach shots, may safely face the most difficult course, with entire confidence in his success.

From experience, and from the known opinions of golfers of the highest eminence, I am inclined to advise brother golfers to try a 'Forrester centre-balance'; but after all, one may go back to an anecdote related in your own columns and say, in the caddie's words, 'There's no muckle wrang wi' that end o' the club.

I am, Sir,
AN OLD GOLFER.
Edinburgh, March 14th 1892.

Note: Forrester's centre-balanced cleek had a rounded back with the weight concentrated above, rather than in the true centre of the blade, causing the ball to fly very low.

Golf
20th March 1891

CARRUTHERS' PATENT CLEEK

To the Editor of Golf
Sir,
Having heard considerable discussion recently upon Carruthers' New Patent Cleek, and being unable to give my own opinion, not having seen the Patent, I determined to do so, and for that purpose called upon the inventor. I am not at any time in favour of new inventions in the shape of clubs, because, with all the supposed improvements, the result of one's play is not in keeping with them. In truth, were all the intended benefits derived from every new patent club, I should not like to predict what the game would ultimately become. In course of conversation with Mr. Carruthers I was fingering away with some of his cleek heads, and found them so well balanced that they stood upon a smooth table in playing position without support. The very moment I saw his driving cleek I could see at a glance what its capabilities were, provided that the other end was all right. There are all kinds of clubs, driving cleeks, putting cleeks, lofting irons, heavy irons, and niblicks; and his latest is a neat little cleek also of perfect balance, and so small that two of the heads go easily into the watch-pocket. Mr. Carruthers is also very careful with the handles and has them all made of fine tough white hickory, with the spring where it ought to be. But the great treat is to try one – I mean as a driving cleek. There is, I am certain, a surprise awaiting anyone who has yet to try it; for in the

flight of the ball, just at the moment when you are expecting it to begin to fall, it begins to rise as if while in the air receiving some fresh impetus. The ball leaves the cleek with a pleasant feeling to the hands, making little noise, and if the strokes are played easily (which they must be on account of the extra spring) the ball travels off as if played from a driver. With apologies for taking up so much of your valuable space.

I am, Sir, &c.,
R. J. B. T.
Edinburgh, May 22nd, 1891.

Golf
29 May 1891

Mr R. J. B. Tait ('R.J.B.T.'), who died in 1893, was a noted Aberlady golfer who had been the crack local player on Luffness green, his love and excellence in the game being an inheritance of the third and fourth generations. According to the Reverend John Kerr in his book, *The Golf Book of East Lothian,* he was also a writer who had an enormous fund of golfing and other local historical lore. For some years, he was proprietor and occupier of the old Aberlady Inn, the name of which he changed to the Golf Hotel. His father was joint-owner, with Mr John Croall of Edinburgh, of the stagecoach that ran between North Berwick and Edinburgh. (When the Bruntsfield and East Lothian clubs met at Gullane in June 1863, they dined at the Golf Tavern and were driven away to Edinburgh in a 'coach and four'. Gullane was 'by no means the most accessible of greens, and it is not reached without some little trouble' wrote *The Scotsman* newspaper almost thirty years later. A new rail branch line to Aberlady and Gullane was eventually opened in 1898 but its extension to North Berwick remained at the planning stage.)

Professor P. G. Tait

Another well-known family who shared the same Tait name with equally strong connections to golf and Luffness around the same time, but probably was not related, was headed by Professor P. G. Tait, professor of physics at Edinburgh University from 1860–1901. He established the importance of spin in dictating the flight of golf balls, and wrote a series of papers on the physics of golf in the period 1887–1896. In his younger days the idea that spin could bring benefits, especially in relation to the lifting force in the flight of the ball, was considered fanciful but after the completion of his studies he said: 'I understand it now, too late by 35 years'. He also wrote:

> I have been very, perhaps even unnecessarily, cautious in leading up to this conclusion – I have the vivid recollection of the 'warm' reception which my heresies met with – from almost all good players to whom I mentioned them. The general feeling seems to be one in which incredibility was altogether overpowered by disgust.

When Willie Park Jun. applied for a patent on 14 December 1889 for his new lofter design, which was to become the first ever patent for an iron golf club when the complete specification was accepted on 25 January 1890, he and his patent agent, W. R. M. Thomson of 96 Buchanan Street, Glasgow, used Professor Tait's important findings to support his application:

> This innovation has reference to and comprises certain improvements in the construction of the head or blade of golf clubs and has for its object the striking of the lower part of the ball under its centre thereby causing the ball to revolve or spin in a backward direction while being propelled forward by the stroke of the club which has the effect of stopping the ball more suddenly when it falls on the ground and counteracts the tendency of the ball to roll forward on alighting.

Professor Tait's third son, F. G. Tait, who worked with his father in developing his conclusions on backspin, was British Amateur Champion in 1896 and 1898, runner up in 1899 and tied for third in the Open in 1896 and 1897. It was a great tragedy that, when serving with the Scottish Black Watch Regiment during the Boer War, he was killed by a sniper's bullet at only thirty years of age. A contemporary account, which appeared in *The Scotsman's* edition of 30 April 1900, gives a moving description of the loss felt by his fellow members at New Luffness:

> The spring meeting of this popular club was held over New Luffness course on Saturday and brought out an unusually large muster of members. The principal interest centred in the scratch competition for the Leconfield gold medal, which was won for the first time in 1895 by the late Mr. F. G. Tait.
> After luncheon an interesting function took place in the clubhouse when a beautiful platinotype of the late Mr. F. G. Tait,

presented to the club by Mr. John Kerr, Gilmerton, Unionist candidate for East Lothian, was unveiled by Lady Mary Hope in presence of Mr. M. W. Hope of Luffness, Master Hope younger of Luffness, and a large company of members together with a few ladies. The portrait is a bust of the late Mr. Tait in uniform as an officer of the Black Watch, and the enlargement (which is on a 25 inch plate from a photo by Mr. Marshall Wane) was entrusted to Mr. W. Crooke, Princes Street, Edinburgh, who had been remarkably successful in producing a most pleasing portrait of the celebrated golfer. Mr. Kerr, in asking Lady Mary Hope to unveil the portrait said he was deeply sensitive of the honour the club had conferred on him in allowing him to present a portrait of the distinguished golfer whose career had been brought to so early and glorious close in South Africa. Mr. Tait, he said, was a frequent player over New Luffness being one of the original members of the club, and in mourning his loss, they regarded him, not only as the most outstanding Scottish golfer, but also as a prince of good fellows. Lady Mary Hope, in unveiling the portrait, said – before unveiling Mr. Tait's picture I must say a few words about the young hero we have met together to honour, who has so often played on these links, and taken part in our competitions. We were all proud of him, and deeply we mourn his loss. The same qualities that made him one of the finest golf players in the world, and that endeared him to all his friends showed themselves in another field, when he went to fight in South Africa. Whatever he did, he did with all his might and this was the secret of his success. Everyone liked him; everyone had a good word for him. Golfers may come and go, but we shall never see a finer golfer, a better soldier, or a kinder friend than Freddy Tait. I am much gratified at being asked to unveil this picture, which I believe is considered a very good likeness. Her ladyship then unveiled the portrait. Mr. Armour accepted the portrait on behalf of the club, and said they were much indebted to Mr. Kerr for his gift. On the motion of Mr. Richard Clark, a hearty vote of thanks was accorded to Lady Mary Hope, which was acknowledged by Mr. Hope of Luffness who said no-one had the welfare of the club more at heart than Lady Mary.

Improvements in Play 1890–1900

In 1903 Harold Hilton, the legendary amateur golfer from Hoylake and prolific writer who became editor of *Golf Illustrated*, wrote an article, which appeared in *Outing* magazine, on why the standard of golf play had improved so much from about 1890 or 1891. He ascribed this to the introduction of the bulger and the better-balanced, shorter-headed iron clubs. The following is an extract from his article:

> Between the years 1880 and 1890 there was little difference in the winning scores in big competitions. They were somewhat on a par with those of the 'sixties and 'seventies, when the condition of the links was nothing like so good. But from 1890 the play of the game was improved by leaps and bounds; that unerring guide, statistics, proves it, and cannot be gainsaid. It may be that the links nowadays are kept in much better order, but, on the other hand, the material from which the implements are made is not superior; the present great demand precludes that; but I candidly think that more than a fair proportion of the improvement is due to the alteration in the shape of wooden clubs, which, in the hands of an expert, allows hard hitting with accuracy; which, in addition, allows balls to be played successfully out of lies that were impossible with the old fashioned clubs.
>
> Again, we find a similar state of affairs in connection with iron implements. I can remember the time when an iron made by Wilson, of St. Andrews, was considered a 'pearl beyond price'. Nowadays they may be said to represent 'old iron'. It has been a most rapid change, as Wilson irons were much esteemed only seven or eight years ago; but as with the wooden clubs, it was generally found that a shorter head was more serviceable; not only did it drive farther, but it was an implement with which it was easier to play from indifferent or heavy lies, as when lying in such a position it is necessary to hit the ball, not swing at it; and the old fashioned iron, long-headed and comparatively cumbersome, was a difficult weapon to wield in this fashion. So the iron club of the 'seventies and the 'eighties had to give way to the modern invention.

According to Peter Georgiady, in his book, *Collecting Antique Golf Clubs,* virtually every manufacturer made club heads on the Carruthers' principle in the ensuing two decades. He also includes the Carruthers' patent amongst the ten most important patents of the nineteenth century, all of which were registered in the 1890s – possibly the single most influential decade of club design.

Chapter 5

The Carruthers' Patent

T he duration of the period of patent protection in 1890 was fourteen years and the continuance of the patent was conditional on the payment of annual renewal fees, which in total over the fourteen-year period amounted to £150 (approximately £10,000 in today's value). This meant that the cost of registering the patent, the cost of renewing the patent each year, the fees for the patent agents' services and the development and marketing costs in bringing the invention to the market represented a considerable investment.

Thomas Carruthers employed a London patent agent, in addition to Johnsons of 115 St Vincent Street, Glasgow, named F. W. Golby of 36 Chancery Lane, London WC, whose office was situated close to the Patent Office in Chancery Lane. This firm, in addition to other services, renewed the Carruthers' patent each year whereupon the Patent Office issued a Certificate of Payment or Renewal that was stamped with the amount of the payment and with the seals of the Patent Office and F. W. Golby, Carruthers' London patent agent. An example of one of the annual renewal certificates is shown here to the right.

Annual Certificate of Payment or Renewal for Patent No. 19684, required to maintain the inventor's rights under Patent Law

Applications for Patent Protection

During the 1890s the momentum to register patents gathered pace as inventors rushed to protect their new designs under patent law. This increase, not unnaturally, was proportionate to the steep rise in the popularity of the game of golf witnessed by the many new golf courses being laid out. New players were coming into the sport, implements in the form of golf clubs and golf balls were more easily available and there were more club makers, ball makers and golf magazines. By the end of the century a vast industry had developed around the game of golf.

The Carruthers' patent dated 3 December 1890 was one of the early golf club patents. It was the fourth invention for an iron club to be patented and the sixth for a golf club if one excludes inventions that included 'catch-all' applications. The first for an iron club was Willie Park Jun.'s concave face lofter, patented on 23 March 1889. The only invention specifically for a golf club patented before Park's lofter was Thomas Johnston's vulcanite wood in 1876. Although George Forrester took out a British design registration for his 'Concentrated' irons in 1889, it was never patented.

The original patent document (see Appendix 3), bearing the red seal of the Patent Office in Chancery Lane, London, is still in existence along with the documents of Provisional and Complete Specifications and Certificates of Renewal. This Carruthers' patent document may be the oldest surviving original golf club patent document in existence.

The Carruthers' business, throughout the fourteen years of the patent's protection period, provided by patent law at that time, maintained a firm control over the supply of the product of his invention. Carruthers, at 5 Gillespie Place, Edinburgh, granted manufacturing rights for his metal club heads to James Anderson of Anstruther, probably on an exclusive supply basis.

Infringement

During the period 1890–1904, the protection period, only one case of patent infringement is definitely known to have occurred. This concerned Thomas P. Waggott, an innovative club maker who made clubs in Musselburgh and had a shop in Aberlady between 1893 and 1915. He was a fine golfer who himself patented several designs. In an interesting occurrence, he voluntarily withdrew from sale a model cleek he had invented with a drilled hosel because he found after the fact that it might possibly infringe the earlier Carruthers' patent.

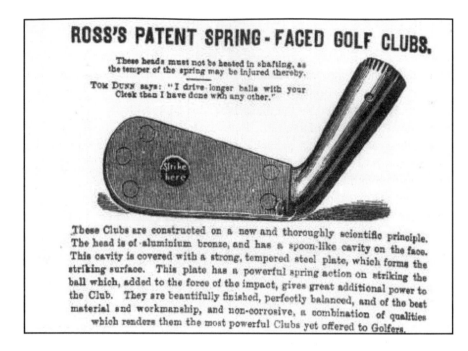

ROSS'S PATENT SPRING-FACED GOLF CLUBS,

These heads must not be heated in shafting, as the temper of the spring may be injured thereby.

Tom Dunn says: "I drive longer balls with your Cleek than I have done with any other."

These Clubs are constructed on a new and thoroughly scientific principle. The head is of aluminium bronze, and has a spoon-like cavity on the face. This cavity is covered with a strong, tempered steel plate, which forms the striking surface. This plate has a powerful spring action on striking the ball which, added to the force of the impact, gives great additional power to the Club. They are beautifully finished, perfectly balanced, and of the best material and workmanship, and non-corrosive, a combination of qualities which renders them the most powerful Clubs yet offered to Golfers.

The Golfing Annual 1895/1896: Ross's Patent Spring-Faced Golf Club

Golfing Annual of 1895–1896 displayed an advertisement for Ross's Patent Spring-Faced Golf Club, which is shown above. The head was made of aluminium bronze with a spoon-like cavity covered with a tempered steel plate and secured by five circular rivets. What is interesting, however, is that it had a short socket with what appears to be a depiction of the shaft extending right through to the sole of the club and similar to the Carruthers' patent. This particular version of Ross's club was seemingly abandoned for he later developed a revised club in 1896 with a longer socket without the through-bore design. In this later design the plate was held in place by only three rivets.

Another possible infringement concerned the Carruthers' trademark 'Perfect Balance' which he used continually in his advertisements from 1891 to 1906. This concerned the 'Maidenhead' putter patented by Alex R. Simpson, under a British registration dated 10 March 1900. The putter had an unusual square socket with 'no bend in the socket to take the eye off the ball'. The blade was formed with a socket at one side that projected from its face so that it lay entirely in front of the blade. The socket was square and short with the shaft extending completely through it. Simpson's advertisement, shown overleaf alongside a Carruthers' advertisement, (both of which appeared in *Golfing* on 27 December 1900) also used the same Perfect Balance term in its description. Simpson dropped the term in future advertisements, confining his description to 'the shortest socket club made' and 'no ugly crook'. Despite its initial popularity, the Maidenhead putter was only manufactured for a very short time.

There were a number of patented golf club inventions manufactured and sold during the last decade of the nineteenth century, to which reference is made in golf periodicals, that bore some similarity to the Carruthers' short socket invention – at a time when golf developments and new inventions were racing on to the market to an eager public. Although the Carruthers' patent was not infringed, other than as stated above, at least one patented invention must have come very close to the mark.

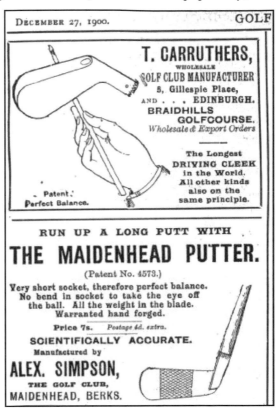

Golfing, **27 December 1900: advertisements for Carruthers' clubs and Alex Simpson's Maidenhead Putter, Patent No. 4579**

Robert Anderson's Socket Invention for Wooden Clubs

Nobody would contest the validity of Robert Anderson's patent, whose socket invention was an important advance in wooden club design, but the following account shows just how closely the principles of his invention related to the Carruthers' patent.

When Robert Anderson of Princes Street, Edinburgh, patented his new invention of a socket-head wood with the shaft running straight down into the head in 1891, a review appeared in the 19 February 1892 issue of *Golf*. In describing the merits of the new wooden-headed golf club design direct comparison was made to the Carruthers' socket for metal playing clubs and the application of the same principle to wooden-headed golf clubs:

THE 'ANDERSON' GOLF CLUB

Messrs. R. Anderson and Sons, fishing-rod and golf-club makers, 67 Princes Street, Edinburgh, have recently brought out a new golf club, which will undoubtedly rank with the bulger, the Carruthers', and Forrester cleeks, and the Park lofting-iron, as one of the soundest and most serviceable of permanent improvements in the game. The firm has long been known as one of the best makers of fishing rods and gear, and a few years ago we believe that it gained a prize medal at one of the Exhibitions for the superior excellence and finish of its golf clubs.

The improvement in the club under notice consists, speaking briefly, in the application of the principle of the Carruthers' socket to wooden clubs. The neck of the wooden club is considerably shortened as compared with the older pattern of club; and the weight of wood, instead of being distributed up the shaft of the club by means of an elongated neck, is concentrated more in a line with that portion of the club which gives the impact to the ball. Hence in the 'Anderson' club the neck towards the heel of the club is a trifle thicker, but not so thick as to destroy the symmetry of the club, or to render it either unsightly or badly balanced. This wooden neck is hollowed out right through to the sole, and the shaft, instead of being glued to the head by means of an outside splice is fixed in the interior of the socket. The shaft, therefore, runs right through the neck, and appears, like the Carruthers' cleek, with the shaft protruding from the sole of the club. It is at once obvious that a much juster distribution of the weight of the head is obtained in the hands of the player, while the shaft by the security of its fixing in the socket renders the club at once better balanced and less liable to fracture from a badly-driven ball off the heel. But the curtailment of several inches of useless wood at the tapering neck of the club and its utilisation as part of the driving force of the club is not the only advantage of the 'Anderson' club. The six inches of 'whipping' on the splicing of the club is rendered unnecessary, and a small tie of an inch and a half at the top of the join is enough both for security and for preventing oil and wet from loosening the glue. Hence the risk of having loose play club-heads owing to the failure of the glue at the unprotected half-inch at the bottom of the present form of club is hereby entirely obviated. We think, however, that both Messrs. Anderson and Mr. Carruthers ought to rub a little pitch, creosote, or some other protective compound on the sole end of the shaft, so as to guard to the utmost extent against wet entering a chink and causing rot. We do not say that the safeguard is absolutely necessary, but it is merely a precautionary hint thrown out for consideration, and in order to disarm the hostility of critics who might be disposed to urge this lack of protection as a disadvantage to the use of both forms of clubs.

The advantages claimed for the 'Anderson' club are three – strength, balance, driving power. Owing to the manner in which the head is fixed it is claimed by the patentees that the neck is unbreakable; by the abolition of the splicing above referred to, that the balance is improved; and by adopting the interior socket that a better spring is imparted to the lower end of the shaft in driving the ball. We have recently subjected two clubs – a straight-faced driver and a bulger – to a thorough test, and we frankly admit that the claims just enumerated are not pitched a bit too high. We did not, of course, attempt to break the neck of the club by driving balls off the heel; the clubs are too handsome and valuable for an experiment so rash, but one has only to look carefully at the bulldog neck to see that strength and durability are, so to speak, enshrined therein. We cheerfully bear testimony, however, to the balance of the club. In the present form of driver the spring in driving a ball is obtained on the twelve inches of the shaft just above the splicing; below that the club is, of course, as rigid as an oaken staff. The 'Anderson' club reverses this order of things, and the inventors have undoubtedly been right in their conception as to the portion of the shaft, which was most serviceable in lending carry and distance to the drive. In this club the spring is obtained quite close to the short neck, and not so near the player's hands as at present. The change in the locality of the spring gives the player greater control over the direction of the ball, and certainly a greater initial velocity and carry. This was tested in a fairly strong head wind, and also with the wind blowing across the line of flight of the ball. The driving power was increased certainly to the extent of ten or a dozen yards carry ... (*Golf*, 19 February 1892)

Anderson's patent of 1891, unlike the Carruthers' patent for short socket iron clubs, was slow to be accepted and the use of the design principle in golf club manufacture did not become common until after the turn of the century, following the catalyst of later parallel patented designs by Charles Spinks and George Forrester. Anderson did not benefit financially from his invention, but along with the Carruthers' patent granted in 1890, it proved to be one of the landmark improvements in the development of golf clubs.

The common principles of the two patents remain in use by golf club manufacturers to the present day, the earlier relating to iron clubs and the later to wooden clubs:

- Shortened socket with no loss of length of shaft
- Redistribution of weight to the impact area
- Better balanced club
- Greater leverage and spring
- Improved fitting

It does seem remarkable that the Carruthers' patent was registered on 3 December 1890 and that the Robert Anderson patent was registered only three months later on 3 March 1891. Not only did the patents have a very short period of time between their registration dates but Carruthers and Anderson also used the same patent agent – Johnsons, 115 St Vincent Street, Glasgow.

It is interesting to note that Robert Anderson described himself as 'Fishing Tackle Manufacturer' of 67 Princes Street, Edinburgh, Scotland, on his patent application and not as a golf manufacturer. In a similar vein Tom Carruthers described himself as 'Dairyman' when he registered his provisional specification. Significantly, when he registered the complete specification nine months later, he described himself as 'Merchant'.

The omission of the words 'golf club manufacturer' no doubt reflects the fact that, at this time, the two patentees' main trade was as stated in the registration documents and that their golf businesses were smaller, but growing, activites. In Carruthers' case the change to describing himself as 'Merchant' reflected the rapidly changing contribution that his golf business was making to his overall business interests. One month later he is described as 'Golf club-maker' in the 11 September 1891 issue of *Golf* in their announcement that 'Mr. T. Carruthers, Golf club-maker, Edinburgh, has just laid out a Golf course for Mr. Alfred Rothschild at Tring.' Although a celebrity in his running days, he continued to describe himself as a 'working tailor' on official documents even when his running exploits became a full time occupation.

Another interesting observation is Carruthers' address, recorded as 5 Gillespie Place, Edinburgh, in the County of Midlothian, North Britain. The term 'North Britain' rather than 'Scotland' was often used in the 1890s as part of an address. Two Scottish newspapers, *North British Advertiser* and *North British Daily Mail*, published in Glasgow since 1847, carried the term in their titles. Carruthers himself regarded the whole of Britain as his market which certainly proved to be correct as his patented clubs were to be sold in large numbers throughout Britain and, later, overseas. Perhaps his view also reflected previous experiences as a professional runner when he travelled widely throughout Britain to compete at the major venues. James Anderson also used Anstruther, 'NB', in 1900 advertisements, as did Charles Spinks of Pirrie Street, Leith, in 1891, 'sole patentee of plane for shaping golf club handles', who supplied shaped shafts to the trade. Carruthers and Anderson were members of the Bruntsfield Allied Golf Club, but not at the same time.

Carruthers, although he was also an innovator in the design of wooden clubs, is better known for his ground-breaking iron club technology for which he used James Anderson of Anstruther to supply his metal club heads. Both he and Robert Anderson were no doubt spurred on by the insatiable demand from the masses of new golfers for better implements in their quest to master the game. James Braid, five times Open Champion, however, said that there was nothing new about Robert Anderson's new design for wooden clubs. The following is an extract from the biography, *James Braid,* written by Bernard Darwin describing Braid's childhood at Earlsferry in Fife:

> The difficulty about golf was to get any practicable kind of club. The best that could be done was to pick up by good fortune an old discarded head and a derelict shaft and if possible unite them. 'People nowadays,' he says, 'talk about the modern system of socketing the shafts of wooden clubs on to the heads, as if it were a recent invention, whereas the caddies of my generation certainly socketed the shafts of the clubs that they made for themselves in this way, the method being the simplest possible, namely, boring a hole through the head and fastening the shaft in it as tightly as possible.' *(Reproduced by permission of A. P. Watt Ltd. on behalf of Lady Darwin, Paul Aston and Ursula Mommens)*

In his youth Harry Vardon used a similar technique for fixing the shaft to the head of the club as he explains in his biography, *My Golfing Life*:

> We decided that we must use as hard a wood as possible, and as the wood from a tree which we called the Lady Oak was suitable for our purpose, another important difficulty was satisfactorily overcome. First of all we cut a thick branch from the tree, sawed off a few inches from it, trimming this piece as near as we possibly could to the shape of the heads of the drivers of those players for whom we had been carrying. As splicing was impossible, we agreed that we must bore a hole in the centre of the head, to enable us to fix in the shaft sticks. These were made of thorn, white or black, and when they had been trimmed and prepared to our satisfaction we proceeded to finish off our club. To make a hole in

the head we had to put the poker in the fire and make it red hot so as to allow the shaft to be fitted in. Then after tightening it with wedges, the operation was complete.

Set out below is a Lunn & Co. advertisement from 1891 that features Carruthers' Patent Socket Irons and the 'Anderson' Patent Golf Clubs.

LUNN & CO.,

Golf Outfitters,

OXFORD CIRCUS; 257, REGENT STREET, LONDON, W.

The Balfour

Perfect in bounce,

Per dozen, 12/-

Golf Balls.

flight, and shape.

Per dozen, 12/-

THE "BALFOUR" GOLF CLUBS.

The Finest Selected Scotch Make.

Sole London Agents for PETER PAXTON, Eastbourne.

CARRUTHERS' PATENT SHORT SOCKET IRONS.

THE "ANDERSON" PATENT GOLF CLUBS.

The Golfing Annual 1891/1892: **Lunn & Co. Oxford Circus, London: advertisement featuring Carruthers' Patent Short Socket Irons and The 'Anderson' Patent Golf Clubs**

Other clubs with similar features

George Nicoll of Leven and Robert Wilson of St Andrews both developed and brought cleeks to the market that bore similarities to the Carruthers' patent but neither infringed his patent. This is what the trade press said about the new iron clubs:

> A new cleek has recently come into the market. It is the patent of Mr. George Nicoll, of Leven, and consists of a leather face on the centre portion of the blade of the cleek that strikes the ball. The socket is also a little shorter than the ordinary club, resembling to some extent Forrester or Carruthers' clubs, though the shaft does not come through as in the last-mentioned club. The blade is also thickened at the back to add to the driving power, and the blade generally is short and compact. When the weather and the green are dry the leather face undoubtedly gives a better grip to the ball, and prevents the skidding that is so noticeable in playing with a smooth-faced iron club. For putting it is also very serviceable. Peter Paxton is the sole agent for the club south of the Tweed. It is undoubtedly a useful improvement, and is meeting with widespread recognition among Southern golfers. (*Golf*, 8 December 1893)

> Mr. R. B. Wilson of St. Andrews has put yet another patent club on the market, which he calls his A1 driving cleek. A1 because it is much after the same idea as his A1 putting cleek, which was noticed in these columns some time ago, in that it has no hose. The shaft passes through the end of the blade, which is thickened to allow of this, to the sole of the club, resembling in this the 'Carruthers' cleek, which, however, unlike Mr. Wilson's idea, has a hose. (*Golf Illustrated*, 9 February 1902)

Early United States' Golf Clubs and Makers

Golf's popularity spread to many countries across the globe in the last decade of the nineteenth century, none more so than to the United States' Atlantic coast, giving rise to big business opportunities for those British manufacturers who were able to meet the great demand coming from home and overseas. Even when the new American golf equipment companies were able to supply their home demand, opportunities remained for British exporters with innovative designs.

In the May 1895 edition of *Scribner's Magazine* Henry E. Howland wrote:

> The nurseries for golf in the United States are many and varied, and increasing so fast that the tale outruns the telling. The first one, established at Yonkers on the Hudson, some five years ago, by Mr. John Reid (of course a Scotchman) bears the name of St. Andrews, in honor of the Royal and Ancient Golf Club of the East Neuk of Fife, in the shadow of 'Auld Reekie,' the clustering point for the great mass of golfing history and tradition.

Country Clubs played a major part in the development of golf in the United States. Many golf courses were attached to country clubs, whose members had taken the game with them in summer months. Professionals from Scotland were engaged as club makers, most of the golf clubs sold by them being imported. In a report of the 1899 American Open Championship it was stated that in the five years since the first (unofficial) Championship in 1894, won by Willie Dunn, 'Scotland and England have been ransacked for their best, and they have come.'

Horace Hutchinson's comments on the importation of golf equipment were made in 1896 in *Outing* magazine at a time when a number of famous names were about to establish themselves as golf club manufacturers.

> When the States, in the early stages of her golf ... have got their golf into something like organised order, Americans will probably reflect that the importation of clubs from Britain is rather analogous to the importation of Welsh coal by a Newcastle man, for the great bulk of the hickory used in the making of shafts comes originally from America.

One of the first of the early companies which began selling to the golf trade to meet the fast-growing demand in the 1890s was A. G. Spalding & Bros., for whom the Carruthers' patent design clubs became an important part of its business.

Spalding (Boston, Chicago, Philadelphia), founded in 1876, combined the two great American pastimes of baseball and golf. They began importing clubs from Britain for American distribution extensively from 1893. They had a strong retail presence in Britain with stores in Edinburgh, London, Birmingham and Manchester. Their London operation was opened around 1900 and by the following year had started a manufacturing facility.

They opened a factory at Dysart near Kirkcaldy, Fife, not far from St Andrews, around 1905 with a forge where they also carried out the final assembly of clubs. Their principal market was Britain, but clubs stamped with the Dysart 'anvil' cleek mark were also shipped to America. Spalding exported golf products to Britain from their factories in America but they also purchased British-made items for sale on both sides of the Atlantic.

> According to J. M. Cooper, the well-known collector who specialises exclusively in Spalding clubs and items, the first Spalding brand clubs offered were simply stamped 'Spalding' in block letters. Iron heads were forged in Scotland, probably by James Anderson of Anstruther, and assembled by craftsmen, many of whom were Scottish immigrants in the Chicopee and Chicago factories.
>
> Never content to only make ordinary clubs, Spalding was always looking for items of extraordinary character. In 1897, they were assigned the patent rights for the wood-face cleek designed by James Cran, also produced with a steel face and known as the spring faced cleek. Other patents to which they owned exclusive rights were the Sharpe double faced iron, the step faced lofter designed by Willie Park, Jr., Verslage's guttie faced metal wood, the Seely fork-hosel design irons and the curious perforated steel shaft of Alan Lard now known as the 'whistler'. They also made patent clubs to which their rights were less exclusive: Willie Dunn's one piece woods, J. Youd's lead faced putter and Thomas Carruthers' drilled-hosel cleek. (*Compendium of British Club Makers* and *North American Club Makers* by Peter Georgiady)

James Anderson of Anstruther was in the vanguard of the British exporters to America and, when his son took over the reins following the death of his father in 1895, he expanded his forging business and exported extensively to America.

In 1896 it was reported in the *Derby and Derbyshire Gazette* that Messrs Robert Forgan & Sons had visited the United States with a view to developing their business, for whom J. & G. Heywood were the local agents. They reported back that the Americans were manufacturing their own clubs and retailing them at much cheaper rates than those imported from the old country but also that they were much inferior to those made in Great Britain. Their report's conclusion accords with the view given elsewhere that as the indigenous manufacture of golf equipment grew to meet the quickly growing demand, so too did the importation of golf clubs with extraordinary characteristics such as the Carruthers' patent through-bore short socket design.

Tom Carruthers advertised his patented short socket irons in the trade press continuously from 1891 until 1906. The advertisements show that by

1894 his business was primarily directed to 'wholesale and export markets'. During those years Spalding would likely have been his major overseas customer.

Short socket irons, incorporating Carruthers' patented design, were sold by every one of the early American club makers of the 1890s: A. G. Spalding & Bros., Wright & Ditson, Bridgeport Gun Implement Company, MacGregor (Crawford, McGregor and Canby Company), and J. H. Williams Company. Spalding, like both Wright & Ditson and Bridgeport Gun Implement Company, imported most of the early clubs they sold.

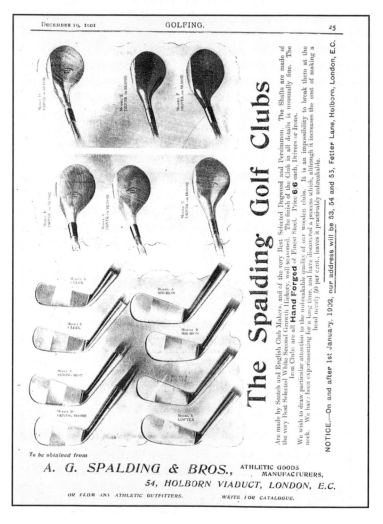

***Golfing,* 19 December 1901: A. G. Spalding & Bros. advertisement, including a Carruthers' Patent Short Socket model termed the 'A' Cleek**

In Britain the Spalding advertisement on the previous page that appeared in *Golfing* of 19 December 1901 shows a Carruthers' short socket model, termed the 'A' cleek. It is an example of clubs sourced from Carruthers by the Spalding organisation. The following words are included in the caption below the illustrations of the clubs: 'The Spalding Golf Clubs … Are made by Scotch and English Club Makers … Iron clubs are all Hand Forged'.

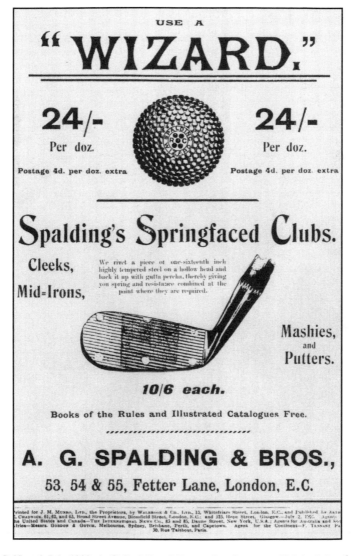

Golfing, **2 July 1903: A. G. Spalding & Bros. advertisement which includes their Springfaced Iron Clubs with Carruthers' Patent Short Socket**

The advertisement of 30 July 1903 on the previous page which appeared in the same magazine, displays Spalding's Springfaced Clubs with the Carruthers' short socket design. Carruthers, because of the legal protection provided to him by his short socket patent, which did not expire until the end of 1904, may have had a licensing agreement that allowed Spalding to incorporate his short socket design into their springfaced design.

The contribution that Carruthers' short socket invention made to Spalding's British and American business was substantial. J. M. Cooper's book *Early United States Golf Clubs by A. G. Spalding & Bros., Wright & Ditson and Bridgeport Gun Implement Co.* catalogues over 500 of their golf clubs sold from 1893–1932. A number of the clubs illustrated in his book in the period 1893–1906 are of Carruthers' short socket for metal playing clubs design and include the following:

(1) The Spalding, Hand Forged (cleek), 1897–1900;
(2) A. G. Spalding & Bros., Makers, Model A, Hand Forged (cleek), 1899–1901;
(3) A. G. Spalding & Bros., Makers, Model B, Baseball Mark, Trade Mark, Hand Forged (deep faced mashie), 1901–1905;
(4) A. G. Spalding & Bros., Makers, Model B, Baseball Mark, Trade Mark (crescent cleek), 1898–1901.

In addition Carruthers' design clubs were sold by another A. G. Spalding & Bros. Group Company called Wright & Ditson which bore the following markings:

(1) Standard (cleek), 1897–1903 and are referred to in their advertisement as 'hand-forged and vastly superior to other grades: made by golf experts: all our standard clubs are 1 dollar each.'
(2) A. H. Findlay, Wright & Ditson, Makers Model 4 (cleek), 1899–1905.

Scotsman, Alexander H. Finlay, was a professional golfer and the company's designer whose name appeared on a range of clubs. He was famous for his record of playing twenty consecutive holes in exactly four strokes each at the Hoosic, Whisick Golf Club, situated in the vicinity of Boston. A. G. Spalding & Bros. also used the Carruthers' short socket design for other clubs within the Spalding range manufactured before 1904, the Spalding Model Springface Series (1902–1904) for example.

J. M. Cooper's book also contains pictures of clubs sold by the Bridgeport Gun Implement Company (BGI), the third United States company to offer golf equipment in 1897, that shows a Carruthers' patent design club marked 'Bridgeport Trade Mark 'B.G.I. Co.' Conn. USA' (mid iron), 1898–1904.

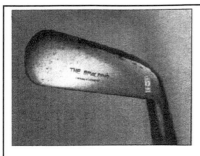

1897-1900
The Spalding Convex Back Cleek with the Carruther's Type Hosel
FACE SMOOTH # 1
SHAFT STAMP The Spalding
RARITY 4

Spalding Irons: 1899-1901

AGS&B Model A Cleek With Carruthers Type Hosel (drilled through the sole)
FACE SMOOTH #1
SHAFT STAMP A.G. Spalding & Bros.
RARITY 7 as a club

1901-1905
AGS&B Model B # 18 Deep Face Mashie With The Carruthers Type Shaft Fitting
FACE LINED # 2
SHAFT STAMP A.G. Spalding & Bros.
RARITY 6 as a club

1898-1901
Carruthers Type Shaft Fitting Crescent Cleek With Ribbed Back And Baseball Mark Added
FACE SMOOTH #1
SHAFT STAMP A.G. Spalding & Bros.
RARITY 7 as a club

Carruthers' Short Socket design clubs: A. G. Spalding & Bros. 1897 to 1905

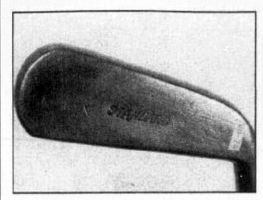

Wright & Ditson
Standard Cleek, Carruthers Shaft
1897-1903
FACE SMOOTH # 1
SHAFT STAMP W & D # 3
RARITY 6

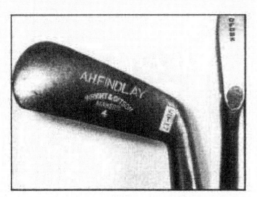

Wright & Ditson

Findlay Model 4 Cleek With Carruthers
Type Shaft Shown At The Right
1899-1905
FACE SMOOTH # 1
SHAFT STAMP W & D # 2
RARITY 6

BGI Co. # 125½ Mid-Iron With Carruthers
Type Shaft (Heavy)
1898-1904
FACE SMOOTH # 1
SHAFT STAMP BGI Co. # 125½
RARITY 6

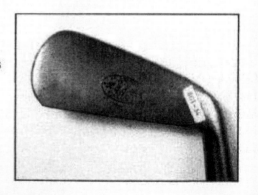

Carruthers' Short Socket design clubs: Wright & Ditson and the Bridgeport Gun Implement Co.
1897 to 1905

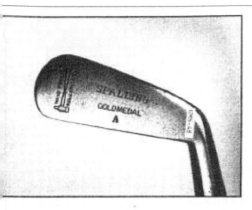

1906-1909
Gold Medal A Cleek With Carruthers Type Shaft Fitting And Short Hosel
FACE SMOOTH # 1
SHAFT STAMP AGS&B Gold Medal
RARITY 6 as a club

Gold Medal Cleek (L) With The Carruthers Type Shafting
FACE SMOOTH # 1
SHAFT STAMP AGS&B Gold Medal
RARITY 5 as a club
1912-1918

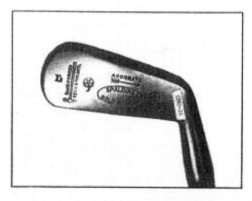

1912-1918
Gold Medal Cleek, With The Carruthers Type Shaft Fitting
FACE # 8
SHAFT STAMP AGS&B Gold Medal
RARITY 5

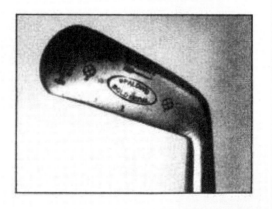

Carruthers' Short Socket design clubs: A. G. Spalding & Bros. 1906 to 1918

The preceding illustrations are copies of Carruthers' Design Clubs from J. M. Cooper's book, *Early United States Golf Clubs by A.G. Spalding & Bros., Wright & Ditson and Bridgeport Gun Implement Co.*

After 1904 Spalding continued to use the Carruthers' short socket for metal golf clubs design on their Gold Medal 'A' cleek (1906–1909) and Gold Medal cleeks (1912–1918).

The Carruthers' short socket for metal clubs invention was not registered in the United States.

Post–Patent Protection Period

When the protection period provided by the patent expired in 1904, the short socket metal clubs made by Carruthers continued to be advertised nationally by him and also by some large London stores but other manufacturers were now free to copy the design and incorporate it in their own clubs. From 1904 until the present day the design principles of his invention have been widely used by other manufacturers, some of which are mentioned below.

1. Thomas Stewart of St Andrews was the most respected of the old cleekmakers during the wood-shafted era. He was renowned for the high quality of his club heads. In the twentieth century he produced copies of clubs used by well-known amateur and professional golfers and he also produced copies of many popular patentees' clubs including, Thomas Carruthers' short hosel irons, Hugh Logan's Genii series and both Smith's and Fairlie's patent anti-shank irons. 'Carruthers' pattern cleeks' are listed for sale in Tom Stewart's 1930 catalogue.

2. In 1907 Ernest Newbery registered a design for his 'half-moon' irons, having a pronounced semi-circular weight at the top of the back of the club, which incorporated Carruthers' short socket invention.

3. Robert Simpson of Carnoustie adopted the trademark 'Perfect Balance' that Carruthers had consistently used since 1891, when he (one of the famous six Simpson brothers) obtained a patent in 1907. He used similar principles to George Forresters' inventive developments, introduced over ten years earlier, that concentrated weight to the back of the club.

4. The writer owned a set of Wilson Fluid Feel irons in the 1970s that incorporated similar principles to the Carruthers' short socket design.

5. In 1984 Callaway had a stand at the Open Golf Championship at St Andrews where they proclaimed their new S2H2 through-bore

technology (short straight hollow hosel). David Neech, Sotheby's Golf and Sporting Consultant, tells how he pointed out to the Callaway's representative on the stand that a similar golf club design had been developed by Thomas Carruthers and patented by him in 1890 (although the protection period had long since expired). The Callaway's representative apparently expressed surprise whereupon David retrieved a Carruthers' short socket cleek from Sotheby's stand, which Callaway promptly purchased. Later they asked if he would acquire another Carruthers' short socket iron for them and this was duly despatched. Callaway is today still incorporating its short straight hollow hosel design in some of its iron clubs.

An Age of Experimentation and Inventiveness

To be patentable an invention has to be new, involve an inventive step and be capable of industrial application. This means that the invention must take the practical form of an apparatus or device, a product such as some new material or substance or an industrial process or method of operation. In the Victorian age great achievements were nurtured by the *laissez-faire* political philosophy. This freedom brought about great advancements in industrial processes and wealth that also inspired the creative talents of innovative golf club makers, although some golfers expressed alarm at the rapidity of change and innovation believing that the game of golf itself, and its fundamental values, were threatened.

> ... many indignant protests from conservative minded players, who asserted as some of them do even yet that this innovation (the introduction of the iron-headed club, named the cleek, by Allan Robertson circa 1840) would completely destroy the Royal and Ancient Game as it always had been played. (*Golf,* 9 April 1897)

Many of these inventions record for posterity the historical development of the game during the 1890s. A great number of newly-patented clubs never reached the market, their applications having been abandoned by their inventors. Many did, but few were successful. The Carruthers' short socket for metal playing clubs is one of those special inventions. It was undoubtedly one of the biggest-selling patented golf clubs of its time.

The Royal & Ancient introduced rules governing the legality of golf club design in 1908. Up until this time golf club designers and club makers had been unencumbered in giving free rein to bringing their creative, bold and free-thinking ideas to the market. The 1890s witnessed what was probably the most exciting and influential period of golf club design, many of whose technological advances can still be recognised in today's golf club industry.

In those days the golfing public was the only arbiter and it was eager to test the benefits claimed by the makers of being able to improve skill and competence around the golf course. Many of these new innovators received provisional patent approval for their new ideas and put them into production but a great number also fell by the wayside, never reaching the stage of applying for approval of their complete specification, once golfers had exercised their judgment.

Scepticism abounded, however, in some quarters and the following is a selection from the many letters published in contemporary golf periodicals:

> As a golfer of the old school, and one saturated with its best traditions for nearly thirty years back, I am perplexed and distressed at the continual innovations being introduced into the game … If the object of the game were merely to get the ball round the course in the fewest number of strokes, irrespective of the weapons used, then no doubt many ways could be devised which would produce better results than the ordinary Golf Club. Might not one have drivers with catgut faces, or dynamite cartridges, and as for putting (as a 'beginner' aptly queried in the papers the other day), is there anything to prevent one using a billiard cue on the putting green? No doubt one would be surer at short putts with a billiard cue (applied as one gracefully lay on one's stomach) than with a putter. What is the reply to that beginner's query? None, I fancy except that though the rules do not forbid it, it is not golf.
> (*Golf*, 9 December 1892)

> Were the shape of clubs once defined, and 'regulation' measurements adopted, limiting the extremes of length, width, and depth of wooden, and iron club-heads; also prohibiting the attachment, or insertion, of the shaft in any other way than to, or into, the neck (i.e., the lateral prolongation of the head) we should not only get rid of the numerous and unsightly abominations masquerading as golf clubs, but … we should hear no more discussion as to what position a player should, or should not adopt … We shall soon have the 'Hockey-knockers' – to give the wielders of these ghastly shaped clubs a name – clamouring for a square hole on the putting green!!
> (*Golf*, March 1894)

I was playing a few days ago against a scratch player and a member of several clubs, and had brought to the ground with me a couple of new patent drivers. You may imagine my astonishment when he remarked that if he had known I was going to use them he would not have played; which remark was reiterated after halving the first hole. (*Golf*, 20 April 1894)

A golf club looks, and ought to be a simple thing; two pieces of wood, some string, and there you are. Nothing shows the astounding spread of the game more surely than the amazing variety of woods, which are employed by the club maker ... They all drive 15 yards further than any two of the others ... And yet some old-fashioned players cling to the belief that the art of driving must be mastered by the man, not by the club. (*Golf*, 11 November 1898)

Some golfers can never resist the temptation to produce a special club, ball, boot-stud, spat or what not for the medal or bogey round. The ordinary driver, cleek, iron and putter are not considered good enough for a competition, so the patent bell-metal bulger, the adjustable brassey, the paper-faced cleek, the convex mashie, and the parallellopipedon putter are ostentatiously put into the bag, much to the amusement of the cynic, and greatly to the disgust of the overburdened caddie. Ten years ago 'patent' clubs swarmed; nowadays, in spite of the enormous increase in the manufacture and sale of golfing material, you seldom see one. By 'patent' of course we mean not every harmless necessary driver or iron which embodies some useful feature worth registering, but those 'cranky,' 'faddy', weird-looking abortions. (*Golf*, 9 December 1899)

Further information on the story of the evolution of the cleek and patent drivers is given in Chapter 8.

End of the Century Reviews of the Carruthers' Patent Short Socket Clubs

When the new short socket iron had been in use for a number of years several accounts from golf professionals of the day gave considered views of the Carruthers' patent clubs. These accounts were a testament to its enduring qualities, the technical merits of which are as sound today as they were well over one hundred years ago.

Firstly, William Aveston of the Royal Cromer Golf Club of whom J. H. Taylor said in his book, *Golf My Life's Work*, that beside himself in 1895, there were only the brothers Vardon, Harry and Tom, and Willie Aveston privileged to carry the banner to challenge the supremacy of the Scottish professionals.

The following summary is based on an article that appeared in the 2 December 1896 edition of *The Golfer*.

William Aveston was born in Holyhead, Wales, in 1873. His family moved to Cromer where his father was in charge of the lighthouse that was situated on the very Links with which Aveston's own name was in due time to be so closely associated in golfing memory. He showed such remarkable aptitude for the game that he was sent, first to Oxford, and thereafter to Yarmouth where he learned club-making under George Fernie. When Fernie left, Aveston, although only seventeen, was immediately appointed professional at Cromer, his home town. Royal Cromer golf club was under the direct patronage of the Prince of Wales.

He attributed much of his rapid improvement in the game to having played a good deal with his great friend J. H. Taylor who won the Open at his second attempt at Royal St George's at Sandwich, the location of the first Open to be held outside Scotland. He preferred the bulger to the older shape of wooden club and the only patent iron club that he used was the Carruthers' cleek, in which he had thorough belief.

The next review was published in *Golfing*, 27 February 1899.

A well known professional not a hundred miles from Glasgow, happened to remark to me, one day last week, that he made no special things in clubs, and that, moreover, he did not believe in 'patents'. He modified this latter statement by saying there were, to his mind, two exceptions, as far as patents were concerned, one of those being Carruthers' Patent Socket Irons.

It does a man good to hear one in a trade speak well of another, and while mentally consigning the professional with whom I was conversing to a much higher position in my estimation, I resolved to call upon Carruthers and investigate his speciality.

As luck would have it, I found Mr. Carruthers at his residence near to Bruntsfield Links, Edinburgh, and completely – very completely – did I learn the scientific lesson of the principles upon which his famous irons are built up. To begin with, they are called 'Perfect Balance' Irons, and when I myself took a 'head' and balanced it easily upon the pencil with which I took my notes, the easy grace of workmanship became apparent.

Most golfers, I dare say, will have seen, at one time or another, a Carruthers' 'patent'. In the first place, the shortening of the socket has enabled the weight to be better distributed and the centre of gravity in the socket-iron is right behind the ball. The shaft runs right down and out at the heel, and, owing to the shortening of the socket, has a better spring. A Carruthers' cleek is unequalled for long driving, and possesses the merit over a brassey that – to the majority of golfers, at any rate – it is a surer club.

The following article appeared under the heading 'Golfing Trade Notes by Tee Caddie' in *Golfing*, January 1899:

Another cleek of name, a driving cleek, is that of Carruthers, Edinburgh. It is equal to a brassey in length of drive, and is, to many players, a much surer club. Carruthers' patent cleek is one of the oldest of the patents, and has been tried on many links, and always highly spoken of.

Horace Hutchinson, the outstanding amateur golfer and respected golf historian and prolific writer, who won two British Amateur titles in the 1880s, wrote about Carruthers' breakthrough in club design in *The Badminton Library: Golf* in 1898 in the following terms:

Considerable improvements have been introduced lately into the making of cleek heads. A while back the great trouble was to get a cleek head thick enough in the blade. They were all apt to bend from hard hitting in one place. But now we have cleeks that are thickened and rounded at the back of the blade. The 'Forrester' cleeks and irons are of this round backed sort. The 'Carruthers' cleeks and irons carry the principle of massing the weight behind the point of impact a little further, for in them the shaft runs right through the 'hose'. This dispenses with some two inches of the length of 'hose', and the weight thus saved is added onto the blade … The power of long driving with the cleek has doubtless been a factor in the disuse of spoons. Douglas Rolland, of Elie, and Mr. John Ball Jun. of Hoylake, can both drive with a cleek very nearly up to their ordinary driver shot.'

Chapter 6

Clubs and Marks

A good indication of the golf clubs that were available to Bruntsfield's golfers from Tom Carruthers' golf shop in the 1880s was given in the first part of Carruthers' 1892 price list headed 'List of Ordinary Clubs' and in correspondence published in *Golf* dated March 1891, both of which are set out in chapter 3. Towards the end of the 1880s Tom was experimenting with new wooden and iron golf club design concepts.

When he patented the famous short socket for metal golf-playing clubs' design in 1890, which effectively re-balanced the iron club, giving it more weight behind the 'sweet spot', it was so successful that he brought out a whole new range of clubs incorporating this invention. These clubs are included in the second part of the Carruthers' 1892 price list headed 'List of Patent Clubs', reproduced on the page opposite. The patent clubs, the 'transitional' wooden clubs and the 'test-bed' designs are considered in this chapter as well as the accreditations attached to the well-known golfers mentioned in the price list.

Hilton and Ball, Simpson, Rolland, Sayers

The right hand side of the 'List of Patent Clubs' bears the claim 'All the Best Players are now using my Patent Short Socket Iron Clubs' and continues:

> Messrs Hilton & Ball, who were first and second respectively in this year's Open Championship, both used them, and to illustrate the frequency of their use, it may be mentioned that Mr. Ball, played 49 strokes with the Cleek out of a round of eighteen holes. His round was 74. Also Archie Simpson and Douglas Rolland, who tied for the St. Ann's-on-Sea Tournament, both use them.

No higher accreditation could have been given, for these players are legends in the history of the game. The Open Championship referred to above was

LIST OF PATENT CLUBS.

Driving Cleeks, ...	7/-
Playing Cleeks, ...	7/-
Putting Cleeks, ...	7/-
Gun Metal Putting Cleeks,	7/-
Round-faced ,, ,,	
Round-faced ,, Irons,	7/-
Driving Irons, ...	7/-
Sand ,, ...	7/-
Lofting ,, ...	7/-
Round-soled Irons, . .	7/-
Driving Mashies, . . .	7/-
Mashies, ...	7/-
Niblicks, ...	7/-
Patent Wood Driver, Centre Balance, ...	5/-
Left-handed Cleeks, &c.	

All the Best Players

Are now using my

PATENT

SHORT

SOCKET

IRON

CLUBS

—❖✱❖—

Messrs **HILTON & BALL**, who were first and second respectively in this year's Open Championship, both used them, and to illustrate the frequency of their use, it may be mentioned that **Mr BALL** played 49 strokes with the Cleek out of a round of eighteen holes. His round was 74. Also **ARCHIE SIMPSON** and **DOUGLAS ROLLAND**, who tied for the St. Ann's-on Sea Tournament, both use them.

BERNARD SAYERS, the Celebrated Golfer, says:—"I now play regularly with "The Carruthers Patent Cleek," and I find it the best I have ever seen. I can drive quite as far with it as with a Brassey, and for a long shot up to the hole side—which of all others is the shot of most importance in golf—I consider your Cleek unequalled."

T. CARRUTHERS,
5 GILLESPIE PLACE, EDINBURGH.

Page 2 of Carruthers' 1892 Price List: List of Patent Clubs

the Championship held in 1892. It was the first to be competed for at the Honourable Company of Edinburgh Golfers' new course at Muirfield, East Lothian. An account of that Open Championship, published in *The Scotsman* of 23 and 24 September 1892, recorded John Ball's considerable expertise with his Carruthers' cleek:

> Mr. Ball was in his strongest long game. He played his iron with deadly effect, and his putting, though now and then just a little short, was on the whole very accurate. The crowd at the home green recognised the excellence of his play by a hearty round of applause, and his 74 at once established him as a favourite for the cup.

To commemorate his success in the Open Championship Hilton was made a life member of the Royal Liverpool Golf Club and the Formby Golf Club. Ball achieved his third victory in the Amateur Championship in 1892 and was runner-up with two of the foremost professionals of the day – Hugh Kirkaldy, the previous year's winner who tragically died five years later at the young age of twenty-nine years after a long and lingering illness, and Sandy Herd. Hilton narrowly failed to equal Ball's unique Open/Amateur double of two years earlier when Ball defeated Hilton at the 17th hole in the final of the Amateur.

> Both Hilton and Ball were members of the Royal Liverpool Golf Club at Hoylake and their influence on amateur golf cannot be over-emphasized. Between them they dominated the amateur game of that era and were also a major influence in the professional game, both winning the Open Championship as amateurs. Ball won the Amateur Championship eight times between 1888 and 1912 and was runner-up twice. He won the Open Championship in 1890; the first Englishman and the first amateur to do so and also won the Amateur in the same year. Harold Hilton's record was just as impressive. He won the Open Championship at Muirfield in 1892 (the first year that the Open was played over 72 holes) and again five years later. He is the only amateur apart from John Ball and Bobby Jones to win the title. Hilton won the Amateur Championship four times, was runner-up on three occasions and won the US Amateur Championship in 1911, the year in which he also held the British title. He became the first editor of *Golf Monthly* magazine launched in the same year. (Royal Liverpool Golf Club)

Archie Simpson was a brilliant match player who in 1887 challenged 'any man in the world' at one hundred pounds a side. The newly crowned Open

Champion, Willie Park Jun. accepted the challenge and lost by eleven holes. He was runner-up in the Open Championship in 1885 and also in 1890 when he lost out to John Ball.

Douglas Rolland, a cousin of James Braid, was one of the most famous of golf's uncrowned kings. He was runner-up to Jack Simpson, brother of Archie Simpson, in the 1884 Open Championship held at Prestwick and again in 1894 when he was runner up to J. H. Taylor at Royal St George's. Around this time John Ball issued a challenge from Hoylake to play any amateur in a home and home match. It was taken up by Rolland who finished nine up at Elie and added further to his lead at Hoylake. Another thirty-six hole match was played between the two the next day when John Ball became five up with six to play and then incredibly lost all the last six holes and the match.

The St Ann's-on-Sea Tournament refers to an 'open' tournament for amateurs and professionals run by the Royal Lytham and St Anne's Golf Club. The first tournament was held in 1890 and the second tournament, open to professionals and amateurs, was held two years later in 1892 when Archie Simpson and Douglas Rolland tied for first place. Frank Fairlie, a well-known player and patentee of his popular anti-shank iron, won the amateur prize.

The bottom left of the price list page already shown carries the testimony:

> Bernard Sayers, the Celebrated Golfer, says: 'I now play regularly with 'The Carruthers' Patent Cleek,' and I find it the best I have ever seen. I can drive quite as far with it as with a Brassey, and for a long shot up to the hole side – which of all others is the shot of most importance in golf – I consider your Cleek unequalled.

Ben Sayers was born in Leith and became the professional at North Berwick. He finished in a three-way tie for the Open Championship at St Andrews in 1888 only to be edged into second place with David Anderson when it was discovered that Burns' (the winner) score was incorrectly calculated. He participated in every Open Championship from 1880 to 1923 and went on to establish a successful golf club-making business.

Carruthers' Wooden Clubs

Carruthers' earliest-surviving wooden clubs that bear his mark date from the 1880s.

LONG-NOSED WOODEN CLUBS

The graceful long-nosed wooden driving putter photographed here, bears the mark 'Carruthers'/Patent' on the crown. This is the only Carruthers' wooden club that the writer has seen with this unique mark. Its workmanship is of the highest quality.

It is believed that the club shown here may be the only surviving example of Carruthers' patent application No. 22045 dated 17 December 1891 for 'a new or improved method of loading all wooden golf-playing clubs', which is fully dealt with later in this chapter.

A Long-Nosed Wooden Driving Putter

It has a full brass sole plate to protect the sole of the club from damage when striking from hard lies, such as the stony paths or roads or hard gravel to be found at Wimbledon Common or Blackheath, and its hardened rubber-faced insert, fixed with twelve brass pins, also protected the face of the club from the impact of the rock-hard guttie ball as well as helping the player to 'get more feel on his putt' when the club was used on the green. Its thick hide leather grip also served in this regard. The club is stained, reflecting the fashion at that time, and varnished. The club has a lead weight showing on the back of the head and is very heavy, weighing 435 grams.

Vulcanite, which was hardened rubber, was a durable elastic material that featured in the first ever patent for a golf club when in 1876 Thomas Johnston patented a club head 'consisting in the employment of the well-known preparation of India-rubber called vulcanite or ebonite in the construction of such club heads.' It was Goodyear who, in 1839, first cured or vulcanised rubber, and, after undergoing this treatment, the rubber acquired a high degree of resilience.

Willie Park Jun. provides the following description of the driving putter in his book, *The Game of Golf*, published in 1896:

> The driving putter is really a driver with a short stiff shaft and a deep face, more upright than an ordinary driver and flatter than an ordinary putter, and it is used for playing long putts and also for driving against a head wind. The shortness and stiffness of the shaft ensure accuracy, and the less tendency to pull or heel the ball.

Carruthers' Durable Hardwood Wooden Clubs

During the last quarter of the nineteenth century traditional hardwoods such as holly, apple, thorn, acacia, and hickory (often steamed into shape and sold as 'compressed') were used for wooden club heads but when the softer beech wood was introduced there was a continuous debate on the merits of hard versus soft woods, the latter being susceptible to cracking on the club face.

Carruthers introduced a new harder wood known as 'Sylviac' which had extraordinarily good properties. This was a Brazilian wood, Silvia Itauba, from the upland forests of the lower Amazon, and which was formerly prized for shipbuilding.

It was a very hard wood, waterproof, durable and resistant to attacks from fungi and termites. Textures were fine to medium. The wood was only susceptible to slight warping, was easy to work with by hand and had an excellent reputation for resistance to decay. Its colour was yellowish with a greenish hue when fresh, becoming brown or olive on exposure.

The following reference to Sylviac appeared in *Golfing and Cycling*, 27 October 1898:

Those who know the value of Sylviac in club-head making may be pleased to know that the other day the good ship 'Vedamore' was the bearer to these shores of 500 selected pieces of prime Sylviac wood. The consignment is now being converted into sawn and bent club-heads by the well-known government contractors, Messrs. Joseph Owen and Sons, of Stanley Road, Liverpool.

The 'Carruthers/Sylviac/Edinburgh' mark that appeared on the crown of the Carruthers' durable hardwood wooden clubs

TRANSITIONAL WOODEN CLUBS

Clubs called 'transitional' wooden clubs, marked the transition from the traditional long-headed wooden club to the more compact shorter wooden-headed club that became known as the bulger because of its convex-shaped face. By 1890 the bulger with its short broad head and convex face was being used. In 1896 Alex Patrick, the club maker, reported that three-fourths of all woods in use were bulgers. (*The Golfer*, 12 August 1896)

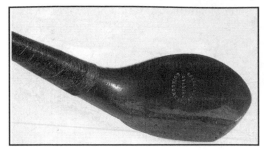

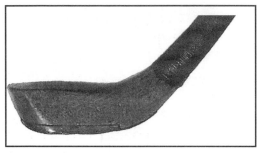

The three examples of Carruthers' transitional wooden clubs all date from the late 1880s and therefore pre-date his 1892 price list. Each club has 'Carruthers/Sylviac/Edinburgh' marked on the crown, with scared neck-joint construction.

The club on top left is a rare left-handed early transitional driver, made from the 'Sylvia Itauba' Brazilian hardwood with a vulcanite hardened rubber insert designed to protect the face of the club, and the shock on the player's hands, from the impact of the hard 'guttie' on the face of the club and also to improve its driving qualities. The dark vulcanised fibre, sometimes used instead of horn, was certainly an improvement on the horn's brittle substance and the brass pins, to secure it, were better than wooden pegs according to Horace Hutchinson.

The club in the centre left is a transitional brassie with a slight concave face. It has a full brass sole and underneath the brass is a horn insert base showing in the leading edge.

Examples of Carruthers' transitional clubs which pre-date the Carruthers' 1892 price list

Brassies, introduced circa 1880, were initially made with a horn covered by a brass sole plate but later the brass plate was screwed directly onto the wooden sole without the horn.

Willie Park Jun. said in 1896:

With regard to brassies, I would point out that some makers, considering the brass sole to be sufficient protection to the club head, omit the usual bone with which all wooden clubs should be protected at the bottom of the face, but players should not accept such clubs. Without the bone the wooden face gets hammered in by repeated strokes and the result is that the brass sole, being left projecting, cuts the ball, not to say the turf of the links. See, therefore, that the brassie has bone in it.

The lower left club on the previous page is a late transitional driver, its

Sylviac head covered with a darker wood stain.

BULGER WOODEN CLUBS

On the left is an early 1890s' bulger brassie with full brass sole plate, fixed over a horn insert by six brass screws. The club has on the crown the mark 'Carruthers/Sylviac/Edinburgh'.

Carruthers also made later bulger-type wooden clubs of modern head design. The bulger-type wooden club shown on the lower left is a socket head wood with the shaft running straight down into the head, resembling in style the famous Anderson patent. This patent was the first wooden-headed club patented and commercially produced with a socket neck of 'through bore construction'. The invention is described more fully in Chapter 5. This club also is marked with 'Carruthers/Sylviac/Edinburgh' on the crown. It shows a clear line where the top of the socket meets the shaft and is of an innovative design. The line indicates that a small shoulder, used to abut the top of the

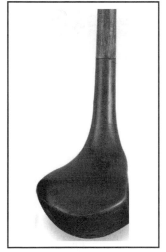

Top: **Bulger Brassie Club.**
Left: **Bulger Socket Head Club**

socket neck, was built into the shaft. The traditional method of applying whipping to the neck has been dispensed with and the appearance of the club greatly improved, in the style of modern club design. The example shown is a post 1895 example.

Patent Application Number 22045

On 17 December 1891, Carruthers made a patent application No. 22045 for 'a new or improved method of loading all wooden golf-playing clubs'. The invention concerned loading or running the lead more into the centre of the head in order that the balance or centre of gravity would be at the centre of the club head, hence providing 'centre balance'. Although the new club did not proceed to complete specification stage, it probably went into limited production. The long-nosed putter shown earlier is one such example, marked 'Carruthers'/Patent' on the crown. It is also probable that the 'Patent Wood Driver, Centre Balance' club listed in Carruthers' price list was another product of this invention.

Messrs Thornton & Co., Princes Street, Edinburgh, the well-known golf ball makers, later received patent office approval for the provisional specification of their own central loaded golf club invention. In April 1893 they advertised their 'Central-loaded Putters' at 5s. each, but this patent was also abandoned, no doubt because its modest commercial prospects had been recognised.

Patent Application Number 5781

On 24 March 1892, Carruthers made patent application No. 5781 which was described as 'a new and improved wooden golf club having metal on sole and face'. It is probable that a limited number of wooden golf clubs were made and distributed in order to test the demand for this innovation, designed to combat the damaging effect that the gutta percha ball and hard and wet ground conditions could have on many of the timbers used in the construction of wooden golf clubs at that time

Damage to golf clubs was a particular problem for golfers in the gutta-percha golf ball era because of its hardness. Golf club makers made great efforts to combat its damaging effect by bringing out a number of innovative remedies to combat the problem.

THE PATENT OFFICE,

25, SOUTHAMPTON BUILDINGS,

CHANCERY LANE,

LONDON, W.C., 2

30 Dec: 189 *1.*

Sir,

In conformity with the provisions of the "Patents, &c., Act, 1883," I hereby give you notice of the acceptance of your Application with a Provisional Specification for a Patent for *"A new or improved method for loading all wooden golf-playing clubs."*

No. *22045,* dated *14 Dec.* 189 *1.*

Mr J. Carruthers

I am, *Sir,*

Your obedient Servant,

H. READER LACK,

Comptroller-General.

N.B.—A Complete Specification must be left at the Patent Office within 9 months of the date of application, if a patent is desired.

This Complete Specification must be prepared upon Form C, stamped £3, must bear the number and date of the application, and must end with a distinct statement of the invention claimed.

If the Complete Specification is not left at the Patent Office within the prescribed 9 months, an extension of time for 1 month more may be applied for upon Form U, stamped £2.

At the end of 10 months, if no Complete Specification has been filed, the application will be regarded as abandoned.

Forms C and U may be purchased in London at the Inland Revenue Office, Royal Courts of Justice (Room No. 6), or may be obtained at a few days' notice through any Money Order Office in the United Kingdom, upon prepayment of the value of the stamp.

W B & L (142ka)—14917—20000-4-91

Letter of Acceptance for Patent Application No. 22045 from the Patent Office for 'A new or improved method for loading all wooden golf-playing clubs'

The gutta-percha ball was rock-hard and caused damage to the club head, particularly when wet. Clubs were often faced with thick leather inserts, or alternately, when the beech was damaged, they were repaired with leather patches. This not only protected the wood but also cushioned the shock of the ball. Thick grips also helped in this respect. Patches made of other materials were sometimes used, for example, a piece of harder wood on putters, and later vulcanite (hardened rubber). Metal was also used – 'the mules' patent was for a metal face plate screwed onto the entire face of the club. (*Golf Implements and Memorabilia* – Kevin McGimpsey & David Neech)

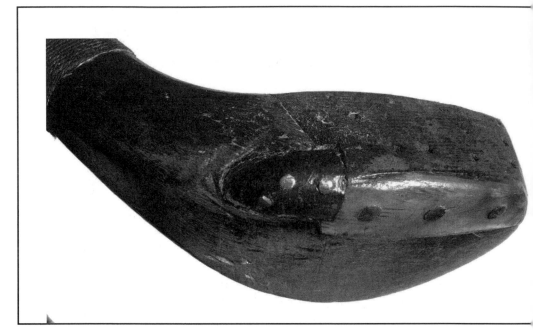

A fine illustration of a Carruthers' Transitional Club showing a small wooden patch repair towards the heel of the club fixed with 3 brass pins

In an article that appeared in *Golfing,* 9 February 1899, J. H. Taylor, Open Champion 1894–1895, cautioned against the use of leather faces:

The reason why a leather face is less desirable in a wet weather club is a very apparent one. As soon as the face gets sodden and spongy, it naturally loses its driving powers and the ball has a very great tendency to 'skid and duck'.

The integral metal face/sole of the Carruthers' design was very much an innovation before its time for the 'Cuirass' patent was well received some ten years later when it was patented by the London Golf Company. The choice of the word 'Cuirass' by the patentee was entirely appropriate as *Chambers Twentieth Century Dictionary* gives the following definition: a defensive breastplate and back plate fastened together. The following article published in *Golf Illustrated*, 27 November 1903, gives the clue to its relative success:

> One of the latest and best of new clubs is the 'Cuirass' driver, made by the London Golf Company Ltd., 13 Copthall Avenue, E.C. It is a well-recognized fact that the new rubber balls fly relatively further from metal than they do from wood, as compared with gutty balls. Why this should be so is not quite clear, but the fact remains, and the makers of the 'Cuirass' driver have accordingly fitted a ribbed face of finely tempered and elastic steel to the ordinary driver. The steel covering also turns over on to the sole of the club and takes the place of the horn, the whole 'Cuirass' being one piece of metal. With this club we find that a rubber-cored ball can be driven quite as far as from a wooden one, and with a lower trajectory and consequently greater run. These clubs are beautifully balanced and finished and as the 'Cuirass' renders the club practically indestructible, they are well worth the 10s.6d. charged for them. On wet days and on wet courses the advantages of the 'Cuirass' are obvious.

Golfing, 15 October 1903, reported that Lindsay G. Ross, the professional and club maker at Streetley, Sutton Coldfield, produced and sold 'Ross's Patent Angle Plate' which was designed to be fitted to existing drivers or brassies with a metal plate, possibly similar to that of the 'Cuirass' and the clubs made from Carruthers' patent application No. 5781 of 24 March 1892. Lindsay Ross was also the first professional to be appointed at the Braid Hills Golf Course in Edinburgh, opened in 1889, and became the co-owner of the Golfers Rest, one of the first of two purpose-built golf clubhouses which stood adjacent to the Golfers Tryst, another purpose-built golf clubhouse, first owned and constructed by William Frier, golf club maker, and then by Thomas Carruthers in 1899. This episode and its significance in the history of golf in Edinburgh are covered in a later chapter.

Patent Application Number 7992

On 28 April 1892, Carruthers made patent application No. 7992 for the 'Medal' golf club. It is believed that this innovation may have been for the use of metal in golf club construction. The complete specification was never submitted but it is always possible that some rare example of this club may exist.

The identification of golf clubs for which their inventors received patent office approval for provisional specifications, but for which a complete specification was never submitted and therefore the patent process was abandoned, may never be known. The only clues are contained in a few key words in the patent application, as the patent office did not retain copies of the provisional specification.

Golf club makers often used the word 'medal' in advertisements if a particular club, shown at an exhibition, won a prize for its novelty or standard of workmanship. For example Robert Forgan, established in 1856, golf club makers to HRH the Prince of Wales, stated in their 1891 advertisements that they had won a gold medal at the International Exhibition of Art, Science and Industry, held in Edinburgh in 1886. Thornton & Company, golf ball and club makers of 78 Princes Street, Edinburgh, similarly proclaimed in their 1891 advertisements that they had won a gold medal at the 1890 International Exhibition of General Inventions &c. held at Craiglockhart, Edinburgh. In later years club makers also used the term 'medal' in marketing new club designs such as Robert Simpson's 'Medalist' drivers and mashies in 1914 and Spalding's 'Medal' wood which had a steel plate.

The fact that this patent application was made within one month of Carruthers' patent application No. 5781 for 'a new and improved wooden club having metal on sole and face' indicates that, as well as using the hard rubber called Vulcanite on the face of wooden golf clubs, he was experimenting with the use of metals to overcome some of the disadvantages caused by the hard gutta-percha ball.

The 'Medal' golf club may have had similarities to Thomson's metallic-faced golf club, which, it was claimed transferred the weight from the back of the club, as well as having improved strength and durability. It was described in *Golf*, 25 March 1892, as follows:

> Mr. William Thomson of 2 Roseneath Terrace, Edinburgh, who some time ago patented a combination golf cleek and iron club, has invented a metallic-faced golf club.

The last invention consists of having the weight of metal taken from the back part and placed on the front or face of the club, and fitted into the head in a circular shape, and held in position with screw-nails. The metal on the face is made rough, so as to cause it to grip the ball to stop. The advantages claimed for this club are chiefly durability and strength, and it is also claimed that the club is made on principles more scientifically accurate than an ordinary wooden club in as much as the weight is taken from the back and placed more in a direct line with the shaft.

Carruthers' Patent Iron Clubs (Patent Number 19684 dated 3 December 1890)

The following section describes each of the clubs listed in Carruthers' Price List dated 1892.

DRIVING CLEEKS, PLAYING CLEEKS AND PUTTING CLEEKS

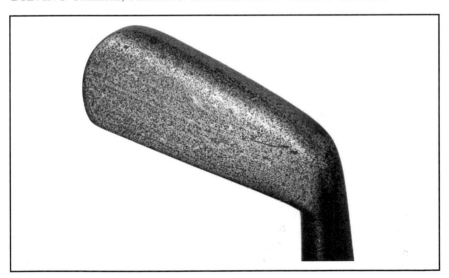

Carruthers' 1890 Patent Short Socket Driving Cleek

The iron head of the cleek has a straight and narrow face. The spoon and baffy were gradually replaced by the cleek as iron clubs became more popular. The cleek was considered by some to achieve a surer shot than the brassie. It could achieve greater distance than all the other iron clubs.

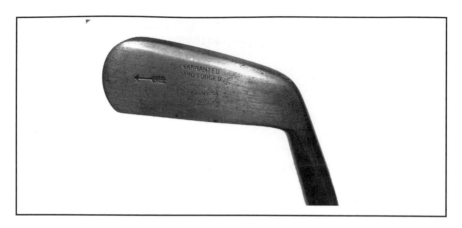

Carruthers' 1890 Patent Short Socket Playing Cleek

Carruthers' 1890 Patent Short Socket Ladies' Playing Cleek

The cleeks shown are Carruthers' 1890 patent clubs with short sockets, drilled through. The cleek shown on the the previous page is an early example of a driving cleek. The blade is tapered and the bottom of the blade is thicker than the playing cleeks shown in the other two pictures. The shaft of the driving cleek bears the name 'Philip Wynne/Tooting' on the shaft indicating that this professional bought the head from Carruthers and fitted the shaft and the grip himself. Wynne was a professional at Tooting Bec at the same time as Peter Paxton (1898–1900), who had an outstanding reputation as a golf club maker. The driving cleek has no markings on the back of the club whereas the playing cleek at the top of the page bears the traditional 'Carruthers'/Patent/Edinburgh' mark with 'Warranted Hand

Forged'. The playing cleek is also stamped with Anderson's arrow mark. A Carruthers' family heirloom, the club originally belonged to Tom Carruthers, the maker of the club.

The bottom club shown on the previous page is a fine example of an unusual ladies' round-soled playing cleek that has the letter 'L' on the back of the club alongside the mark of the seller of the club, 'J. Preston & Sons / Leamington'. Carruthers, wrote D. G. Robertson of the Brunswick Golf Club in March 1891 when commenting on Tom Morris' new round-soled cleek, had been selling round-soled lofting irons for some years past so this application of the through-bore patent design to the ladies' cleek was a natural development. To find the markings of the seller, or no marks at all, is common in Carruthers' patent clubs as he only put his own mark on the clubs sold from his own shop, and as his business was mainly devoted to the wholesale and export markets from about 1894 onwards, his own markings are fairly rare.

Carruthers' 1890 Patent Short Socket Bent Blade Putter

The Putting Cleek began to be used in the 1880s for short shots around the green where the ground was flatter but the grass longer and uneven. It differed from the iron putter in that its face was slightly laid back. The shaft was stiff, shorter and more upright.

The putter shown is not a putting cleek but is a bent blade smooth-faced Carruthers' 1890 patent putter with a short socket drilled through. The design is most unusual because the bottom of the socket stops approximately half an inch above the bottom of the club. This was designed to remove any tendency for the socket of the club at the heel to catch the ground before striking the ball. Because the blade is set well back behind the line of the

125

shaft, the player is able to see the whole of the ball and the face of the putter much better than with an ordinary putter.

The putter bears the traditional 'Carruthers'/Patent/Edinburgh' mark on the back along with 'Warranted Hand Forged' below it. This club belonged to John Carruthers, Tom Carruthers' third son, and dates to about 1900.

GUN METAL PUTTING CLEEK

'Centre Balance' Gun Metal Putter

Whereas gun metal putters (an alloy of copper and tin in the proportion of about nine to one, once used in the making of cannon) became popular in the 1890s, the putting cleek had become popular in the previous decade. The only alternative to the putting cleek at this time was the gun metal putting cleek which was a heavier metal that helped to give a firmer stroke.

ROUND-FACED PUTTING CLEEKS/IRONS

Pete Georgiady wrote the following about a Carruthers' round-faced putter in an e-mail sent to the author:

> Some years ago I had a most unique Carruthers' putter. Besides being short hosel, through bore design, it had a roll face (convex) for imparting topspin. Alas, I sold it at least a dozen years ago.

The quality of the picture of this round-faced putter overleaf does not show it to its best advantage. In 1892 James Anderson of Anstruther brought out his Kurtos putter and it is possible that, taking into account their close working relationship, the Carruthers' round-faced putter incorporated the Anderson design, which wasn't patented.

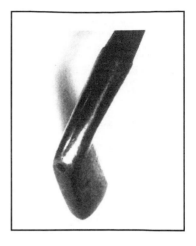

> In shape it somewhat resembles an ordinary cleek, only it presents a round or convex face to the ball, and shows no edges to disturb the eye of the player. It is claimed for the new club that it will ensure a perfect run for the ball, as its formation ensures that it will neither top the ball nor cause it to jump, as is often done by an ordinary flat-faced putter'. (*Golf*, 27 May 1892)

Carruthers' 1890 Patent Short Socket Round-Faced Putter, the face of which was probably similar to that of James Anderson's Kurtos putter

The round-faced putting iron would have used the same principle. It had a deeper face and was designed to cater for more grassy lies.

DRIVING IRONS, SAND IRONS AND LOFTING IRONS

These irons were deeper in the blade than the cleek. They had different weights and degrees of loft to suit the particular shot and the shafts were shorter. Whereas the cleek was designed for distance, the iron clubs,

Carruthers' 1890 Patent Short Socket Lofting Iron

especially the lofter and sand irons, were designed to give more elevation. The example shown is a Carruthers' 1890 patent lofting iron with short socket, drilled through. It bears the traditional 'Carruthers'/Patent/Edinburgh' on the back with 'Warranted Hand Forged' below. A Carruthers' family heirloom, it originally belonged to Tom Carruthers, the maker of the club.

ROUND-SOLED IRONS

The letter dated 7 March 1891 from D. G. Robertson, Captain of the Brunswick Golf Club, entitled 'The Cleek for Cupped Balls', previously referred to in an earlier chapter and which commented on a round-soled cleek designed by Tom Morris, contained the statement that ' ... Mr. T. Carruthers, Edinburgh, had regularly sold round-soled lofting irons to golfers for some years past'. These irons, dating into the 1880s, would not have been of short socket, through-bore design, as the Carruthers' short socket patent irons were not patented until 1890.

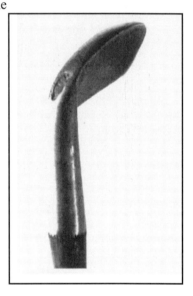

As the subject of the correspondence clearly indicates, this club was especially adapted to play a ball lodged in a small hollow with a cup-shaped structure and also for balls resting on hanging lies.

The picture shown is an example of the Carruthers' 1890 patent smooth-faced round-soled lofting iron with a short socket, drilled through. It has a curved sole with a straight top line and a concave face. The traditional 'Carruthers/Patent/Edinburgh' mark is stamped on the back, along with the mark 'Braddell & Sons Belfast', a sports' goods firm established in 1811, which began making golf clubs in the early 1890s. It has the letters 'J. J. R.' carved on the shaft. The club dates to the early 1890s.

Carruthers' 1890 Patent Short Socket Round-Soled Loftimg Iron

DRIVING MASHIES/MACHIES

The mashie was developed from the lofting iron, becoming popular in the latter half of the 1880s. It was designed to give more loft and was popularly used for pitching the ball onto the green. The driving mashie, however, has less loft than the mashie and was used off the tee at long par three holes or into a strong wind.

The picture below is of a Carruthers' 1890 patent deep-faced mashie with a short socket, drilled through. It bears the traditional mark 'Carruthers'/Patent/Edinburgh' on the back with 'Warranted Hand Forged' in small letters above it. It is also stamped 'Mashie' and bears the Anderson arrow marks that dates the club to post 1895. This also is a Carruthers' family heirloom which originally belonged to Tom Carruthers, the maker of the club.

Carruthers' 1890 Patent Short Socket Deep-Faced Mashie

NIBLICKS

The niblick was used to extricate balls from very bad lies, such as a cart rut, sand lies or deep hollows. The head is heavy, very small and round and was used when no other club would be effective.

The picture overleaf on the left is an early Carruthers' iron niblick or rut-iron with short socket, drilled through, with no markings on the back of the club. This club, listed in Henderson and Stirk's book *Golf in the Making*, would certainly appear to date before 1890, the year of the Carruthers' patent. The metal at the point where the socket joins the shaft is much cruder than the example shown on the right.

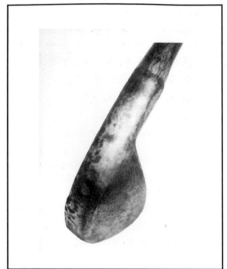 

Carruthers' 1890 Patent Short Socket Niblicks

The immediate success of the Carruthers' short socket invention confirmed its importance as a technological advance in the evolution of iron clubs. It marked the culmination of the heavy work programme which had brought such a wide range of new clubs ready for sale in a relatively short time from the date when the patent was registered on 3 December 1890, the effective date, and acceptance of the final specification on 12 September 1891. The effort required by the initial development, the patent process, and collaboration with Andersons of Anstruther who had to adapt their production methods for the new club, would have been considerable. As it also cost a large sum of money Carruthers must have been very confident that this development in club technology, which he was bringing to the market, was robust. It is possible that he had already brought this innovative design to fruition and had made and tested the concept 'on the green' without the protection provided by the registration and acceptance of a provisional specification by the patent office. Although at first sight this seems a risky strategy it must be remembered that the concept of patenting a golf club innovation had not yet taken a firm hold before the 1890s.

While the club above (left) bears all the hallmarks of a 'pre-patent' club it is impossible to confirm this without further information. Nevertheless, it is interesting that a Carruthers' cleek was sold at auction in March 2001 which had an added backweight, two inches by one inch in size, professionally affixed to the back. Maybe this was one such experimental club used to evaluate the application of added weight to the striking area in the development stages of his patented design.

The right-hand picture on the previous page shows a Carruthers' 1890 patent smooth-faced niblick with a short socket, drilled through. It bears the traditional mark 'Carruthers'/Patent/Edinburgh' with the words 'Warranted' above his mark and 'Hand Forged' below the mark. The owner's initials are also stamped on the back.

Post-1892 Carruthers' Golf Clubs

The two 1892 Carruthers' Price Lists of his Ordinary and Patent Clubs relate only to that window in time, and whereas this provides a historical insight into his range of clubs, we know that his product range evolved, in response to changes in club design in the industry, over the many years in which his business thrived. His bulger-type wooden clubs with through-bore socket design and the bent blade putter are examples but he also produced an interesting concentric design cleek, shown below, that has the weight concentrated behind the ball-striking area and tapering to the top edge and heel and toe.

Carruthers' 1890 Patent Short Socket Concentric Cleek

Marks on Carruthers' Patent Short Socket Iron Clubs

Jeffrey Ellis explains the history of marking clubs in his book, *The Clubmaker's Art,* as follows:

> Prior to the 1890s, a mark on a club, if there was one, identified the club's maker or owner. Not many pre-1890 irons exist, and few of them are marked. After 1890 it became common practice for golf professionals to purchase – either finished or raw – club heads, shafts, and grips and then assemble or otherwise prepare them for sale. Irons were then marked with information relating to the maker, the seller (a professional or a retail establishment), or both.

In accordance with the general practice of the day no 'Carruthers' mark of identification was stamped on the iron clubs sold from his shop until the late 1880s. Examples of his iron clubs, as listed in his price list 'List of Ordinary Clubs' (non-patented), bearing his mark are very rare, but those that do survive are marked 'Carruthers/Edinburgh'. His iron club heads were sourced from James Anderson of Anstruther and some rare examples of Anderson's 1880s' period iron clubs that can be identified are marked only with the name of the cleekmaker on the club head: 'Anderson Anstruther'. Such clubs were sold to golfers through outlets such as the Carruthers' shop at Bruntsfield Links.

The following article from *Compendium of British Club Makers* by Peter Georgiady describes the cleek marks used by Andersons of Anstruther:

> James Anderson died early in life in 1895 and was succeeded in the business by his son Alexander. Alex did a fine job of growing the company from his father's moderately sized shop to a large volume production company making hundreds of thousands of heads yearly. The Andersons used several cleek marks over the years. James' first mark appeared in about 1875 or 1880 and was used up to his death in 1895. It is the classic Anderson-Anstruther name in a circle measuring only ½" diameter, usually stamped in the centre of the back of the club head. Alex then switched to a similar mark with a double circle, which he used for about 15 years before reverting to the original design his father used, only in a slightly larger 5/8" size circle. It was Alex who began to use the 'arrow' cleek mark for which the firm is now so famous.

None of the Carruthers' patented short socket metal club heads sourced from Anderson appear to have been marked with either of the Anderson circular logos and only some bear the 'arrow' mark. This was probably a condition of the supply contract.

Carruthers' short socket patent clubs that bear marks other than his own 'Carruthers'/Patent/Edinburgh' mark, are numerous for the following reasons: The Carruthers' selling strategy for his patented short socket golf clubs was to provide an advantage to golf professionals and others selling direct to the public by providing them with the option to have their own mark solely stamped on the back of the metal club head. After all, as well as being a club maker, he also had had a retail outlet at his shop for many years, at 5 Gillespie Place, and also at the Braid Hills Golf Course from 1899. He knew how this stamp option appealed to the trade and, if more clubs were sold as a result, it would in turn boost his own sales. Therefore, neither the cleekmaker's mark (Anderson) nor Carruthers' own mark appear on club heads, except when he, himself, sold direct to the public, in which case he would add his own mark. The golf professionals and agents, who themselves sold direct to the public, would add their own unique mark which would normally be the only name to appear on the club head. It was a strategy that proved to be popular with those operating within the golf trade who could therefore have their own mark only on the back of the inventor's readily recognisable club head (the short socket and the visible end of the shaft appearing on the sole of the club head). As we shall see in Chapter 7, Tom Carruthers' main business was supplying his patented short socket clubs for the wholesale and export volume markets from 1893–1894 onwards. His direct sales to the public were limited in comparison and this accounts for the rarity of club heads marked with the 'Carruthers'/Patent/Edinburgh' mark.

In marketing his new invention Carruthers probably provided a complete choice of service to his customer: a metal club head only could be supplied, either unmarked, to which the customer could later stamp the club head, or have it stamped with the customer's own proprietary mark by Anderson for no extra charge; or a complete club could be fitted with the shaft and grip in Carruthers' own workshop.

James Anderson of Anstruther

An article that appeared in *Golf*, 15 July 1892, summarises the history of James Anderson, the famous cleekmaker:

Over thirty years ago Mr. Anderson entered on business as a smith and farrier, in a quaint roadside cottage at the outskirts of the burgh, and chiefly with his own hands forged the horseshoes and shod the horse, like 'John Smith o'fallow fine' occasionally turning his hand to the making of Golf-cleeks and irons, a job not unlike the forging of a horseshoe; but for many years this was a small affair. In the best of times, when he had turned out 500 cleeks in a year he had done a big stroke of business; but the finely-made cleek led to continued increase of trade. To meet the demand Mr. Anderson introduced machinery into the polishing of the work, but all the forging is done by hand. A large building, erected by an old naval doctor for a museum, came into the market, and to it Mr. Anderson removed, only to find it not half large enough. Other buildings for forges had to be erected, and now he has 14 forges constantly turning, and more than double the number of men and lads are employed. The polishing and finishing necessitated increased machinery and this is driven by 12 horsepower Otto gas engine. With all this increase in production, the same high quality of article is maintained. Mr. Anderson, in his blue flannel shirt, with his bushy black locks, and burghley frame, is constantly in the work, nothing escaping his eye, which largely accounts for his success.

No accurate account can be given of the number of cleeks turned out, but about 16 tons of the finest iron is used and it is computed that this yields over 40,000 clubs in a year, sent to all parts of the world, Bombay having been one of the earliest customers. Forrester's centre-balance cleeks, *Carruthers* and other patents, are all made by Anderson, who though not a golfer,

Golfing, 15 March 1900, James Anderson's advertisement

has a keen sense of what tool is needed. He has never taken out a patent until this year when he registered a new putter, which he intends shortly to have in the market, the main feature being a rounded face.

As can be seen from the preceding passage Tom Carruthers was an important part of James Anderson's business. It is estimated that the number of Carruthers' golf club heads produced in his forges during the period when Tom was actively engaged in the golf business ran well into six figures. His patented short iron socket for metal golf clubs accounted for most of these sales and represented about two and a half years production from Anderson's forges at Anstruther measured in terms of his 1892 output.

Identification of Carruthers' Patented Short Socket Iron Golf Clubs

The following points help in the identification and dating of Carruthers' patented short socket iron clubs made in the period covered by the patent 1890–1904:

*   The design is readily identifiable – the club head has a short socket, being about two inches shorter than the length of other sockets when patented in 1890, and the shaft appears out through the heel of the socket onto the sole of the club.

*   As Anderson of Anstruther was the manufacturer of Carruthers' club heads in Britain some club heads carry the Anderson arrow mark but none appear to have been stamped with either of the two 'Anderson/Anstruther' circular marks. (In the post patent protection period after 1904, Anderson continued to forge the Carruthers' patent design for Carruthers and also for themselves, which they sold using their own circular mark).

*   Although American golf manufacturers turned out their own ranges of clubs in quantity from about 1896/97 onwards they still imported large numbers of clubs from Britain's best makers. Amongst these was Carruthers who was still exporting his clubs/club heads to the United States in 1899. The extent to which the Carruthers iron club heads for this market in the period up to 1904 were locally forged by cleekmakers such as J. W. Williams of Brooklyn, New York, maybe under license, and assembled by makers such as BGI and MacGregor, is unclear but James Anderson retained a strong presence.

* The club heads bear the seller's mark, e.g. golf professional or retail store. This includes the Carruthers' clubs sold through his own retail outlet, as opposed to wholesale, which are marked 'Carruthers'/Patent/Edinburgh'. Note the use of the possessive case apostrophe, Carruthers' Patent, after his name, which Carruthers strictly adhered to, not only in stamping his mark on the back of his patent irons, but in all his advertisements and literature such as price lists.

* Because most of the Carruthers' patent clubs were sold wholesale or for export, there are many different individual marks on clubs. Some of these include clubs stamped with the mark of well-known names such as Harry Vardon, Totteridge, Tom Ball and Craigie of Montrose and not so well known professionals such as W. A. Wood, Cheltenham.

* There are Carruthers' patent clubs that have no markings whatsoever, either because marks have been worn away by continual removal of rust by excessive emery paper rubbing or because they were clubs sold to the trade and never stamped with the seller's own mark

* Some Carruthers clubs are stamped 'Warranted Hand Forged'. According to Peter Georgiady the appearance of these words stamped on the back of iron clubs can be dated to post 1896 or 1897:

> By 1900 most British made irons had the warranted statement, in response to an anticipated import threat from American club manufacturers who, like MacGregor, were already supplying British makers with rough turned persimmon heads ready for finishing.

Golf Bags

Although Tom Carruthers handed over the day-to-day management of his golf business to his second son, Thomas Jun. when in his sixty-fifth year, he continued to apply his inventive mind to the game and on 1 October 1908, he applied for a patent for a new design of golf bag which involved 'the application of a spring attached to a moveable rod with a footplate attached thereto for the purpose of making a self supporting golf bag.' On applying pressure to either a hand or foot knob the spiked rod was inserted into the ground. When the bag was removed from the ground the spring drew up the rod into the bag. His patent No. 20,706 was accepted on 12 August 1909 on filing the complete specification.

N° 20,706

A.D. 1908

Date of Application, 1st Oct., 1908
Complete Specification Left, 31st Mar., 1909—Accepted, 12th Aug., 1909

PROVISIONAL SPECIFICATION.

"Improvements in or relating to Golf Club Bags."

I, THOMAS CARRUTHERS, 5 Gillespie Place, Edinburgh, Golf Club Maker, do hereby declare the nature of this invention to be as follows:—

Carruthers' Patent No. 20706 for 'Improvements in or relating to Golf Club Bags'

Carruthers' 1892 autumn catalogue gave a full page spread to a new golf bag, 'designed and manufactured by a golfer of twenty years experience, and recognised by all players as the most perfect bag in the market.' This was the golf club bag, designed by David Stocks, later to become captain of the Warrender Golf Club, who applied and was given approval for his provisional patent application on 12 May 1892. He received acceptance of his complete specification on 11 March 1893 and was issued with letters patent. Stocks' first advertisement appeared almost immediately afterwards in *Golf*, 7 April 1893, but it is interesting to see that Carruthers was selling the golf club bag six months before the Stocks patent was granted. He had good judgement for this golf bag was still being advertised ten years later.

STOCKS' PATENT
GOLF ÷ CLUB ÷ BAG

(Protected by Royal Letters Patent).

Designed and Manufactured by a Golfer of 20 years' experience, and recognised by all Players as the Most Perfect Bag in the Market.

>⟶※⟵

The Bag is of the usual size, and is fitted with a Tube and Rod by which the Bag is made to stand upright.

The rod slips up and down the tube, and by a slight pressure on the Ball at top fixes the Bag to the ground upright, thus avoiding all unnecessary stooping, and giving the player a quick and easy selection.

To lift the Bag, pull the rod upwards, when it disappears into the tube, leaving no unsightly or dangeroos point protruding.

The Bag is fitted with a large and handy pocket *inside*, to hold Cap and Balls.

The Straps are arranged to form Handle or Shoulder Strap as desired.

Has neat straps outside for waterproof coat or umbrella.

Bag will not tilt, as is usual, when filled with Clubs, and, from the nature of its construction, feels lighter and more readily carried in the hand.

If a caddy is engaged, it can be made an ordinary Bag by simply withdrawing the rod.

Will repay the extra outlay in one day's golfing.

Designed specially to suit Greens where Caddies are not readily got or are an expensive commodity.

DAVID STOCKS,
BAG AND LEGGING MANUFACTURER,
20 NIDDRY STREET, EDINBURGH.

Stocks' Patent Golf Bag, 11 March 1893

Chapter 7

Advertisements 1891–1908

The first advertisement for Carruthers' patent socket irons appeared in *Golf*, 13 March 1891.

CARRUTHERS' PATENT SOCKET IRONS.

Perfect Balance, 7s. each. Only to be had from the

Patentee, T. CARRUTHERS, 5, Gillespie Place, Edinburgh.

For description of this Cleek, see Golf, Feb. 27th.

The phrase 'Perfect Balance', soon to be established as his trademark, appeared consistently in all future advertisements for the next sixteen years. The selling price of 7 shillings each (20 shillings to the pound in those days) was for the complete club, that is to say, with the shaft and grip fitted.

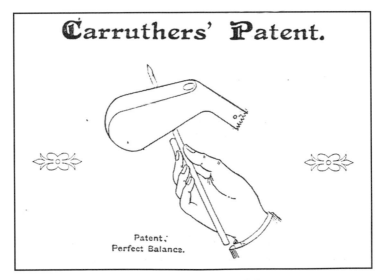

Carruthers' Patent: Perfect Balance

The words 'Only to be had from the Patentee, T. Carruthers, 5, Gillespie Place, Edinburgh' refer to his shop which housed both his dairy business and his golf outlet where he made, sold and repaired golf clubs as well as selling and re-making gutta-percha balls and golf equipment. More importantly, the advertisement's wording proclaims the exclusive rights and control given to him by the provisions of the patent. 'For description of this Cleek, see *Golf*, Feb. 27th.' draws attention to the extensive first published reviews by the respected commentators J. G. McPherson and Gregor Macgregor that appeared in *Golf*, 27 February 1891. These reviews are reproduced in Chapter 4.

The advertisement in *Golf* was interestingly preceded, in the same column and on the same page, by the letter, dated 7 March 1891, quoted earlier, from D. G. Robertson, Captain of Brunswick Golf Club, which substantiated the existence of Carruthers' golf business during the 1880s with the following phrase: 'I also know that Mr. Anderson of Anstruther, is at present making round soled lofting irons for Mr. T. Carruthers, Edinburgh, who has regularly sold them to golfers for some years past.'

On 20 March 1891, only a week after his first short narrative advertisement, his second advertisement for patent socket iron clubs appeared in *Golf*. This was the first advertisement to carry his 'Patent. Perfect Balance' design trademark incorporating an illustration of the 'perfect balance'. The quoted prices are '7s. each; or Head alone, 5s.' His 'patent iron clubs' carried a premium to his 'ordinary iron clubs', which he sold ready shafted for 5s. each.

The final phrase in the advertisement 'Trade supplied on Special Terms' is significant, indicating widespread demand following the good reception and interest that his newly-patented club had

Golf, **20 March 1891: Carruthers' rushed advertisement**

created. The presentation of the advertisement bears all the hallmarks of a rushed job for not only is the illustration upside down but his name has the letter 'U' missing.

His next advertisement, which appeared in the same magazine on 3 April 1891, comprised a simple short statement. This excluded the illustration shown in his previous advertisement, no doubt to allow more time and to ensure that the mistakes couldn't be repeated. On the same page it is interesting to note the advertisements of the following list of other illustrious club makers: A. Forgan, P. Paxton, D. McEwan & Son, R. Forgan & Son, Alex. Patrick and W. Park Jun.

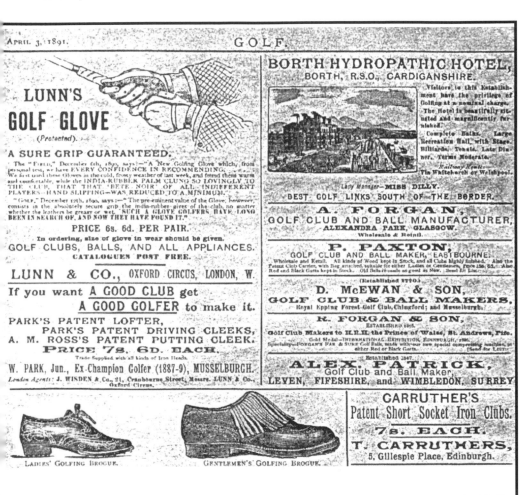

Golf, **3 April 1891**

When *Golf's* edition of 17 April 1891 appeared, the Carruthers' Perfect Balance trade mark was back in the display where it was to remain in all Carruthers' advertisements for the next fifteen years, the longest running golf trade mark advertisement of its time.

Golf, **17 April 1891**

On the right hand side of the page of advertisements shown below is a typical Carruthers' display with the 'Perfect Balance' trademark and the phrase 'the longest driving cleek in the world', that was to appear in all future Carruthers' advertisements.

Willie Park Jun. stated in his book, *The Game of Golf*, published in 1896, that it was necessary to buy a patented driving cleek to get the best club. Clearly referring to the Carruthers' patent he wrote:

> The socket of the cleek i.e. the part into which the shaft is fitted should be short and light so as to enable more weight to be put into the blade … The general principle is the weighting of the blade behind the point of impact of the ball and all driving cleeks are made more or less on this principle or a modification of it. There is no doubt that these cleeks enable a longer ball to be driven than can be done with an ordinary cleek …

The magazine advertisement which is reproduced below dated 16 October 1891 carries a large advertisement for Lunn & Co., Oxford Circus, W. (London) which features George Twist's patent mechanical putter, the first

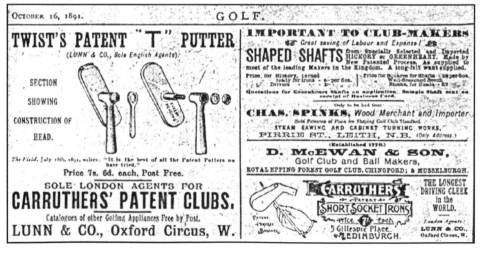

Golf, **16 October 1891**

adjustable club to be patented, and immediately below 'Carruthers' Patent Clubs' are advertised with the statement that Lunn & Co. are his sole London agents.

The Lunn and Carruthers' advertisements for his patent clubs signified an important development – he now had the formidable support of one of London's major golfing retailers, right in the heart of the most exclusive and popular shopping centre of the capital at Oxford Circus. Lunn & Co. were always in the vanguard of promoting popular new golf equipment in the 1890s, which they consistently advertised in the golf journals, and were agents for Peter Paxton, Tom Carruthers, R. Anderson & Son and Willie Park. They were also the exclusive sellers of the Balfour line of clubs, Balfour being the popular amateur golfing Member of Parliament.

The association with Lunn & Co. established Carruthers at the forefront of the commercially successful patentees and club makers during the 1890s. At the same time Carruthers was also selling clubs direct to the public, for example, 'short socket irons price 7/- each', from his golf shop at 5 Gillespie Place.

Whereas Lunn's advertisement claimed sole London agency rights to sell the Carruthers' patent clubs, Carruthers' own advertisement did not attribute sole rights to them. This was more correct, as he proceeded to appoint further London agents to promote and sell his patent clubs on a non-exclusive basis.

The Carruthers' advertisement of 16 October 1891 finally became his established format until the beginning of 1893, although important wording changes were introduced indicating the direction in which his business was moving.

The Carruthers' advertisement of 20 May 1892, which appeared in *Golf*, signified another landmark business achievement with the use of the words 'to be had from all leading club-makers'. This short phrase meant that in the space of just over a year his existing 'trade' distribution chain had been extended to cover the major golf centres.

Golf, **20 May 1892**

Securing a wide distribution network, which included golf professionals and a number of other manufacturers ('the trade') and leading golf stockists ('the agents'), could not have been accomplished single-handed for, in addition to the tasks of golf club design and manufacture, the administrative burden must have been onerous. However, one of the advantages of fathering a large family of eleven children meant that assistance was available. In the early 1890s four of Tom Carruthers' grown-up daughters – Agnes, Jessie, Lizzie and Maggie – still lived at home in Bruntsfield, Edinburgh. All in their early twenties, they ran the dairy business and assisted in the administration of the golf business at 5 Gillespie Place. Three of his daughters were to remain

**Carruthers' daughters, Lizzie and Maggie, and his grandson Tom,
the author's father (circa 1915)**

unmarried and their father gifted the property at 5 Gillespie Place, Edinburgh, to them in 1922 'for love, favour and affection which I have and bear my daughters Agnes, Jessie and Lizzie …' The family also employed a domestic servant to assist with running the household.

Tom Carruthers was extremely active in putting in place the foundations of his growing golf business in the early 1890s and travelled extensively during this period. That he was never content to turn down a business opportunity might be indicated by a report in *Golf*, 11 September 1891, that 'Mr. T. Carruthers, Golf Clubmaker, Edinburgh, has just laid out a Golf course for Mr. Alfred Rothschild at Tring' (Halton, Buckinghamshire). It is not known, however, whether Carruthers designed any other golf courses.

Upon inheriting the Halton Estate in 1879, Alfred de Rothschild commissioned William Rodgers to design, and Cubitts to build, 'an English Chateau modelled on modern French lines'. Construction was completed in 1883. There was never any intention to take up permanent residence in Halton House; it was built purely as a weekend home, providing an escape from the City and enabling the family to indulge in their passion for hunting, and later, Alfred de Rothschild's own enthusiasm for golf. Born in 1842, Alfred Charles de Rothschild was at one time Governor of the Bank of England.

The original course designed by Tom Carruthers for Alfred Rothschild consisted of six holes. It included a par six hole with the tee on the site of the present clubhouse and the hole finishing on the site of what is now the first green. Shortly after the First World War the land was acquired by the War Office for use as a training camp for the fledgling RAF. During the Second World War, when Henry Cotton was stationed at Halton, he added a further three holes. Now extended to eighteen holes, the Tring Golf Club is today known as Chiltern Forest Golf Club.

As well as being active in establishing a distribution and marketing network for his growing golf business and laying out a new golf course for Alfred de Rothschild, Carruthers was able to find time to patent three new designs for which he was issued letters of acceptance for his provisional specifications from the Patent Office as follows:

1. 22045 – 17 December, 1891 – A new or improved method for loading all wooden golf playing clubs.
2. 5781 – 24 March 1892 – A new and improved wooden golf club having metal on sole and face.
3. 7992 – 28 April 1892 – The 'Medal' golf club.

In early 1893, the Carruthers' business took another important step in cementing its distribution channels in the Metropolis when Tom secured the services of John Wisden & Co. 21 Cranbourn Street, London, W.C. as agents, which added to the strength of his existing London agents, Lunn & Co. at Oxford Circus. In the following year Wisden opened a new golf showroom which was to become 'London's greatest golf depot'.

Lunn & Co.'s advertisement in *Golf*, 13 January 1893, still represented themselves as sole London Agents for 'Carruthers' Patent Short Socket Irons' but John Wisden in an advertisement in *Golf*, 24 March 1893, also proclaimed itself as 'Sole London Agents for All Best Makes'. (See p. 147)

Included in an extensive list of many of the foremost club makers of the period were 'Carruthers' short socket cleeks, irons and mashies 6/6 each.' The full list comprises Tom Morris, Robt. Forgan, D. McEwan, Alex. Patrick, Willie Park, P. Paxton, D. Anderson, T. Carruthers, G. Forrester, F. Fairlie.

> John Wisden & Company was one of London's premier sports outfitters and one of the first and most complete golf houses in London. Wisden's claimed to be the first house in London selling modern golf clubs back around 1874. In the heyday of the 1890s, they sold clubs from all the best makers and the latest patentees. The sole proprietor in the 1890s, Mr. Henry Luff, was an acquaintance and frequent golfing partner of J. H. Taylor.
>
> After many successful years of being an agent for others' clubs, most of which were sold with the Wisden name stamped on the shaft, they produced their own brand called Wisden's Royal (1906–11) with an escutcheon mark. Their store was an unofficial shrine of cricketing history, displaying the bats used by famous cricketers of the past century. (Peter Georgiady, *Compendium of British Club Makers*)

The following is an extract from an article entitled 'Wisden's' which appeared in *Golfing* six years later, 23 November 1899:

> Cases upon cases, and racks from the floor to the ceiling filled with picked clubs presented a splendid collection of choice specimens of such makes as those of Cann and Taylor, Peter Paxton, R. Forgan, Auchterlonie, J. and D. Clark, Anderson, Simpson, Ben Sayers, Tom Morris, Patrick, Braddell, Dickson, Forrester, *Carruthers*, Harry Vardon, and Andrew Scott.

Carruthers' *Golf* advertisement, 7 April 1893 (page 148), appeared alongside an advertisement for Thornton & Co. of 78 Princes Street, Edinburgh, India rubber manufacturers who were successful in the ball making business. They

Top: Golf, 13 January 1893. Bottom: Golf, 24 March 1893

Golf, 7 April 1893

also sold clubs and accessories and their advertisement included their central-loaded putter that was described in the previous chapter:

> Messrs. Thornton & Co., Princes Street, Edinburgh, the well-known golf ball makers, have at present a very fine stock of their seasoned 'Match' balls. They have 10,000 dozen (120,000) of thoroughly seasoned balls, carefully finished and painted. (*Golf*, 5 June 1896)

By 1893 the level of demand for Carruthers' patented clubs had grown with such speed that the basement workshop premises at 5 Gillespie Place ran out of space. Not only was he now supplying wholesale to 'all leading club makers' but he was also selling to the public directly from his golf shop, 'price 7/- each', and through a number of agents. The climax to the overwhelmingly successful reception of the Carruthers' patented range of short socket clubs was when Hilton and Ball, legends in the history of golf, both used them so brilliantly in finishing first and second equal respectively in the 1892 Open at Muirfield (see previous chapter). Ball's prowess with the cleek was proverbial. In late 1892 Carruthers' price list proclaimed that 'All the best players are using my patent short socket iron clubs.'

New Workshop in Leven Street, Edinburgh 1893

It was at this point that Carruthers moved his golf club-making activities and reinstalled the workshop at 41 Leven Street, Edinburgh, only a short step away from 5 Gillespie Place, which was retained for his golf shop, dairy and business address. This was a two-story building, which also housed the 'Auld Toll Tavern', where tollgates to the town once stood outside. To be able to cope with the high levels of demand flowing from the universal success of his patent short socket iron clubs Carruthers was forced to re-assess and reorganise his business to meet the challenge. However, he decided that, if he was to be able to keep up with rising demand at home and also to service the new opportunities presented by exports, especially to the growing North American golf industry, he had to make changes. To achieve this he switched much of his piecemeal retail sales that were tying up valuable resources to other retail outlets, which were appointed agents, such as Thornton & Co. of Princes Street, Edinburgh (which also had branches in Glasgow, Leeds, Bradford and Belfast) – much as he would have liked to carry on these sales himself. From now on he would re-brand himself as a 'wholesale golf club manufacturer', concentrate his efforts on meeting the needs of the trade and the agents at home and take up the opportunities presented by the growing popularity of golf overseas.

Golf, 10 July 1894, carried the following advertisement for Benetfink & Co., 89, 90, 107 & 108 Cheapside, London. Adding Benetfink to the list of agents promoting Carruthers' patent clubs in the Capital marked the widespread popularity and availability of his golf clubs. Benetfink was an ancient London retailer of sporting goods that sold its own makes of clubs as well as selling those from major makers.

GREAT CITY DEPOT for Forgan's, Carruthers', Forrester's, Park's, Ayres', Slazengers', The 'Clan' &c., Golf Clubs. Agents for Brougham's Patent Aluminium Golf Drivers, Garden and Marine Golf, and the new game, Puttinshu. A large stock of well-seasoned Silvertown and 'A1' Balls always kept. Sports and Games Catalogue Free by Post. – BENETFINK & CO., 89, 90, 107, & 108, CHEAPSIDE, LONDON, E.C.

Carruthers redesigned his advertising display to bring it into line with the changes that had taken place in his golf business. The changed strategy was set out in his new style advertisement (overleaf) published in *Golf*, 7 September 1894. The text retained the phrase 'The Longest Driving Cleek in the World' but added 'All other kinds also on the same principle' and it also showed his trademark and illustration – the 'Patent Perfect Balance' golf club.

The introduction of the new phrase 'All other kinds also on the same principle' was a reference to the extensive range of patented clubs available in addition to the famous driving cleek. This range was probably quite similar to his 1892 price list of patented clubs.

The reference to 'Works' did not now only apply to 41 Leven Street because he was once more installed in new overflow workshop premises. This workshop was located on Bruntsfield Links at 26A Wright's Houses not far from his former family home at 32 Wright's Houses (1877-1879) and next to the old Golf Tavern Hotel (Hotel) which still stood at Nos. 27 and 28 Wright's Houses. The Golf Hotel was soon destined to disappear under the progressive redevelopment of Wright's Houses, begun in 1885. The building at Nos. 30/31 Wright's Houses still remained, but as a Tavern only, and it too would undergo renovation. His other immediate neighbour at No. 26 was William Davies, joiner and cabinetmakers, who may have provided contract services to Tom Carruthers, as could Peter McLaughlan, joiner, at No. 36 Wright's Houses, but this cannot be verified. Carruthers terminated his occupation of the workshop premises at 41 Leven Street in 1895 when 26A Wright's Houses became his sole workshop for the next four years.

Golf, 7 September 1894

The remainder of the wording of the advertisement marked the material change that his business had undergone. The advertisement states 'wholesale and export orders'. From this point on he would concentrate his efforts on supplying the UK through trade and agency outlets. The growing importance of demand from overseas markets, especially North America, was signalled by the introduction of the word EXPORT into his advertisements.

> Throughout the 1890s the leading British club makers were doing an increasing export business to the USA and the British Empire. (Henderson & Stirk, *Golf in the Making*)

By 1894 exports to overseas markets were assuming an important element of Carruthers' total sales. *The Golfer* reported in August 1897 that a recent edition of the *New York Sun* stated the following:

> One point that shows the extent to which golf is played is that a firm that sold 50,000 of imported golf balls during 1896 has planned to sell double the number this season and this is but an item, for as the song says, there are others selling golf balls. The demand for golf balls from the United States has amazed the foreign manufacturers. The sale of golf clubs both imported and of home manufacture is also enormous.

There were only a couple of golf courses in existence in the United States about 1890 but ten years later this had risen to over 1,000. Golf clubs were all initially imported from Scotland but by the end of the decade five US golf club-making companies were addressing the need for a home grown industry. The Carruthers' patent short socket design clubs were sold by every one of those early U.S. club makers.

Reference has been made to J. M. Cooper's book, *Early United States Golf Clubs,* and its impressive catalogue. This book includes many pictures of the Carruthers' range of short socket irons sold by Spalding, Wright & Ditson and The Bridgeport Gun Implement Co. (BGI).

The following notes give a brief account of the early American golf club makers, much of which has been derived from the book, *North American Club Makers,* by Peter Georgiady.

A. G. Spalding & Brothers
Spalding's first catalogue of golf clubs in 1893 was probably all imported from Scotland and by 1896 they were selling a range of golf clubs bearing their own mark as well as importing from the best Scottish manufacturers.

Wright & Ditson Co
'From 1890 to about 1894 or 1895 clubs sold at the Wright & Ditson Company were all imported from Scotland. Goods from

James Anderson of Anstruther, Tom Morris, Robert White and Robert Forgan were among the early shipments … It was about this time that the A. G. Spalding & Brothers Company bought a significant but silent interest in Wright & Ditson. Many early Spalding clubs are identical in form to Wright & Ditson clubs since they were produced in the same factory.' Spalding provided the supply of unmarked clubs to them and Wright & Ditson stamped their own marks on the iron and wood heads before selling them to the public.

Bridgeport Gun Implement Company

'B.G.I. offered its first golf clubs in late 1896 or 1897. It had an aggressive marketing and advertising plan rivalling Spalding and Wright & Ditson, its chief competitors. Business showed a marked improvement when the firm hired Willie Dunn in 1897 to design clubs and supervise manufacturing.' In addition to J. D. Dunn's one-piece wood, B.G.I. made a 'fork splice' driver, short hosel, Carruthers-style cleek, and several gunmetal putters. Most pre-1899 golf clubs sold by B.G.I. were imported or made by Spalding before the J. H. Williams Co., Brooklyn, New York, became its major supplier.

J. H. Williams Company

'The first iron clubs forged in the United States were probably hammered at the works at J. H. Williams in Brooklyn, New York. Most of the irons sold by B.G.I. were sourced from Williams as well as heads for MacGregor and several, other early, companies.'

Examples of these clubs exist today: a smooth-faced cleek, circa 1900, in Carruthers' short socket design, with 'Metropolitan' stamped in large block lettering on the back, sold at auction in April 2002; the Carruthers' short socket cleek, shown to the right, which bears the Williams name and is marked 'forged from steel', came up at an auction in June 2004.

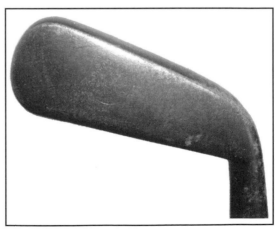

J. H. Williams & Co., Brooklyn, N.Y., Cleek with small diamond mark, incorporating the Carruthers' 1890 patent short socket design

Crawford, McGregor and Canby Company

'MacGregor produced high quality clubs throughout its first 10 years but at a relatively low volume,' They made wood heads initially until 1900 when Willie Dunn was hired to design clubs including irons and putters. Over the years they used a variety of marks on their range of clubs, including MacGregor series irons with the Carruthers' short socket design (1900–1905). Examples of these clubs exist today. For example, a 'circa 1900' Carruthers' smooth-faced cleek with the MacGregor small double circle mark around a shamrock was sold at auction in March 2001.

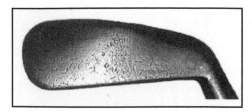

A 'J. MacGregor Cleek' with Shamrock Mark (circa 1900) incorporating the Carruthers' 1890 Patent short socket design, stamped with the their small double circle mark

Chicago Golf Shop, Inc.

'One of the most famous golf factors in America; this large golf house was a distributor of MacGregor clubs in Chicago and an agent for just about every important Scottish maker. They did a large business in both Forgan clubs and James Anderson irons.'

In an extract from *Golfing*, 16 March 1899, where the photograph opposite of Mr. T. Carruthers, Edinburgh, formed the front cover of this edition of the magazine, the writer wrote:

> Mr. Carruthers has done a great trade with his patent clubs, and up to the present has sold over 35,000 driving cleeks. There is always a demand for them and only the other day he received a large order from New York.

The second sentence is very significant because, although the United States indigenous golf club manufacturing industry was expanding towards the end of the nineteenth century, imports of Carruthers' short socket irons still continued to be strong in 1899, the forged heads being supplied by Anderson of Anstruther. The Carruthers' patented clubs were very successful and their distinctive character accounted for the continuing demand coming from the big manufacturers on the other side of the Atlantic.

Vol. VII. No. 195. MARCH 16, 1899. ONE PENNY.

Mr. T. CARRUTHERS
Edinburgh

[SEE PAGE 8.

Cover of *Golfing,* 16 March 1899, with photograph of Thomas Carruthers

The identity of the New York customer mentioned on page 154 in relation to 'the large order from new York' would have been one of those referred to in the following notes, each of which had a presence in New York.

1.   A. G. Spalding & Bros., Nassau Street, New York, (also the location of their eastern warehouse) who had a couple of stores in New York City.

2.   J. H. Williams Company, Brooklyn, New York.

3.   William Dunn Jun. was born at Blackheath where his father Willie Senior, a considerable golfer, was the professional and club maker. He emigrated to the United States. In 1891 he laid out the Shinnecock Hills golf course, New York, where he was the keeper and ran a thriving golf club shop before moving on to the Ardsley Casino Country Club, Dobbs Ferry, New York. Soon afterwards he opened a retail shop in New York City.

4. Slazengers was originally a British company which made as big an impact in the American market as it did in Britain. 'Formed in London in 1881, this company was established as a manufacturer and seller of tennis equipment ... They began offering golf clubs in the late 1880s and by the 1890s were equipped with their own brand. These earliest Slazenger clubs were assembled in their workshop beginning in 1891 with iron heads coming from James Anderson (Anstruther).' In the mid 1890s Frank Slazenger opened the company's store in New York City and was advertised as being the 'oldest golf house in the U.S.'.

5.   Messrs Park & Son: Willie Park Jun. opened a store in New York City in the late 1890s that was managed by his brother Mungo.

From September 1894 to the end of 1900 the Carruthers' golf business kept to its strategy of supplying wooden golf clubs and a full range of short socket iron clubs from the workshop at Bruntsfield Links to the wholesale and export markets. Over the counter sales were maintained, on a much reduced scale, from the shop at 5 Gillespie Place, where all the administration was looked after. The wholesale market represented the golf professionals in the major golf centres, other golf club manufacturers and the well-established retail outlets in Britain. The overseas market was essentially North American.

During this period two of Tom Carruthers' sons, Thomas Jun. and John, who were born in 1880 and 1882 respectively, and were trained as joiners after leaving school, began working in their father's golf business. The certificate of marriage of Thomas Carruthers Jun. who worked full-time in the business, described his occupation as 'golf club maker'. His younger brother, John, worked part-time. This was described in a letter from his son written in 1975 to his own son (the author). 'In his youth he worked at his trade in the morning. The afternoon was spent golfing at the Braid Hills. The evenings were devoted to club making in his father's workshop situated in Wright's Houses (Bruntsfield Links) which made up his wages.'

This studio photo shows John Carruthers (seated on the right) as a young man with other club members circa 1898. John was Tom Carruthers' third son and the author's grandfather. The identity of the club is not certain but it is definitely a Braid Hills based golf club, possibly the Edinburgh St Andrew club which rented accommodation at the Golfers Tryst clubhouse from Tom Carruthers and which ceased to exist in 1912.

Much of Tom's son's work involved preparing and fitting shafts and grips to his father's patented iron clubs. The design of a Carruthers' short socket iron meant that the club maker could get a better fitting shaft owing to the socket being open at both ends. When the club maker had selected a roughly shaped shaft, he tapered the end, fitted it into the socket and drove it down until it came out at the sole where the excess was cut off flush with the sole and secured with a rivet inserted near the top of the socket. The grain of the shaft would be set in line with the shot at right angles to the head. Once fitted, the shaft was shaped with a spoke-shave tool and sanded by hand to obtain the required degree of stiffness and to optimise the degree of whip at the correct distance above the socket. To obtain the right balance he had to take account of the type of iron club he was making, the weight of the head and the desired amount of spring in the shaft. He then cut the top of the shaft to the desired length. Once the shaft was fitted, shaped and cut to length, pitch and linseed oil were applied to bring out the grain and to provide protection against the elements. The grip would be fitted using split strips of cowhide or sheepskin leather and wound round the upper part of the shaft and secured at its upper and lower ends by a small tack. Earlier clubs often had thicker grips, built up by layers of linen strips or 'listings', under the leather grip, to obtain the desired thickness for the grip. Waxed thread whipping was wound round the lower, and sometimes the top, of the grip, to give additional security to the leather grip and then it was coated with varnish. If required, the Carruthers' mark would be stamped on the back of the club's head.

During this period, 1894–1900, J. Lillywhite, Frowd & Co. was added to the list of London retail agents stocking Carruthers' short socket iron clubs. Their advertisement that appeared in *Golf Illustrated,* 25 October 1901, states 'Golf Clubs by all the leading makers including Alex. Patrick, J. & D. Clark, Forgan, Forrester, Carruthers, Simpson, Scott, Auchterlonie, &, &.'

Peter Georgiady in *Compendium of British Club Makers* states that:

The 'Carruthers'/Patent/ Edinburgh' stamp used on 1890 Patent Short Socket Iron Clubs sold direct to the public

Long a landmark retail store in London's fashionable Piccadilly Circus shopping district, Lillywhites was once a leading supplier of cricket, football, hockey, tennis, croquet, polo and golf goods for metropolitan area golfers. Along with John Wisden & Co. they were one of the two premier West End sports depots with a strong clientele drawn from military and clubmen.

They advertised continuously and offered clubs from many leading makers as well as other golf accessories. Among the lines they sold included clubs by George Nicoll, D. & W. Auchterlonie, Bob Simpson, George Forrester, Robert Forgan, J. & D. Clark, Braddell & Son, Alex Patrick, Thomas Carruthers, J. & W. Craigie and James Anderson, one piece hickory clubs from the United States, Schenectady putters and Mills aluminium sets. Lillywhites enjoyed sole distribution rights to the patent Butchart V-groove splice woods and were a special agency for Mills clubs, circa 1898–1935.

According to *Golfing*, 9 April 1903:

The famous house of Lillywhite, Frowd & Co. have gradually and substantially increased their clientele among clubmen and others in the West End of London, until at the present day their stock and resource is a bye-word among those whose business and pleasure carry them frequently to the neighbourhood of the Haymarket.

Golf Illustrated, **25 October 1901**

The next variation of the Carruthers' advertisement appeared in *Golf, 27 December* in 1900. The advertisement signalled another change of premises and direction. Out went 'works – Bruntsfield Links' which was replaced by 'and Braid Hills Golf Course'.

When the popularity of golf in Edinburgh led to severe congestion at Bruntsfield, Edinburgh Town Council initiated steps to curtail golf activities severely. Musselburgh was then the only other golf course in the County of Midlothian. After much lobbying by the golfing community the Town Council purchased land at the Braids, on the south side of Edinburgh, constructed and subsequently opened the Braid Hills Golf Course on 29 May 1889. Two privately owned clubhouses were constructed and opened in 1892. One of these clubhouses was built for William Frier, golf club maker, described as 'Golfing Clubhouse, Tea Room and Shop selling golf equipment'. When William Frier fell into financial difficulties Tom Carruthers acquired the premises on 31 October 1899, converted part into a workshop and moved out of 26A Wright's Houses, Bruntsfield Links. The story of the Golfers Tryst and the Braid Hills Golf Courses is described in chapter 9.

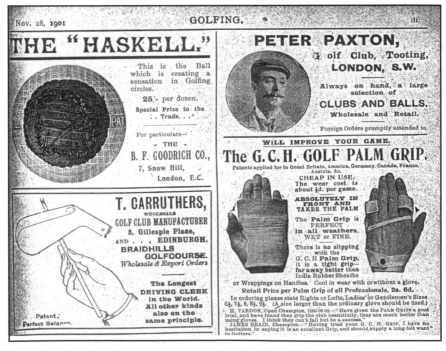

Above the Carruthers' advertisement from *Golfing,* **28 November 1901, which includes a reference to his new premises at the Braid Hills Golf Course, is one of the very first advertisements for the new 'Haskell' rubber-cored ball that was to replace the 'guttie'**

Coburn Haskell was an American golfer from Cleveland who had often turned over in his mind the possibility of improving the 'guttie' ball by the use of alternative materials in its construction. With the help of a friend who worked for the B. F. Goodrich Co. he developed the new rubber-cored ball. It was not an immediate success but once teething problems were overcome by the introduction of a new cover, the new ball was to revolutionise the game in much the same way as the 'gutta-percha ball' had when it replaced the 'feathery' fifty years earlier. It was double the price of the 'guttie' at 25 shillings per dozen and old 'gutties' could be re-made for 3 shillings per dozen! The following article which appeared under the title, 'Dearer Golf Balls – Proposal to return to the Guttie', in the *Edinburgh Evening Dispatch* on 21 April 1910, reveals how the price factor of the Haskell ball caused some sections of the golfing community to reflect on its adoption. Within the comments are some interesting observations about golf courses that echo the feelings of some parts of today's golfing community with regard to the introduction of new technologies:

Dearer Golf Balls - Proposal to return to the 'Guttie'

With rubber becoming as precious as radium, and a further rise in the price of golf balls not only possible but, according to some in the trade, probable, the moment is surely opportune (remarks the *Daily Chronicle)* to consider the question of returning to the old 'guttie'. It would be tragic to have to part with the lively rubber-core, but the solid old-fashioned 'guttie' at least has the merit of being unaffected by the fluctuations of extraneous things like markets.

Such a good opportunity of settling the question of balls will probably never occur again. St. Andrews are said to be trying to evolve the definition of a golf club. Why should they not also fix a standard ball?

As a matter of fact, if St. Andrews had been true to their traditions when the rubber-cored ball was first introduced from America, golfers might now have been supremely indifferent as to the price of rubber. At the time when the new ball made its appearance in this country, the Professional Golfers' Association strongly opposed its introduction. Braid, Taylor and Vardon were the leading men in the professional ranks who condemned the invention, and Mr. J. L. Low and Mr. S. Mure Fergusson were its strenuous opponents on the amateur side.

A meeting was held in Edinburgh to consider the matter. The views of the P.G.A. on the subject were before the meeting, but neither the opinion of the professionals nor the arguments of Mr. Low and Mr. Mure Fergusson carried any weight. St. Andrews, usually so grave and dignified, so keenly suspicious of anything with a touch of newness, were fascinated by the resiliency of the Haskell. They flirted with the young thing from the States. Now we are all in the toils of the rubber-core, which governs the situation. The thing gave its users so many obvious advantages over those who remained faithful to the 'guttie' that it was not long before its use became practically universal.

Any proposal to make the 'guttie' the standard will, of course, be met by the objection that links are now laid out for the longer-flying rubber-core. It will be said that, in many cases, it will be impossible to rearrange courses to suit the old ball. The objection seems reasonable enough on the face of it, but it must not be forgotten that even now there is no fixity of conditions. At any moment a ball may be invented which will add twenty, thirty, or any number of yards to the drive. Contrivances for adding to the flight of a ball may be introduced at intervals, and if the standard be not fixed the courses will naturally have to be altered to meet the requirements of each new invention.

Another article entitled 'American Balls and British Golfers', that considered the consequences that might flow from the introduction of the new rubber-cored ball, was written in 1903 by Horace Hutchinson, the well-known golfer and commentator. It included the following interesting observations:

There has been vague talk of standardizing the ball, which means barring everything but the 'gutty'; but people's wish to play with the ball that is most agreeable is too strong for such a step as this. Still something is being done – something in the way of lengthening courses by putting back the tees, of making the courses more difficult by multiplying bunkers – and that, no doubt, is the way that things will adjust themselves, until the inevitable time shall come when some pernicious genius shall invent a ball that will go absurdly far, in which case restrictive legislation as to the implements of the game will become a necessity. In the meantime the result is rather to bring back the game to the condition in which it was in the time of feather balls; not because the feather balls were at all more elastic than the 'gutty', but because courses were at that time much more narrow, and the sides of the courses were fringed with whins that made the punishment of crooked play quite dreadful. The result of widening the courses has been to put a premium on very hard hitting and far driving more or less irrespective of direction. It has made the game less one of skill than one of strength, speaking with relation to what it used to be. The new ball, by giving increased value to skill and less to strength, compared with the relative values of those gifts in playing with the 'gutty', has done much to re-establish the old proportions. We accept the American invention, as Britons will, of course, with grumbling, but with gratitude down in our hearts. (*Outing*)

Carruthers continued to advertise in the trade press until 1906. John Wisden & Co. were still advertising Carruthers' patent short socket irons in 1908.

JOHN WISDEN & CO.

Have the Finest Selection of Golf Clubs in the World.

MILLS' ALUMINIUM CLUBS.

Sole London Agents for CANN & TAYLOR'S CLUBS

We have always a good stock of the following makers' clubs :—

FORGAN, SCOTT, | CARRUTHERS' PATENT IRONS
BRAID, PATRICK, | GIBSON, BUTCHART,
FAIRLIE and GEO. LOWE PATENT CLUBS.

Our stock of Golf Balls includes among others :—

Kite, Colonel, Ace, Buzzard, Final, Dunlop, Macintosh, Craigpark Special, Climax, and Captain.

We are Special London Agents for :—
The CRAIGPARK "SPECIAL" and "TONIC" BALLS.
Canvas and Leather Caddy Bags, and Travelling Trunks.

21, CRANBOURNE STREET, LONDON, W.C.

Wisden Advertisement, 5 March 1908

By this time Tom Carruthers had handed over the management of his golf business to his second son Tom Jun. in 1904. In the years leading up to the Great War in 1914 the country and the golf game entered into a period of uncertainty and Tom's golf business, based on his privately-owned clubhouse (Golfers Tryst), came through into peacetime but it was not unscathed.

Chapter 8

The Evolution of Golf Clubs: the Cleek and Patent Drivers

Two great pieces of golfing history from contemporary accounts of the evolution of golf clubs feature in this chapter. The articles, written in the 1890s, are reproduced almost in their entirety in order to retain their historical perspective.

The first article entitled 'The Evolution of the Modern Club – The Cleek' appeared in *Golf*, 9 April 1897, and is supplemented by additional information at the end of the article. It sets out the important contribution that Carruthers' short socket patented design made to the development of the cleek.

THE EVOLUTION OF THE MODERN CLUB -- CLEEK

The introduction of the iron-headed club by Allan Robertson was probably intended to supply the long-felt want of a lofting or approaching implement which would not wear out so quickly as the baffy spoon and other wooden clubs, and apart from this consideration, it would commend itself for the negotiation of awkward lies. In this latter capacity especially the iron club came into more general use and favour, and by degrees supplanted the wooden spoon and baffy, their places being taken by the cleek and iron; this result, however, was not arrived at without many indignant protests from conservative-minded players, who asserted, as some of them do even yet, that this innovation would completely destroy the Royal and Ancient Game as it always had been played, just as the bulger and other modern heresies are doing now. So far as the royalty is concerned differences of opinion may arise, but nothing could be more emphatically ancient than the general appearance of these new forms of golf club, judging from the specimens which have come down to us of the 'Iron' in its original form. The name itself is suggestive, in its lack of qualification, of the primitive simplicity and rugged outline, which characterised this valuable weapon in the early days of its career. No distinction had then been finely drawn between the driving, the medium, and the lofting iron, and still less had the wonderful developments of the latter, and its hybrid offspring, the mashie, entered into the minds of our golfing forefathers. True it is that the amount of loft on the iron varied a great deal, even in those days, but that was, no doubt, due more to accident than to design, the successful junction of head and shaft occupying more of the maker's attention, the facilities for the manufacture of head and socket being probably limited to the use of an ordinary blacksmith's forge.

To these limitations may no doubt be ascribed the peculiar clumsiness and hideous form of the old iron club, the socket of which seemed to swallow the lower end of the shaft, and always represented about half the weight of metal in the whole head, tending to lose driving power and create bad balance, amounting to positive unwieldiness, from the amount of weight and its clumsy distribution. Later on, when club making became a solid profession and a lucrative business, and the demand was in advance of the supply, more attention was turned to the manufacture of iron clubs, the general shape of which had varied but little from that of the originals, although experience in construction had lessened the amount of metal necessary to produce a firm junction between head and shaft. This diminution of the weight of the socket or 'hose' of the iron was carried on until the short socket was introduced several years ago; very little, however, was heard of this form of improvement until Carruthers still further emphasised it by again reducing the length of the socket, and at the same time running the shaft right through the head so as to leave the end exposed, thus overcoming the former objection to the short socket by providing a greater length of shaft inside of, and in gripping contact with, the former. The name of 'Centre Balance' given to this and similar iron clubs shows that the improvement intended was a scientific one, and an advance in the right direction, although there are differences of opinion as to the advantages to be obtained from their use. Dickson's Patent 'Simplex' was another method of taking weight from the socket to put into the head; in it the 'hose' is replaced by a claw-hammer grip, which gives greater length to the shaft and at the same time does away with the exposure of the end of the latter, with the open end of the grain, to the wet, which is apt to destroy the shafts of Carruthers' patent clubs inside their sockets.

Nearly all the more modern forms of cleek and iron are now made with comparatively short sockets, and the average club-maker will tell you of one point which he considers is gained by this method, namely, that for the same length of club there is more shaft in the same proportion as there is less socket, and consequently (in his opinion) more driving power. This cleek driving power has become a perfect craze, and is one of the most modern features of modern Golf; it is almost universally condemned by the conservative professional fraternity, who ask, with some reason, why you carry a brassie if your patent cleek is equally effective. Professional players, however, who are also club makers, cannot afford to carry their conservatism into their business. This is evidenced by the advertised qualities of certain patent cleeks, and the craving for long cleek shots is fully realised and carefully fostered by the makers, who specially draw attention to length of carry, one patentee having even gone so far as to introduce a steel spring into the socket of his cleek, so as to get spring from grip to head. One of the most, if not the most, powerful of driving cleeks, is Anderson's patent. This cleek has the central socket at the back of the head, and the shaft is also made longer in proportion by reason of the shortness of the socket, the centralisation of the weight of the head being further emphasised by the upcurving of the ends of the sole, which gives the club the general appearance and want of beauty of a gardener's tool. It is a matter of ease to accustom oneself to the use of this club, notwithstanding its peculiar shape, but a drawback to its use is that the old form of cleek is difficult to handle afterwards, owing to a developed tendency to heel; this, of course, is no real argument against its utility, but it is a fact which has to be taken into consideration with regard to iron play, as the latter may be similarly corrupted. One especially marked feature in the more modern cleeks is the concentration of the weight of metal in the head, this being effected by shortening the latter and at the same time giving greater depth to the face. Wilson's 'Mashie' Cleek exemplifies this tendency to a marked degree, being, to all intents and purposes, a driving mashie, shafted for use as a cleek, and admirably adapted for many shots which could not be successfully accomplished with the latter club, owing to the shortness of the head which permits its easy introduction into 'cups' and the depth of the face which allows more margin in ' getting down' to a heavy-lying ball.

Numerous, and generally hideous, are the cleeks with excrescences at the back of the head. These are also designed for long shots, but more reasonably for negotiating heavy lies, in which capacity the cleek naturally supersedes the brassie. The centralisation of the weight of the head, resulting from the presence of these bumps on the back of it, although pandering to the popular taste in the 'long carry' direction does not by any means tend to facility of usage. On the face of an ordinary club a target may be drawn, having a small bull's eye representing the spot for correct impact, surrounded by 'inner,' 'magpie,' and 'outer' rings, elliptical in outline, and showing what margin may be allowed for moderate, bad, and abominably bad shots respectively. Now, in a cleek with a patent central hump the concentration of weight is such as to reduce the diameters of these rings considerably, making, perhaps a 'mag' into an 'outer,' and an 'outer' into a practical 'miss.' This, of course, does not of necessity lessen the utility of the implement in the hands of a skilful exponent of the game, but to the majority of players it would prove a serious drawback, far outweighing the advantages gained by extra length of carry.

Forrester, of Elie, seems to be the leading spirit in this phrenological department of club making, having patented cleeks with central bumps and bumps spread over the back of the head, his latest addition to the list being characterised by the abnormal position of the 'knob,' the latter being placed behind the nose of the club in order to counterbalance the weight of the socket, and so promote good direction. Hood has a rectangular lozenge on the back of his cleek, and Park's driving cleek is a combination of all sorts of good qualities derived from the possession of a short socket and an impartially-distributed bulge at the back. Park's 'Spade' was a weird form of cleek introduced some years since; in it the sole was straight, and the upper edge curved down at the ends, aiming, no doubt, at centre balance. The reverse of this form is seen in cleeks with the sole curved up at the ends, facilitating the extrication of the ball from a cuppy lie.

Another improvement upon, or, rather, difference from, the old form of cleek is the modern tendency towards breadth of sole. This alteration is a very marked one, and is partly a consequence of the before-mentioned shortening of the socket, necessitating a greater thickness of head, and partly of the wiliness of the club maker. The great aim of the latter in these days of multiplicity of makers is to produce clubs, which will suit the medium golfer, who is in a majority. Now there is a very intimate connection between his consummation and the breadth of sole of the modern cleek, which arises in the following manner: In speaking of drivers, mention was made of the well-known fact that the lowness of trajectory of a golf ball's flight is inversely proportional to the height above the sole of the centre of gravity of the head. This same rule applies to iron clubs, and its practical exemplifications are much more exaggerated in their case. The broad-soled cleek has its centre of gravity well below the middle of the head, and, consequently, 'throws up' the ball very quickly, producing a high carry, though not a long one. Now the medium golfer, although sometimes able to drive well enough off the tee with a cleek, often, indeed, preferring it to a play-club for that purpose, is very apt to be miserably inefficient with the same club out of a soft or cuppy lie through the green, this inefficiency generally taking the form of driving the ball along the ground, although it may not have been topped. But let the same player essay a similar shot with a comparatively broad-soled cleek; his imperfectly-formed, jerky, hitting swing, which before expended all its, perhaps, enormous energy in making the ball 'duck' along the ground, will now produce more elevation, and, what is to him, perhaps, even a satisfactory shot. Of the two clubs, the old and the new, he will believe in, prefer, and play with the latter; he is satisfied, and so is the club maker.

(C. M. H. *Golf*, 9 April 1897)

The derivation of the name cleek was explained in a letter to the editor of *Golf* on 13 February 1891:

Sir

It has been seriously stated in print that the name 'cleek' has been given to this club in allusion to the 'click' or sound emitted when a golf ball is struck by it. This is erroneous.

Etymology is not based on phonetics: neither need a Scot resort to English. His mother tongue is quite expressive enough. In Scotch a 'cleik' means an iron hook, and the verb to 'cleik' or 'cleek' means to 'catch up' or 'snatch away' with a hook. This name, therefore, is peculiarly appropriate to a club, which is specially intended to sweep away a ball out of a rather uneven or bad lie.

I am Sir, etc. W. G.
Wimbledon Club

Below are some brief notes about the club makers mentioned in the article:

Allan Robertson: 'The greatest golf player that ever lived, of whom alone in the annals of the pastime it can be said that he never was beaten. Born in St Andrews on 11 September 1815.'
(Obituary Notice, *The Dundee Advertiser*, September 1859)

Carruthers: The design principles of the short socket patent of 1890 are covered in the article (concentration of the weight at the point of contact between blade and ball). His trademark was 'Perfect Balance'. It was one of the most important and successful patents of the wooden-shafted era that continues to influence club design more than a century later.

Dickson: John and Andrew Dickson were club makers in Braid Road, Rose Street, and Comiston Road, Edinburgh. They patented a Simplex iron in 1893 but it was only in production for a very short time.

Anderson: Originally manufacturers of fishing tackle with premises in Princes Street, Edinburgh, Robert Anderson patented several unusual clubs. His 'queer-looking' centre-shafted iron clubs were initially well received but their unusual shape ran up against a lot of prejudices and were not widely accepted.

Wilson: Served his apprenticeship with Old Tom Morris in the 1880s. Douglas Rolland was highly successful with Wilson's mashie cleek in the many matches he played and always praised this club.

Forrester: One of the most innovative club makers of the 1890s. The article refers to his 'Master Cleek' but he also produced a 'Ball Back Patent Cleek', 'Centre Balanced Cleek' and 'Concentrated Lofter'. The last-named design has endured to the present day.

Hood: Of Musselburgh and Braid Road, Edinburgh. Better known for his wooden clubs.

Park: 'Undoubtedly the most versatile of all the great golfers of the 19th century. Willie was the best-known club maker in the business over the ten years to 1895. He was a champion golfer, author, course designer, real estate developer, club and ball designer and club maker before he saw his fortieth birthday.' (Peter Georgiady, *Compendium of British Club Makers*). Park's driving cleek was never patented.

The second article entitled 'Patent Drivers' was published on 27 December 1895 in *Golf*. Although Carruthers was better known for his iron club patent design, his Sylviac range of wooden clubs is referred to in the section of the article covering hard woods and durable woods.

PATENT DRIVERS

There are many Patent Drivers, each variety aiming at the introduction of one or more advantages by the peculiarity of its construction. One point almost universally claimed by the patentees is long driving power, due to some peculiarity of balance, material, or general conformation; but endless are the means by which this end, along with the others claimed, is to be attained. There is the driver with 'ballast chambers' for regulating the weight of the head; the India rubber-cushioned face; the double-ended hammer, which if adopted, would go far to justify that opprobrious cry of 'Scotch Croquet' which is such a favourite with the Philistinic anti-golfer; and doubtless the introduction of the extra long carry driver, with a dynamite cartridge in the face, is only a matter of time.

Then the multiplicity of materials used in the construction of the patent driver lends a pleasing variety to their consideration; aluminium, of course has been pressed into the service, along with the more vulgar and ordinary varieties of wood, compressed or otherwise, xylonite, vulcanite, celluloid, iron, brass and steel, not forgetting that the latter has been used for shafts, both as a core to wooden ones, enduing the latter with all sorts of unexpected qualities of suppleness and unbreakableness, and also as simple skewers of toy-like tenuity, having at one end a bloated-looking grip, and at the other an apparently far-gone hydrocephalic case.

All these clubs have their good points, like Mark Twain's horse, but, unfortunately for their patentees, the human golfer, like the cricketer, tennis-player, and athlete generally, has an eye for outline which tells him that the majority of them, though warranted to be joys for ever, will never be considered things of beauty. This factor, appearance, is more essential to successful club-making than is perhaps generally recognised, and although its value is very generally appreciated by the makers of guns, fishing-rods, and cricket-bats, yet there are manufacturers of the implements for other games, such as Golf, who do not seem to have realised that the neat appearance of, say, a play club is more readily recognised than its potential qualities as an implement of the game. This was what rendered difficult the introduction of the bulger and the broadhead, and it may safely be said that their present popular position has only been attained by due regard to their outline and general appearance.

Amongst these patent drivers there is one kind, or rather class, made under several different patents, varying only in details of material or method of construction, in which the shaft is introduced into a hole bored through the head, thus doing away with the 'scare' and the whipping, and the possibilities of fracture connected with the old method of junction between head and shaft. This form of club has several other practical advantages, but it unfortunately labours under the curse of ugliness, which seems so common a characteristic of patent clubs. No better form of club could be put into the hands of any one learning to swing, both on account of the unbreakable nature of the wood-fibre headed variety, and of the fact that there is no inclination to 'heel' with this class of club since this fatal error is due to a tendency to hit the ball with a prolongation of the shaft, which is not provided in ordinary clubs, but in this kind is the normal spot for impact. This, although without doubt the most important advantage connected with the patent, is not what is generally claimed by the makers. 'Having the power behind the ball', and 'long carry' are what they put forward; but these are not worth one-half the above-mentioned properties.

A modification of this form of club, originally patented by Anderson, of Edinburgh, is the same maker's present style of patent driver, the principal characteristic of which is the insertion of the shaft into a hole bored through the head, and its being held there by the wedge arrangement commonly used in axe and hammer heads, assisted by a short neck and whipping. This firm has lately modified their driver-heads by encasing them in specially prepared leather, a very great advantage in diminishing wear and tear. Another departure from the usual method of joining head and shaft is seen in Spinks' patent, in which the shaft is inserted into the head and held tight by a brass ferrule driven over the neck. Both these patents aim at carrying the spring of the shaft right down to the head, which is supposed by club makers to be a great advantage, their contention being that the 'scare' and whipping in the ordinary club are defects in its construction, inasmuch as they curtail the spring of the shaft, and thereby lose driving power. If this is indeed the case then Dunn's patent driver should be more powerful than either of these forms of play club, being made all in one piece with no whipping round the neck, this latter peculiarity producing a curiously cold and collarless appearance in an otherwise beautifully modelled club. This idea was tried by Fernie some six years ago, but it has remained for Dunn to bring it to perfection. Durability of course is one of the qualities of this club, made as it is of hickory; but it has its weak point, and that is the neck, which is soft and pliable, without being particularly elastic, so much so, indeed that it is quite easy to alter the lie of the head by the application of gentle pressure to the neck. It is of course an open question whether this softness detracts from the driving power of the club, or whether it merely has the same effect as a soft face without the disadvantages inseparable from the latter, but this point needs a purely experimental and personal investigation.

Many patent 'play clubs', as the driver used to be called, while of course claiming the usual extra number of yards of 'carry', make a special point of their patriarchal length of life, due, perhaps, to their being bolstered up with steel, or aluminium, or manganese bronze, in the most approved style of modern engineering machine design.

... Any one attempting to make a drawing of a Golf club will at once become aware of the difficulties attending the provision of such an unnatural implement with outlines combining the necessary strength with the symmetry desirable, and in the actual process of manufacture this difficulty of course can only be overcome by long practice. Here, then, arises one of the chief obstacles to the successful production of those Golf clubs, which differ essentially in shape from the normal pattern. Generations of experience have been required to mould into a pleasing shape a lump of beech wood, whipped on to the end of a hickory stick, and some further time will no doubt elapse before a similar result can be attained in connection with many of the patent drivers now in the market. These considerations do not, of course, affect the absolute potentialities of the patent clubs, supposing them to be used by players indifferent to variations from the normal type, but the human golfer as he now exists requires a special education in their use to enable him to make the most of certain of the more advanced forms.

Some eight years ago the first metal-headed driver was made, at the suggestion of a customer, by Messrs. Anderson, of Edinburgh, durability being the primary intention. This head was made of sheet iron, and the difficulty and expense of production were quite sufficient to prevent any repetition of the experiment. Some years after this, another Edinburgh maker tried gun metal for the same purpose, with doubtful success; and this was followed by the use of a white-metal alloy of aluminium, this last idea being patented by Mr. Brougham. This invention was, in turn, modified in detail by Ramsbottom of Manchester, and Braddell of Belfast, the former making for even lengthier life by substituting a material called hornite for the wooden blocks, which formed the face of Brougham's patent. The chief difference between these two forms of the aluminium club seems to be that Brougham's Patent possesses the better shape and model of head, so far as general appearance is concerned; but, on the other hand, Ramsbottom's method of joining head and shaft gives greater strength at this point; and, further, the hornite face extends from top to bottom of the head, whereas Brougham's wooden block is bounded above and below by the metal shell, which is apt to make ugly marks on the ball if half-topped or taken heavy. This latter consideration should, of course, be no disadvantage theoretically, but, taken in conjunction with the shallowness of the head, and the highly practical nature of golfing error, it is a somewhat serious drawback. In driving power there seems but little to choose. Hornite appears to be an excellent material for facing a club, and produces much 'sweetness' of impact. Brougham's blocks, on the other hand, can be made of any wood preferred by the user, and, if necessary, faced with leather, this advantage again, being lessened by a weakness due to the looseness consequent on the alternate expansion and shrinkage of the wood in wet and dry weather.

So far as durability is concerned, it seems probable that aluminium-headed clubs cannot be beaten, as this material, if judiciously alloyed, is very tough, and not at all liable to become brittle. The average golfer, however, with the traditions of the game before his eyes, will naturally turn from a metal-headed play club (as he would from a brassy, were the metal anywhere but where it is – i.e., out of sight) to the alternative forms of longevity in clubs. Of the making of these there is no end, and, further than point out the various well-known forms, and some of their merits and defects, it is impossible for the writer to go, a practical experience of the relative merits of each one requiring a set of lives, each as long as that claimed for the clubs themselves.

The most natural effort in this direction is that which utilises the harder woods, such as holly, apple, thorn, acacia, and hickory, this last being frequently steamed into shape and sold, together with other durable woods, as 'Compressed'. Carruthers' Sylviac, Dickson's Wood-Fibre, Paxton's Oak, Jacobs' Gutta-percha, and Simpson's Unbreakable Head, the 'Woodgrain' unbreakable head of Angus Teen & Co., are further examples of durable material, and one of the latest additions to the list is a head, patented by Robertson, of Edinburgh, made entirely of leather cemented together in layers and waterproofed. This arrangement has obvious advantages, but it remains to be seen whether constant usage will not tend to separate its component parts. Leather being heavier than wood, no lead is required to make up the seven or eight ounces, and this absence of metal improves the balance of the head, and at the same time lends additional strength to the structure. Being waterproofed, the patentee claims for it immunity from the inroads of damp, which of course would be no small additional consideration.

Of the hard-wood heads above mentioned, it may be said that leather faces of sufficient thickness are alone lacking to give them normal driving power, and their durability of course is not to be doubted, although with bad luck in selection, it is quite within the bounds of possibility that a breakable one may be come across. By normal driving power, that of beech-wood is meant, as the writer would not take upon himself, after the multitude of battles which have been fought over it, to dogmatise on the subject of Hard v. Soft Wood for driver heads, preferring merely to use a recognised standard for comparison. Gutta-percha and similar substances, such as vulcanite, have been tried so often in the capacity now under consideration, that their merits have had ample opportunity of making themselves known; but Jacobs' patent head seems to be an improvement in model consequent on careful study of popular types, and as such is likely to win more favour for itself than its predecessors have so far done. One drawback may be mentioned in referring to it, and that is the unfortunate position of the lead, which is so deeply hidden that no alteration in weight can be effected without altogether destroying the balance of the head.

There are, of course, many other forms of patent driver, which, however, differ only in detail from the types above described, and no doubt, their number will be added to before these remarks appear in print.

Chapter 9

The Golfers Tryst, Braid Hills
Golf Course, Edinburgh

Tom Carruthers purchased the Golfers Tryst on 31 October 1899. It was one of two purpose-built, privately-owned golf clubhouses built in 1891 which included a tea room, a workshop and a shop selling golf equipment. The story of the Golfers Tryst and its neighbouring golf clubhouse, named the Golfers Rest at that time, are intrinsically tied to the closure for golf of the historic Bruntsfield Links, where golf had been played for four hundred years, and to the opening of the new Braid Hills Golf Course ('the Braids'), situated two miles to the south of the famous Links. Much of the information about how the Braids came about is derived from an article entitled 'The Story of the Braid Hills Golf Course', published in the 23 April 1903 edition of the *Edinburgh Evening Dispatch*.

Congestion at Bruntsfield Links

As an introduction to the events that led up to the restrictions imposed by Edinburgh Town Council on playing golf on Bruntsfield Links, the following extract from an article entitled 'Golf in Edinburgh', which appeared in *Golf*, 26 September 1890, provides a vivid account of the problems being encountered by both golfers and the public at Bruntsfield Links in the late 1880s:

> About twenty years ago the adjacent estate of Warrender Park was opened up for feuing purposes, and since then the lustre of Bruntsfield Links as a golfing centre has slowly but surely waned, until within the past few years the game has been carried on under conditions far from agreeable to golfers, while to the residents in the neighbourhood it has become a source of actual danger. Among

Edinburgh golfers it was a common aphorism that 'the man who could play golf on Bruntsfield could play anywhere'. There was more significance in this remark than might at first sight appear.

The surrounding neighbourhood is now one of the most densely populated in the city, and as a result of this the links have been sadly cut up by footpaths running in all directions. Almost throughout the entire day there is a continuous stream of pedestrians crossing and re-crossing the line of play, and in such circumstances it may be readily imagined that those who in late years have had the hardihood to attempt the 'far and sure' game on Bruntsfield have had their patience, skill, and nerve subjected to no ordinary test. Each hole in the round of seven had a distinctive danger peculiar to it. A ball played from the first teeing-ground, slightly out of line, brought the unwary golfer into the midst of irate and voluble washerwomen, who regarded the game as an invention of the Evil One, and all its exponents as his agents, against whom they had combined to register an awful oath of implacable enmity. Even when the player had escaped this initial difficulty, the presence of a gang of carpet beaters directly in the line of play was a never-failing source of lively objurgation and discussion as to the golfer's right of way. To shout 'fore' to a Bruntsfield carpet beater was simply to provide him with capital entertainment, the derisive laughter with which it was invariably received indicating that the warning cry was looked upon in the light of an excellent joke. The obstacles to be surmounted at the other holes were not a whit less exciting, and the erratic driver had good reason to congratulate himself if he succeeded in completing the round without bringing down a nursemaid or her infant charge, landing his ball in a baker's shop window, or playing 'two more' off the tramway rails, to the amazement of passing strangers, who regarded the stranded golfer as a mild type of the harmless lunatic.

An account of one such accident which occurred on the Links in 1851 and which involved Bishop Gillis who was Superior of St Margaret's Convent at Whitehouse Loan, is given in *The Chronicle of the Royal Burgess Golfing Society of Edinburgh*:

This gentleman was crossing the Links in a cab on the public road and in the act of reading when a golf ball broke one of the plate glass windows, and passed quite close to his face; very nearly striking one of his temples. Had it done so the consequences might have been of a most serious character, as the violence with which the ball was forced through the window was such that it drilled rather than smashed it in the same way as a bullet propelled by gunpowder might have done, leaving the surrounding parts unstarred and unfractured.

Even the entry for the Bruntsfield Allied Golf Club, instituted in 1856, in *The Golfing Annual* of 1888–89, in which T. Carruthers is shown as a Committee member of the club, drew attention to the attendant dangers in its résumé of the Club Green at Bruntsfield Links.

> As at present existing the round is one of seven holes, two circuits deciding Club competitions. Hazards there are none, the chief difficulty being to avoid collision with passing pedestrians, who use the thoroughfares that intersect the Links.

Accidents of a more or less serious nature were of almost daily occurrence, and as letters began to appear in the newspapers calling attention to the danger that existed to all persons having occasion to cross the Links, it soon became evident that golf on Bruntsfield was doomed. Determined, however, to secure a quid pro quo, and relying upon their rights secured by charter in the event of their being compelled to abandon Bruntsfield, the members of the various clubs began to look about for another suitable green.

Proposals to Restrict Golf

From time immemorial golf had been played on Bruntsfield. As long as Boroughmuir lay on the outskirts of the city the golfers caused no problem. With the growth of the population and the stretching out of the city into the suburbs this was to change. The building of the Warrender Park blocks of houses may be said to have helped to raise the question of the rights of golfers to continue to play a game which other citizens, compelled to cross and re-cross the Links, regarded as little short of a public danger. In 1886 the Town Council inserted a clause in a Private Bill taking powers 'to prohibit absolutely or to restrict or otherwise regulate the playing of the game of golf and all or any other games or game on Bruntsfield Links'.

Golfers' Committee Formed

The Bruntsfield golfers immediately became alarmed. They foresaw in this move by the Town Council the end of their cherished privileges. They were not a large or a wealthy community. The Burgess and Bruntsfield Links

Golfing Societies had already decamped to Musselburgh, for the same reasons that later caused them to move from Musselburgh to Barnton, Edinburgh.

After an initial meeting in the Golf Tavern at Bruntsfield a public meeting was convened, whereupon a Committee was formed to protest to the Council about the injustice that threatened the Bruntsfield golfers' rights and to negotiate with the Council the acquisition of land at the Braid Hills as a municipal property. The election of Mr Hall Blyth to the committee proved to be important, for not only was he well known as a golfer but he was also on close terms with the majority of the Town Council. A civil engineer who had much to do with many of the most important undertakings of the generation, Mr Hall Blyth had distinguished himself as a golfer and had concerned himself with the health of the Royal and Ancient game. In 1885 he was installed as Captain of the Royal Liverpool Golf Club. It was mainly by his efforts that the Honorary Company of Edinburgh Golfers was brought to Muirfield.

The Committee at once set to work. It issued an appeal to golfers throughout the country for support in maintaining in Parliament, if necessary, the rights of the Bruntsfield golfers. It addressed the Lord Provost, Sir Thomas Clark, asking him either to move the deletion of the objectionable clause from the Municipal Bill or to insert a clause giving the Council power to acquire, by lease or otherwise, 'a golfing course in the neighbourhood of Edinburgh – say the Braid Hills, or to expend annually, from the public funds, a sum sufficient to enable the golfers to acquire a suitable course for themselves'. The issue of the circular to the golf clubs brought out in a remarkable way the sympathy of the golfing community. The Thistle and Bruntsfield clubs voted £10 each. St Andrews Ladies' Club sent two guineas. Wimbledon Golf Club expressed its readiness to contribute handsomely to the fund. The Honourable Company of Edinburgh Golfers held a special meeting to consider what they might do to help the movement; and the Burgess and Bruntsfield Links Golfing Societies, which had formerly enjoyed the game on Bruntsfield, heartily joined in the movement. Mr Hall Blyth was appointed Treasurer and started with £60 guaranteed. The ball was fairly set rolling and the Town Council, hitherto hostile or apathetic, began to realise that the opposition of the golfers to their Bill was serious.

There were still many, while acknowledging the right of the Bruntsfield golfers to compensation for dispossession, who considered it doubtful whether the public would go so far 'out of town' for the game. In April 1887 it was intimated that the Council had decided to withdraw the clause in the Private Bill relating to golf on Bruntsfield. Thence forward the golfers and the Council may be said to have worked together. There were periods of friction, but on the whole the Council, while anxious to protect the public purse, showed themselves reasonably willing to conciliate the Bruntsfield golfers. It should not be forgotten, however, that the number of people who golfed in these days was comparatively insignificant. In 1903, when the article about these events was written, there were probably a hundred who pursued the game for everyone who played it twenty years previously. That fact was attested by the extraordinary traffic of golfers on the Braids, which kept the green busy from morning to night. In 1883 there were fewer than forty clubs in Edinburgh. In 1903 they were numbered in their hundreds.

Another public meeting was held in Queen Street Hall on 6 June 1888. It was attended by such a crowd of interested golfers and citizens that although the Committee had only secured a small hall seated for 200 people, before eight o'clock it was apparent that the attendance would largely exceed that number, and accordingly the large hall was thrown open. The followers of the game, who regularly crowded the golf course on Bruntsfield Links in the evenings, deserted it for once. The following resolution was unanimously carried:

> That this meeting, recognising the laudable efforts of the Town Council in time past to provide the means of healthful recreation for all classes of the citizens, respectively urge the expediency and indeed the necessity, of securing the Braid Hills to form a golf course as a substitute for Bruntsfield Links, on which the game has been so constantly and regularly played from time immemorial by a great number of the inhabitants: and that a deputation be appointed to wait upon the Lord Provost, Magistrates, and Town Council to report this resolution and lay the views of this meeting before them.

In a speech supporting the resolution, Lord Shand said that the new golf course would benefit all social classes. Professional men and members of the Law, Medicine and the Church would take advantage of the provision of a public golf course, and every other class of the community would take advantage of it also. No class would give it more support than the hard-worked teachers in many schools, men in banks, offices, and other sedentary occupations. Gentlemen in warehouses, shops, and factories would take advantage of Bruntsfield Links and would, during the summer nights and Saturday afternoons, be found enjoying the healthful game on the breezy slopes of the Braids. He had visited the ground, which it was hoped they might acquire, and he considered that its situation, landscape, beautiful short grass, and magnificent views made the Braids ideally suited for a golfing green.

Proposal to Construct a New Golf Course at the Braid Hills

On 21 November 1888, the Town Council approved the plan to acquire the land at Braid Hills by 25 votes to 15 and on 29 May 1889, the Magistrates and Council, having assembled in the Royal Exchange at 2 o'clock, drove out to the Braid Hills and formally annexed the new municipal property. Lord Provost Boyd drove the first ball with a club bearing a silver inscription, presented to him by Mr William Frier, golf club maker of Bruntsfield Links. The golf course, which had meantime been laid out by Messrs Peter M'Ewan and Bob Ferguson of Musselburgh, was formally opened on 5 September 1889.

The turf was old hill pasture, but the growth was rich, and had it not been for the many who had worked hard to prepare the ground, the task of bringing it into first rate golfing condition would have been infinitely more difficult than it proved to be.

The golfers had now achieved their purpose. The 'Hill' had been purchased and the course had been laid out. The Parliamentary formalities led to no difficulties. All that was required was that the golfing community and the public generally should realise the value of the boon that had been conferred upon them by the purchase of this magnificent recreation ground, and should take full advantage of it. The success of the Braids may be said to have set an example in inland courses. In the 1880s there had been a strong prejudice amongst golfers in favour of seaside courses. It still persisted and it was conceded that the sea air, the short grass, and the sand bunkers were important factors in the ideal golf course. But an upland hilly slope, with well-trimmed pasture and natural and artificial hazards, such as Edinburgh possessed on the Braids course, fell little short of the ideal. *The Scotsman* reported the phenomenal success of the venture in the following terms:

> Today the Braids Hill course is probably the most frequented in the world. From morning 'til night, winter and summer it is never deserted. Even the historic old course at St. Andrews does not get as much work as the Braids course. In the long days of summer 600 players are not an unusual number.

The official figures from *The Scotsman* show at a glance the extraordinary popularity of the golf course with the citizens. The following is the official return of persons playing:

Number of Players

1st July – 31st December 1897 (at 1d per round)	33,893
Year to 31st December 1898 (at 1d per round)	69,787
Year to 31st December 1899 (at 1d per round)	75,153
Year to 31st December 1900 (at 1d per round)	76,807
Year to 31st December 1901 (at 1d per round)	82,687
Year to 31st December 1902 (at 2d per round)	81,821

There is, so far as can be ascertained no course in the world that obtains, and few that could endure, so continuous a traffic. (*The Scotsman*)

The Evening Dispatch Trophy and other Braids' Competitions

In 1903 there were considerably more than 200 golf clubs in Edinburgh, and of these only a small fraction had access to private courses. The Braids was their home. The desire to unite the golfing community in a common annual tournament was a natural sequel to the opening of the course and on Saturday, 9 November 1889, the first tournament open to amateur golfers, members of Edinburgh and Leith golf clubs, was played on the Braids.

The First Braids' Tournament

The first tournament to be played on the new Braid Hills Golf Course aroused considerable interest in Edinburgh. The presence of many notable golfing celebrities and professionals, including old Tom Morris, signified the importance of the occasion. Mr A. M. Ross, the celebrated amateur golfer, won the Kinloch Anderson medal and scratch prize with a score of 84. Tom Carruthers played in the event ending up in equal seventh place with a net score of 86 off a handicap of 11. The following extracts are from an article describing the day's events, which appeared in *The Scotsman,* 11 November 1889:

> The tournament on the Braid Hills, which has been looked forward to with much interest for some weeks by Edinburgh golfers, passed off most successfully on Saturday. The occasion was one of special interest to the golfing community of Edinburgh, and by their presence in such numbers on the Braids on Saturday they showed their full appreciation of the boon they now enjoyed in having such a course at their command. It was not only golfers however who visited the Hill. A large number of the general public were there

including the Lord Provost and other civic dignitaries, including Mr. B. Hall Blyth, C.E. On all hands the greatest interest was manifested in the play and the fortunes of the better-known players were eagerly followed as they wended their way round the course. On all hands, too, was their unanimity as to the excellence of the green, and in this respect the opinion of local golfers was backed up by that of such competent judges as old Tom Morris, young Willie Park, Andrew Kirkaldy, Ben Sayers, and a number of other professionals who paid a visit to the hills in the course of the day. In the matter of weather the tournament was particularly fortunate. The day was just one to thoroughly test the capabilities of the players. The atmosphere was dry and bracing and a strong westerly wind swept across the Hill. This no doubt accounted for the fact that, as a rule, scoring was high. Considering the short time, which had elapsed since the course was opened, it is in wonderful order. To those who went over it then, when laid out in the rough, the change, which a couple of months has brought about, is little short of marvellous.

The Golf Committee, who in their endeavours to secure its success received hearty support from the numerous clubs in the city, promoted the tournament. The Committee very properly restricted the competition to members of Edinburgh clubs, of whom in Saturday's field of 138 players there was a capital representation.

In order that the competition might be completed before darkness, a start had to be made as early as half-past nine, and from that hour 'til two o'clock, when the last of the sixty-nine couples left the first tee, Mr. Peter M'Ewan had his hands full in superintending their dispatch. This work was carried through in the greatest punctuality. About half-past eleven the first couple completed the round, and for the next four hours they came through the pass leading to the home hole in an uninterrupted stream.

The *Edinburgh Evening Dispatch's* edition of the same date reported that:

Great success attended the golf tournament on the Braid Hills course on Saturday. All through the day the ground presented a busy spectacle, and as the afternoon wore on the numbers present were swelled by spectators, among them a large number of ladies, until the attendance reached about 1,000 persons in all. The chief players had such a large following, fully 100 accompanying Mr. A. M. Ross during the latter half of his game.

At the more difficult holes, where the well-driven ball disappeared from sight, boys with red flags were stationed on the eminences, who gave the signal to the successive couples to come on, and watched the fall of the balls. A sub-committee was waiting on the last green, and all disputes were there and then settled. Luncheons, etc., were provided in a marquee (by Mr. Strachan, Forrest Road), and nothing was omitted which could contribute to the comfort of those present. The only untoward element was the wind, which was blowing quite a gale and interfered greatly with low scoring.

Bruntsfield Allied Golf Club Competition

Tom was a regular competitor in club and open competitions and also played in inter-club matches. A report of a Bruntsfield Allied Golf Club special prize competition held on the Braids on Saturday 5 July 1890 appeared in *The Scotsman* newspaper of the following Monday. It is not only interesting to see that Tom Carruthers tied for first place in this handicap club competition but that his son-in-law, William R. Reith, also participated in this event.

> This club held its special prize competition on Saturday on the Braids, the following being the winners, with their scores: – 1 and 2, John Young, 86 less 12 – 74, and Thomas Carruthers, 83 less 9 – 74; 3, James Addison, 82 less 7 – 75; 4, James Swan, 80 less 4 – 76; 5, William R. Reith, 90 less 12 – 78, 6 and 7, Thomas Hogg, scratch 79; J. K. Andrews, 88 less 9 – 79; James Riddell, 86 less 7 – 79. The lowest actual score is that of W. Niven, 78 plus 2 – 80.

Tom Carruthers' second oldest daughter, Euphemia, married William Robertson Reith in 1884. The marriage certificate gives Reith's occupation as 'Mercantile Clerk'. Reith went on to be trained by, and worked, for the Carruthers' golf business as a golf club maker until he moved to take up the position as Eltham Golf Club's first professional in London in 1892. Scottish professionals and club makers were extremely influential in the years when golf's popularity swept across the English counties. Their counsel was eagerly sought in the design of new courses and in making recommendations to fill new positions at the many new golf clubs being created. Tom Carruthers was widely known and respected as a club maker and for having laid out a new golf course for Mr. Alfred Rothschild, and it was he who probably put forward Reith's name for the vacancy at Eltham. One of Reith's sons, A. J. Reith, was assistant to his father at Eltham Golf Club around the start of the First World War and was later the professional at Royal Portrush around 1920–21. Another son, C. H. Reith was at Eltham Warren, Yelverton and North Middlesex golf clubs during the 1920s.

William Reith remained professional at Eltham from 1892 until 1924 when he became professional at Royal Blackheath Golf Club from 1925 until 1926 upon Blackheath's amalgamation with Eltham. He emigrated to Canada in 1926 to take up the position of professional at Pine Ridge Golf Club, Winnipeg. Reith's descendants are still active in golf in America, Bob and his brother Phil Reith being the fifth generation involved in the game as golf professionals. The following is an extract from *Golfing,* 30 March 1899, under the heading 'Trade Notes by Tee Caddie':

> Like father-in-law like son-in-law may, perhaps, be justly allowed if the reasoning conveyed by a simple rule of Logic is applicable in golfing matters. This occurred to me when visiting the Eltham Club and interviewing W. R. Reith, the son-in-law of Mr. Thomas Carruthers of Edinburgh. A good and careful green keeper is Reith, and what he puts in the greens he puts in his clubs and balls in the way of good workmanship.
>
> The 'Eltham' ball is his speciality, and, upon investigation, his private client list for this article is a very large one. Every ball is at least 6 months seasoned before being sent away.

The Third Annual Braids' Tournament

The third annual Braids' tournament took place on Saturday, 24 June 1891. The winner of the tournament was Mr. D. M. Jackson of the Stockbridge Club with a net 80 off scratch. Tom Carruthers competed in the competition, as he had done in the first competition held in 1889, and his score is recorded in 'The best of the other scores' with a net 85 off a handicap of 6. The following extract from *The Scotsman* of 26 June 1891, gives a vivid account of the scene during the course of the competition:

> The day was gloriously fine, and from an early hour in the forenoon till about 5 p.m. there was a continuous stream of golfers engaged in the tournament wending their way round the hills. The lovely weather and the attraction of so important an event in the golfing world brought out crowds of spectators, among whom were a considerable number of the fair sex, whose bright and variegated costumes helped to make the scene still more gay and animated. While on the subject of dress it may be mentioned that there was an unusually large turnout of scarlet jackets on the hill. There seems to be a pretty general opinion that the revival of the bright coloured golfing jacket is a pleasant sign of the times, and it is hoped that an effort will be made to bring back the good old

fashion, and have it generally adopted. Although several very good totals were recorded, the scoring all round was somewhat high when regard is had to the almost perfect weather conditions. There was no lack of the usual incidents peculiar to a competition of this kind. One competitor, for example, played an excellent game till he reached the 'Rockies' (the fifteenth hole). Here a bad drive brought about the most direful consequences, and after a long innings among the whins and sharp-pointed stones, amounting in the aggregate to somewhere about 15 strokes, he lifted the ball and gracefully retired. A scratch player who was known to have a good chance for the lowest actual had reached the sixteenth hole with a score that promised exceeding well. At this point however, he was joined by the inevitable candid friend, who like the proverbial bad sixpence, is sure to turn up when least expected or desired. The information imparted by this indiscreet person had the usual effect, and the next hole to which the veriest tyro rarely takes more than 3, required 6 strokes, an otherwise excellent round being thus partially spoiled. Playing to the second hole, one competitor, whose dress was conspicuous by its scantiness, consisting, as it did, of knickerbockers and a shirt, was, for a time, an object of keen interest to the spectators, who were seated at various points on the hillside. His drive took him into ragged whins about ten yards from the tee. His second carried him into much denser whins a few yards further on. Nothing daunted, he sawed away at the obstruction, doing some really capital clearing work. At length he was seen to make one wild sweep, and the ball soared away in the direction of the hole. As he returned to pick up the remainder of his wardrobe, which he had left at the tee, meanwhile wiping the streaming perspiration from his manly brow, a slight cheer was raised by one or two groups of spectators in recognition of his pluck and perseverance. What a splendid study he would have made for 'Pleasures of Golf!'

Demise of the Braids' Tournament

Although the open tournament, first held on the Braids on Saturday, 9 November 1889, was continued for several years, it had in it the elements of decay. The difficulty lay in adjusting the handicaps to give everyone a fair chance. The committee tried hard by every means in their power to be wholly impartial and perfectly fair in all their handicapping decisions. This was a colossal task and it was no surprise that there was much grumbling and dissatisfaction from a number of the competitors who did not feel that they were being given a fair chance. The committee's decision was largely arbitrary and the multiplication of prizes exposed the competition more and more to the discredit of 'pot-hunting'.

By 1895 the prize list for the tournament comprised as many as fifty of which about half were donated. The full donor's list, which included Tom Carruthers, is set out below. It resembled a roll call of the many organisations associated with golf in Edinburgh and the Braids:

Scratch prize gold medal, *The Golfer*; clubs and cover, Messrs Goudie & Co., Princes Street; clubs, Mr James Smith; plate, Mr Archibald Struthers, 56 Leith Street; box of cigars Mr J. B. Strachan, Abbotsford, Rose Street; tweeds 7 yards, Mr J. Munro & Co., tailors, 19 Maitland Street; 8 clubs, covers and 1 dozen balls, Mr Willie Park Jun., St Andrews Street, Edinburgh; clubs, Messrs Anderson & Son, Princes Street; marble clock, Mrs Kerr, Volunteer Arms, Morningside Road; 3 clubs, Mrs Winchester, Refreshment Room, Braid Hills; golf cover, etc. The North British Rubber Co., Princes Street; 1 dozen match balls, Messrs Thornton & Co., Princes Street; 1 dozen balls, Mr William Allaway, 13 St Andrews Square; 1 dozen balls, Mr D. Stocks, Niddrie Street; 4 clubs and 1 dozen balls, Messrs A. & J. Dickson, Braid Road; 2 clubs, Messrs J. & A. Simpson's, Morningside Road; 6 quarts whisky, Braid Hotel Company, Braid Hills Course; 6 clubs, Scottish Golf Manufacturing Company Limited, Albert Street; 6 clubs and cover, Mr & Mrs Frier, Braid Hills; 4 clubs and cover, Mrs Brown, Golfers Rest, Braid Hills Course; clubs, Mr Thomas Carruthers, Leven Street; 2 clubs, Messrs W. & C. Davidson, Musselburgh; plate, Messrs D. Latimer & Son, Jewellers, Lothian Road.

James Braid, Edinburgh Thistle Golf Club

James Braid, five times winner of the British Open in the period 1901 to 1910, was closely associated with the Braids in the early 1890s. At nineteen he left his home in Earlsferry, Fife, for the first time to work as a joiner at St Andrews where he played with such famous names as Andrew and Hugh Kirkaldy and Sandy Herd, who was serving his last year's apprenticeship as a plasterer. His time at St Andrews had been disappointing for him because his work commitments had not given him enough time to concentrate on his golf, so he moved to Edinburgh in 1891, where the Braids was to become his home course. Braid, in his contribution to the book, *Great Golfers in the Making*, states the following about the Braids:

No turf like it, a course absolutely rich in sporting quality, greens that are magnificent and scenery from every point that is romantically beautiful, and air that makes one feel a good few years younger while playing ... When I went to my work at six in the morning, I constantly met many golfers coming back from the Braids after having had their early round; and on a Saturday afternoon I have gone up there to play at half past one, and have had to wait until half past five before being able to make a start, so great was the crowd waiting at the first tee.

As is the case today, the demand for a game on a good golf course involves a little more than turning up and teeing off. A letter to the *Edinburgh Evening Dispatch*, dated 9 February 1898, described the system at the Braids.

Sir,
The letter signed 'S' in your issue of yesterday will touch a sympathetic chord in many breasts. Your correspondent's experience is that of scores of golfers every Saturday I am sure; and to them the celerity with which the tickets are distributed at a time when the arrivals by the one o'clock train are panting up the steep incline to the first teeing ground must be a source of great perplexity as it has been to 'S'. It puzzled me for long to find that, although on reaching the ground at say 1.15, there were only some 25 or 30 players waiting at the tee and in the refreshment rooms in the neighbourhood, yet the ticket I was supplied with was as much as 100 to 120 behind that of the player driving off. This I say puzzled me for long; but the explanation – or perhaps I should say the partial explanation – was supplied when I discovered the latecomers walking leisurely to the course from the car terminus had their tickets already secured and waiting in the refreshment rooms aforesaid. I am etc.
Fair Field

James Braid joined the Edinburgh Thistle Golf Club which had its home course at the Braids. It was also the main course for numerous other Edinburgh and Leith golf clubs, including those that had formerly played at Bruntsfield Links until 1889 when their right to play there was removed by Edinburgh Town Council. The club welcomed his obvious talents and he played for the team in the Dispatch and Glasgow Evening Times trophies as well as serving on the club's Council. Edinburgh Thistle's tournament winner's board shows that he won the club's Gold Scratch Medal in 1892 and 1893, which was later also won by another of the club's celebrated golfers, Tommy Armour in 1919.

In 1892 he took first place in the Braid Hills' Tournament, open to all Edinburgh and Leith Clubs, in a field of 140. Braid considered this win to be the most notable achievement of his amateur career. A report in *Golf* of 24

June 1892, describes the closing stages of the Braids' Tournament when Braid was the winner:

> Still Mr. King had the honour … and it was only when six o'clock was near that it became known that Mr. Braid of the Thistle was doing even better things. This turned out to be the case, for Mr. Braid, playing a most brilliant game, accomplished the great feat of breaking the record on the green. With the marvellously low score of 73, he displaced Mr. King and at the same time defeated the record score of 74 made a few weeks before in a competition by Mr. W. McLean-Smith of the Warrender. Braid was out in 34 and back in 39, for a total score of 73, and won the Kinloch Anderson medal.

James Braid was not the only Open Championship winner to have been a member of the Edinburgh Thistle Golf Club at the Braids. The distinction is shared by Tommy Armour who won the Open in 1931 (also the winner of the American Open in 1927). Armour was also a member of the Edinburgh Western Golf Club, which like the Edinburgh Thistle Club, played golf at the Braids and rented rooms in the Carruthers' Golfers Tryst clubhouse.

The Dispatch Trophy

In 1890 the proprietors of the *Edinburgh Evening Dispatch* decided to provide a challenge trophy to be competed for annually over the Braids among the clubs of Edinburgh. The trophy was awarded to the winning club and not to an individual. Each Edinburgh club was invited to send two couples to compete in foursome play, club against club. The first competition was held on the first Saturday of April 1890 when twenty-two clubs entered. From this modest beginning the tournament grew so much that numbers had to be restricted by ballot to 128 clubs between 1963 and 1979. The first winner of the tournament was the Edinburgh Thistle Club. One hundred years later, to mark the centenary celebrations when 119 clubs entered the competition, Scotsman Publications presented a centenary trophy for permanent retention by the tournament winners and it was a happy circumstance when the Edinburgh Thistle Club again won the trophy.

The competition not only proved popular with the participating clubs for the public were drawn in large numbers to these exciting annual contests. In 1903 it was reported that some 6,000 or 7,000 must have stood around the first tee, and lined the fairway to the first hole when the final round of the competition was started; and later in the day when the first players were approaching the Valley hole, about 15,000 people were grouped on the surrounding heights. Never in the history of the game, it was reported, had four players been honoured with such a large following. The task of handling the crowd was by no means an easy one for the officials had to appeal repeatedly for more room for the players. In addition to the trophy, the winners received gold badges and the runners-up, silver badges. Two dozen Haskell balls were divided amongst the winners, whilst Messrs R. Anderson & Sons, Princes Street, and J. & A. Simpson, Braid Road, presented clubs which were divided between the winners and runners-up, each member of the teams receiving two clubs. In addition to the above, in 1901, the winners also received two Gunn's patent putters, the gift of Messrs Gunn Brothers, 249 Morningside Road, Edinburgh.

This popular tournament is still held to this day at the Braids.

Edinburgh Thistle Golf Club members photographed on the seventeenth green on 11 August 1894 with the Glasgow Times Trophy won by their team on 7 October 1893 at Troon. The Club Captain James Smith is seated behind the trophy and on his right is James Braid. Standing second from the left is William Frier, the first club maker at the Braids and proprietor of the Golfers Tryst. Standing second from the right is Tom Carruthers.

The Golfers Tryst

When the Braid Hills Golf Course was opened on 5 September 1889 as a municipal course, Edinburgh Town Council made no provision for clubhouses or changing rooms. Hitherto the golfers, members of the many golf clubs who had played over the links at Bruntsfield, had rented rooms at the old Golf Tavern (Hotel), formerly the home of the Edinburgh Burgess

Golfing Society until they had decamped to Musselburgh during the 1870s. The result was that some of the golf clubs retained their rented accommodation at Bruntsfield Links as, with the absence of any form of public transport beyond Morningside railway station, it was literally an uphill struggle to reach the newly-laid-out golf course at the Braid Hills.

At that time golfers made their way to the Braids from Morningside station on foot carrying two or three clubs under their arms. Some lucky ones had bicycles but by and large the majority walked a long way to reach the first tee. In 1897 it was announced that cable cars would be run as far as the Braid Hills Hotel.

Players putt out on the last green during the first Dispatch Trophy competition held in April 1890. In the background is the committee tent with shelter for officials and visitors

The Reverend Dr J. G. McPherson described his walk to 'the Braids' from Bruntsfield Links:

> The first forenoon of the year was piercingly cold, and the roads were covered with ice. The Pentlands were streaked with snow,

which had gathered in the clefts; the sky was leaden and repulsive; yet the hearts of the warriors were not daunted by nature's terrors. It is a hard walk of two miles from Bruntsfield; and even after leaving the main road for the scene of action the steep ascents told severely on the soft frame, untrained for much walking. How in the world the old players can get up for a game is a mystery! Yet golf is generally a craze with veteran players.

The first golf club to take up residence at the Braids was the Warrender Golf Club. This event is described in *History of the Warrender Golf Club* published in 1906:

> It seems not inappropriate that the Warrender should have been the first club to take up its abode at the Braid Hills, the Council having made an arrangement with the tenant of Upper Braid Farm to have the use of his dining-room there as a temporary club-room, and thither the club removed from Musselburgh at the end of 1889.

William Frier

It wasn't until two years later in 1891 that two identically-sized plots of land were sold on which two privately owned purpose-built golf clubhouses were to be constructed. A summary of the feu contract for the plot of land sold to William Frier, golf club maker, recorded in the General Register of Sasines (a historical register of deeds affecting land and property transactions in Scotland), provides a description of each plot of land:

> 105/1000 acre of ground on the west side of a new road formed or to be formed leading from the Braid Farm Road in a south easterly direction by the quarry to the Braid Hills being a part of the lands and Barony of Braid in the parish of Saint Cuthbert's with tiends reserving minerals except that William Frier shall be entitled to quarry stone or sand on said subjects for building thereon.

The two buildings were constructed in early 1891. The Warrender Golf Club was the first tenant of William Frier, the proprietor of one of the clubhouses called the Golfers Tryst and they recorded the event as follows:

> A suitable building having been erected at the western end of the course, the club agreed to lease for seven years a room in the premises belonging to Mr. Frier, club maker, and the opening of the new club-room was celebrated in June 1891 by a cake and wine

luncheon, immediately after a competition for the club gold medal and a silver cup, presented by Councillor Crichton to mark the occasion.

William Frier, born in 1847, was a golf club and golf ball maker recorded in the 1880s as having premises at 34 Wright's Houses, Bruntsfield Links. When Lord Provost Boyd formally annexed the new municipal property at the Braid Hills on 9 May 1889 on which 'the Braids' was to be laid out later in that year, he ceremoniously drove the first ball with a club bearing a silver inscription and presented to him by 'Mr W. Frier, golf club maker, Bruntsfield'. After 'the Braids' opened for golf in 1889, Frier opened a shop a year later at 28 Braid Road, Edinburgh. He was a member of the Edinburgh Thistle and Braids United Golf Clubs.

In March 1896, Frier applied for a patent for a club with wood inserts into the face of the club. It was the forerunner of a similar design granted a U.S. patent in 1910. The following article appeared in *The Golfer* on 3 June 1896:

> A new form of golf club has been patented by Mr. William Frier, club maker, Braid Hills, Edinburgh, the face of which is pierced in three places, into which are inserted pieces of hard wood secured with wooden pins driven through the centre. The middle piece of wood is specially hard, and is placed where the club should strike the ball. For a driver who can use his weapon with reasonable accuracy the club should enable him to send a longer ball than he can with the ordinary weapon.

Disastrous Fire

In May 1894 a disastrous fire took hold at the Golfers Tryst, which caused considerable damage to the building and to the clubrooms of the golf clubs which rented the rooms. The clubs are believed to have included the Warrender and Plewlands Golf Clubs. The *History of the Warrender Golf Club* gives the following description surrounding the event:

> The Warrender sustained the most serious disaster which they have been called upon to endure. As already briefly stated, a fire occurred in the premises on Braid Hills, partly occupied as a clubhouse, on 8 May 1894, causing the total destruction of all the club property there, and as most of the members had boxes in the club room the individual loss to them in the shape of clubs, bags,

balls and golfing apparel was considerable. Unfortunately, through some oversight, the fire insurance policy held by the club for many years had some time previously been allowed to lapse so that the members did not have the satisfaction of recovering even the commercial value of the property destroyed, much of which was of such a character by association and otherwise as could not be replaced. But probably the most highly prized, and certainly the most unique of the possessions, which perished in the flames, was a carved oak chair for the use of the captain, which was presented to the club by one of its members, Mr. A. Forbes. This chair was made from oak taken, when the building was being demolished by Mr. Forbes, from the room in Anchor Close which had been the resort of many literary and other Edinburgh celebrities, including Sir Walter Scott, Robert Burns, and others.

The property deeds of the Golfers Tryst record that William Frier disposed of the property to the Fourth Provident Property Investment Company on 23 April 1894, and that on 26 April 1894, he discharged a bond owing to Martin McCall and James Kidd Andrews, Solicitors, Edinburgh, issued by William Frier on 7 April 1891, for the purposes of purchasing the land and constructing the Golfers Tryst.

From the dates given in the Warrender Club's account of the fire and the General Register of Sasines it seems a stroke of good fortune that the premises had been sold by Frier less than a month before the disastrous fire broke out. The rebuilding of the Golfer's Tryst began almost immediately and *The Golfer* reported in August 1894 that 'Frier's building was being rapidly pushed on and will have an upper flat'. It also reported that 'Mrs Brown, next door at the Golfers Rest, was also putting in an upper flat in rather a picturesque form'.

In any event, whether the dates are a little inaccurate or not, the Golfers Tryst remained in the ownership of the Building Society until 31 May 1897, when it was sold to Martin McCall, Solicitor, residing in Lonsdale Terrace, with consent of William Frier now at the Braid Hills, Edinburgh.

Frier temporarily moved to 29 Wright's Houses, Bruntsfield Links, during the period of rebuilding of the Golfers Tryst and moved back in 1895. He retained his position as clubmaster to the golf clubs which rented rooms in the Golfers Tryst. His wife provided catering services 'refreshments, luncheons, dinners and teas, parties provided for ... ' William Frier traded as a 'wholesale and retail golf club and ball maker' from the Braids, closing his former premises at 34 Wright's Houses, Bruntsfield Links. Frier unfortunately ran into financial difficulties and was subsequently sequestered in 1899.

Towards the end of 1897 the Braids United Golf Club, formed on 22 July that year from ninety-six members of a number of small clubs playing over 'the Braids' at that time, secured rented club rooms in the Golfers Tryst. These clubs included the Braidburn, Comiston, Craiglea, Leamington, Clarendon, Viewforth, and Woodburn clubs. This was made possible by the decision of the Warrender Golf Club, the first club to take up residence at 'the Braids', to find another course and to vacate rented rooms. The club moved to Turnhouse, Edinburgh, to join up with the Lothian Club.

> While finding 'the Braids' in every way suitable for play, it was not many years before the increasing attractiveness of the course, and the growing popularity of the game, drew golfers in such numbers as to seriously interfere with regular play, especially on competition days. This trouble was shared by all the clubs making 'the Braids' their headquarters, and it was felt that if the continued prosperity of the club were to be ensured, it would be necessary to acquire a course for themselves, if at all possible. *(History of the Warrender Golf Club)*

BRAID HILLS GOLF COURSE, EDINBURGH.

The Golfers Tryst and Golfers Rest Clubhouses in 1905 with the houses for the Green Keeper and Park Officer in the background

The above picture shows the Golfers Rest in the foreground immediately next to its neighbouring privately-owned clubhouse, the Golfers Tryst, both constructed in 1891. In the background beside the first tee is the residential accommodation provided by Edinburgh Council in 1897 for the Green Keeper and the Park Officer. At the rear of the clubhouses the low flat structures where the golfers' boxes were situated can clearly be seen along with the workshop premises of the Golfers Tryst. The main two-storey part of the clubhouses housed the clubrooms, refreshment and function facilities. In the distance are the Salisbury Craigs and Arthur's Seat.

Acquisition of the Golfers Tryst by Thomas Carruthers

On 31 October 1899, Thomas Carruthers of 5 Gillespie Place, Edinburgh, acquired the Golfers Tryst from Martin McCall and issued a bond for £550 to him to finance the transaction and to carry out the alterations necessary to convert part of the premises into a new workshop for the manufacture of golf clubs and also to fund the transfer of his previous workshop at 26A Wright's Houses, Bruntsfield Links.

The new Braid Hills Golf Course proved to be an extraordinary success, in that the number of golfers was almost overwhelming. The existence of two purpose-built clubhouses – the Golfers Tryst and the Golfers Rest – the two clubhouses having been built and opened within a short space of time of each other, did not provide any noticeable degree of competition given the demand for rented accommodation from the golfers.

The Golfers Rest

The Golfers Rest, next door to the Golfers Tryst, was owned by Mary McKay or Brown, wife of John Brown, then residing at Ashley Gardens, Edinburgh, but who soon afterwards moved to take up residence in the Golfers Rest, and by Lindsey Goldie Ross, grocer's assistant, of the same address. The contract was dated 7 April 1891. Lindsey G. Ross, born in 1862, was a crack golfer and a member of the Warrender Club. By the end of the year Ross's address showed that he had taken up the position of professional and club maker at Sutton Coldfield Golf Club near Birmingham. In September 1892 he competed in the Open Championship at Muirfield, the first time the competition had been competed for over 72 holes, when Mr Harold Hilton, the amateur from Hoylake, won it. In 1903, Ross patented his Patent Angle Plate that combined a metal sole and face fixed by two screws on the face and two screws on the sole. Ross returned to Edinburgh when he

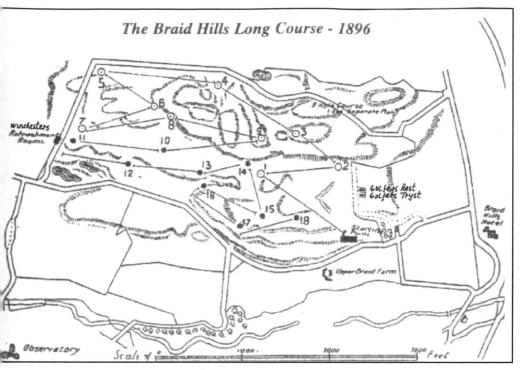

Plan of the Braid Hills Long Course in 1896 showing the Golfers Tryst, The Golfers Rest, the Braid Hills Hotel and Winchesters

took up the position as the first professional at 'the Braids' in 1906. He went back to the Midlands to become the professional at Droitwich for a short spell from 1908–9, and then moved on to Edgbaston Golf Club in Birmingham before joining Aberdovey as professional until 1923.

In February 1897, the committee of the Electric Golf Club, instituted in 1873, which was composed entirely of clerks employed in the Edinburgh's telegraphic department, completed negotiations for the renting of a room in Mrs Brown's Golfers Rest. The Electric Golf Club had previously played golf at Bruntsfield Links before they, like the other golf clubs, had ceased to play over the Links. The Golfers Rest was usually referred to as 'Mrs Brown's Refreshment Rooms' and although she rented boxes to the golfers who rented rooms in Frier's Golfers Tryst following the disastrous fire in 1894, it seems that its main source of income came from its catering activities.

On 12 September 1924, the Golfers Rest was sold to William Smith Gourlay, cashier, 157 Morningside Road, Edinburgh, after which it became 'Gourlay's Tea Rooms'.

The Braid Hills Hotel

The Braid Hills Hotel, Braid Road, opened for business at Braid Road in October 1894. Its first advertisement stated:

> Erected principally for the convenience of golfers.
> Finest site near Edinburgh commanding magnificent views on all sides.
> Clubhouse.
> Applications are now being received for boxes.
> Terms 7/6d. per annum.

It was reported that The Golf Room had about 150 boxes fitted up. The stained glass window plaques were said to have been most artistically finished and the various views exceedingly well presented, the greatest care having apparently been taken with the work. The brothers Kirkaldy and Ben Sayers are among the players depicted on the window plaques in the exercise of the game and St Andrews was of course one of the links portrayed. Messrs Dobbie & Co., of Lothian Road, who had also done tile work at the Royal and Ancient and North Berwick, carried out the work on the windows. The total cost of the hotel was £10,000.

The Braid Hills Hotel still stands today, substantially the same as 100 years ago, with its beautiful window artwork, but its venture as a golf clubhouse was not long-lasting as the golfers were faced with a half a mile upward climb from it to reach the course.

Winchesters

At the far eastern end of the course, an old farmhouse which was demolished in 1946 known as Winchesters, provided refreshments to passing golfers.

The Closing Years

Although the acquisition of the Golfers Tryst proved to be a wise investment over the years, remaining in Carruthers' family ownership until 1946, the golf manufacturing side of the business for the wholesale and export markets was to face difficult times in the years leading up to the start of the First Word War in 1914.

The death of Queen Victoria in 1901 and the impact of the Boer War (1899–1902) eroded the nation's confidence in the assumed invulnerability of the country to continue as 'the workshop of the world'. It was becoming accepted that Britain could not continue as the dominant nation in world trade and was increasingly threatened by the pace of industrial development of rival European and American competitors. The following, seemingly light-hearted, account by Fred A. McKenzie from his book, *The American Invaders: Their Plans, Tactics and Progress, 1901* that appeared in *Britain in the Twentieth Century 1900–1939* contained serious undertones:

In the domestic life we have got to this: the average man rises in the morning from his New England sheets, he shaves with 'Williams' soap and a Yankee safety razor, pulls on his Boston boots over his socks from North Carolina, fastens his Connecticut braces, slips his Waltham or Waterbury watch in his pocket, and sits down to breakfast. There he congratulates his wife on the way her Illinois straight-front corset sets off her Massachusetts blouse, and he tackles his breakfast, where he eats bread made from prairie flour (possibly doctored at the special establishments on the lakes), tinned oysters from Baltimore, and a little Kansas City bacon, while his wife plays with a slice of Chicago ox-tongue. The children are given 'Quaker' oats. At the same time he reads his morning paper printed by American machines, on American paper with American ink, and possibly edited by a smart journalist from New York City.

He rushes out, catches the electric tram (New York) to Shepherd's Bush, where he gets in a Yankee elevator to take him on to the American-fitted electric railway to the City.

At his office, of course, everything is American. He sits on a Nebraskan swivel chair, before a Michigan roll-top desk, writes his letters on a Syracuse typewriter, signing them with a New York fountain pen, and drying them with a blotting-sheet from New England. The letter copies are put away in files manufactured in Grand Rapids.

At lunch time he hastily swallows some cold roast beef that comes from the Mid-West cow, and flavours it with Pittsburg pickles, followed by a few Delaware tinned peaches, and then soothes his mind with a couple of Virginia cigarettes.

To follow his course all day would be wearisome. But when evening comes he seeks relaxation at the latest American musical comedy, drinks a cocktail or some Californian wine, and finishes up with a couple of 'little liver pills' 'made in America'.

Two pioneering studies of the time showed that one in every three or four of the Edwardian town population was living in poverty. The *laissez-faire* doctrine of the Victorian era had swelled the coffers of the nation but at the expense of huge numbers of factory workers who had had to survive on poor wages and often in dreadful housing conditions. It was said by one prominent member of parliament in the House of Commons that when a man got up in the morning he had to put his legs through the window to get his trousers on. In 1904/1905 the country suffered from an economic depression and in the following year an almost revolutionary Liberal government swept into power and a Parliamentary Labour Party took its place as a permanent force in politics.

Churchill proclaimed in 1908 that unemployment was the problem of the hour as trade was again widely depressed. Industrial disturbances and workplace conflicts became widespread up to 1910, in the last years of the Edwardian era, and the country was under what felt like continuous attrition as the effects of railway, coal miners and dock strikes contrasted with the days of the former great Victorian powerhouse.

Looking back in 1923 a prominent parliamentarian wrote of the poorer classes:

> Now they have at least a modicum of education, they are politically as well as industrially organised, and although there is still unemployment and in too many instances, fear of want, yet these grim problems are being tackled with greater knowledge and more humane feeling than ever before. I take these signs and tokens as indications of better things to be. (Arthur Bryant, *English Saga*)

During this period golf's popularity was inevitably affected. The defeat of Prime Minister Arthur Balfour's Conservative government, in power from 1902–1906, was a set-back to the golfing community. This distinguished public figure had done much to popularise golf in England and was a respected ambassador for the sport. He became Captain of the Royal and Ancient in 1894 and once said: 'Give me my books, my golf clubs, and leisure, and I would ask for nothing more.'

It was a fast changing environment, which saw the introduction of many new taxes and impositions on employers such as the theoretical liability for all the risks of his worker's employment. To someone who had thrived in the maelstrom of the sixties they 'would have seemed a revolutionary interference with the laws of supply and demand and a half-way step to wholesale confiscation and communism.' (Arthur Bryant, *English Saga*)

In 1904 Tom Carruthers, now in his sixty-fifth year, handed over the management of his golf club-making business to his son, Thomas Jun., aged twenty-four years.

The year 1904 was also significant for another reason – it marked the end of the fourteen-year protection period for Tom Carruthers' famous short socket patent. Family sources indicate that he wound down the golf club wholesale and export manufacturing side of the business in 1906. This was essentially confirmed when Robert Simpson of Carnoustie acquired the Carruthers 'Perfect Balance' trademark in 1907 and used it in advertising his patented broad-soled concentrated weight round-back cleeks, irons and mashies.

The remaining golf business then comprised retail golf equipment, repair and other services, such as catering, for the members of the various clubs who rented rooms in the clubhouse or played golf on the Braids, under the direction of Thomas Jun. who continued to be listed in the *Edinburgh and Leith Post Office Directory* as 'Thomas Carruthers Jun., Golf Club Maker, Golfers Tryst, Braid Hills Golf Course'.

Carricknowe Golf Course

In 1908 Thomas Jun. took up the appointment of green keeper at Saughton Hall Golf Course (now known as Carricknowe Golf Course), leaving the business at the Golfers Tryst in the hands of his elder brother, Peter. The origins of that course can be traced back to the first year of the twentieth century when Edinburgh City Council acquired the ground for the purpose of constructing a golf course.

The history of Saughton is provided by James Grant in his book, *Old and New Edinburgh:*

> The early origins of the estate of Saughton can be traced back to the Baird family, a branch of the house Auchmedden, who owned and resided on the estate for many generations. The old hall or mansion of Saughton was gable-ended, with crow steps, dormer windows, steep roofs, and massive chimneys, with an elaborate string moulding, and having a shield, covered with initials, above its door. Over the entrance of the house is a shield, or scrollwork, charged with a sword between two helmets, with the initials P. E., the date 1623, and the old Edinburgh legend, 'Blisit Be God For Al His Giftis'.

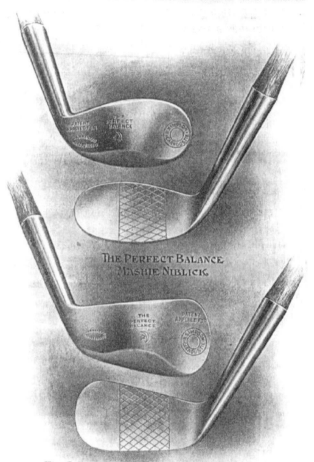

Simpson's advertisement in *Golfing*, 2 May 1907, following his acquisition of the Carruthers'
Perfect Balance trademark in 1907

At that time the clubhouse stood opposite what is now Whitson Crescent and until some years ago protruded into Stevenson Drive. Saughton Golf Course housed the Highland Show and in the 1920s, with the building of the Whitson Houses, it was decided to move the golf course over to the Corstorphine side of the railway. In old maps the area that is now the Carricknowe Golf Course was known as Corstorphine Marches and was bounded by a burn named the Stank. In ancient times the greater part of this now fertile district was a swamp, the road through which was both difficult and dangerous. A lamp was placed at the east end of Corstorphine church for the dual purpose of illuminating the shrine of the Baptist and for guiding travellers through the perilous morass.

The golf course at Saughton was an immediate success. There was no system of advance booking and the 'wait' to get on the course could be up to two hours.

Many clubs played over Saughton, as was the custom in those far off days, using the public clubhouse as their base. In addition to Saughton Golf Club, now Carricknowe Golf Club, there was The Grange; Beechwood; Saughton Hall, the forerunner of Carrickvale; McVities Price; The 'News' and two others whose names James W. Hastings, a former club captain who has provided the historical information about the origins of Saughton Golf Course, is unable to recall. These eight clubs formed a league that survived the First World War, but succumbed in 1939 to the Second World War.

> In those days thousands of golfers would spectate at the climax of important events such as the Craigentinny Quaich, the Dispatch Trophy and the Coronation Trophies – there were two Coronations, one at the Braids and one at Carricknowe. These would attract the best golfers of the day,

Transfer of Ownership to Thomas Carruthers Jun.

When war broke out in 1914 civilians were mobilised into the armed forces. The fighting across the French battlefields caused massive loss of life. At the end of the war the country was crippled financially and had been deprived of almost a complete generation of its finest young men. Golf courses had been ploughed up in whole or part or used for grazing to help the war effort under the direction of the War Agricultural Committee. Many clubs were put under severe pressure to meet their financial obligations as many members had resigned their membership when they were called up to serve in the armed forces. Once the war was over the serving men were demobbed and returned to their families to take up their previous jobs which many employers had held open for them. Tom Carruthers was seventy-eight years old when the war ended and had looked after the Golfers Tryst with his eldest son Peter until the return of Tom Jun., when it was agreed that its ownership would be transferred to him. The transaction was completed on 11 November 1919, but not before it had caused some alarm amongst the members.

An interesting account of events is given in the book entitled *Braids United Golf Club - United for a Hundred Years* by Jim Forson, in which he recounts that the Braids United Golf Club, which rented rooms in the Golfers Tryst, were threatened with eviction. The Club believed that the clubhouse had been sold to an outside third party, but unknown to them, it had actually been sold to Tom's son.

> The situation was resolved on the evening of Tuesday, 14 October 1919, when in the middle of a meeting between the Captain, Secretary and Treasurer in the Braids United Clubrooms, Mr. Carruthers walked in and announced that he had repurchased the Golfers Tryst for £800 (he never divulged the selling price) and was going to run it on the same lines as before. The name of Mr. Bee's (the purchaser's Solicitor) client was never revealed and it does beg the question that either some smart property deal had taken place or Mr Carruthers did not want the Clubs to be treated in such a fashion.

The new owner's name – his son – had obviously not been divulged to the Golf Club members but the selling price was correctly stated! Into the bargain the members of the Club agreed to pay an increased rent for their rooms from 6s. to 7s. 6d. That might of course have been the root cause of this unusual sequence of events.

Following the sale of the Golfers Tryst in 1919 he transferred ownership of the property at 5 Gillespie Place by deed of gift to his daughters, ' ... For love, favour and affection, which I have and bear my daughters Agnes, Jessie and Lizzie ... '

Tom died in 1924, one year after his wife Margaret, mother of thirteen children, eleven of whom grew into adulthood. He never made a will, having divested himself of all his property and possessions in probably the most tax efficient manner, thus providing for the future financial security of his three unmarried daughters who had contributed so much to the efficient operation of his business interests and who had cared for him in his later years.

The *Edinburgh Evening News* carried the following simple obituary notice:

```
4 November 1924
Carruthers at 19 Gilmore Place on 23 inst.
Thomas Carruthers in his 85th year (also at
5 Gillespie Place).
Funeral to Morningside Cemetery.
On Wednesday, at 2'oclock.
Friends wanting to attend kindly meet
Cortege at cemetery gate
```

Shortly afterwards Tom Jun. secured the position of head green keeper at the Braid Hills Course, following in the footsteps of Peter Robinson who had held the post for many years and who became the professional to Edinburgh Corporation. He sold his house at Glendevon Place, situated beside Carricknowe Golf Course, and moved into purpose built accommodation on the Braids. This had been constructed in March 1897 when the Parks Committee of Edinburgh Council resolved to recommend the erection of a public shelter, a caddies' shelter, together with houses for the green keeper and the park officer, as well as a cloakroom, at the pond on the Braids. This was a welcome improvement to the facilities on the course, as the only other buildings at this time comprised a ticket box and a small ladies' pavilion. Tom Carruthers Jun. continued to own and run the Golfers Tryst, as clubmaster to the resident golf clubs, for a further twenty-six years until he decided to retire.

On 26 October 1945, a special council meeting of the clubs then renting rooms at the Golfers Tryst was convened for the purposes of discussing Mr T. Carruthers Jun.'s intimation of his intention to sell the clubhouse. Jim Forson explains as follows in his book:

> Captain W. Banks brought up the question of buying the premises presently occupied by the Edinburgh Thistle, Edinburgh Western and the Braids United Clubs. He asked J. H. Gunn if he would explain to members how the matter stood. J. H. Gunn explained that everything that had been done so far was only verbal. Our position was that we had only two years of our lease to run and the landlord was definitely going to sell ...

A limited liability company was formed, named the Braids Tryst Limited, and the Braids United and Edinburgh Western Clubs subscribed for the issued shares with the balance of the purchase price provided in the form of a long-term loan from the owner, Tom Carruthers Jun., which was finally repaid on 1 May 1956. The transfer of ownership of the Golfers Tryst to Braids Tryst Limited was completed on 23 May 1946.

Although the Carruthers' family no longer owned the Golfers Tryst, the association with the family continued for a number of years as Thomas Jun.'s daughter, Peggy Mackenzie (née Carruthers), took over the duties of caretaker from her mother. Tom Carruthers Jun. died at the Golfers Tryst in May 1961. When his daughter retired in February 1971, this brought to an end the long association between the Golfers Tryst and the Carruthers' family that had begun in 1899.

The Golfers Tryst still stands today at the Braids, over 110 years since it was built. It remains the clubhouse of the Braids United and Edinburgh Western Golf Clubs. Its official address is 22 Braid Hills Approach, Braid Hills Golf Course, Edinburgh.

Opposite: **The Golfers Tryst as it stands today, over 110 years since it was built**

Appendix 1

Historical Gossip About Golf and Golfers by a Golfer

Historical Gossip About Golf and Golfers (believed to have been written by George Robb, Edinburgh, who was a member and former captain of the Bruntsfield Allied Golf Club) was printed by John Hughes, Thistle Street, Edinburgh, in 1863.

Far and Sure

BRUNTSFIELD LINKS

As it may be interesting to some, especially to those who almost exclusively practise the game on Bruntsfield Links, to know something of its history, we here give such information connected with it as we have been able to collect.

Bruntsfield Links originally formed part of the Borough-moor of Edinburgh, which according to Maitland, extended from 'St. Leonards Loning in the Pleasants' on the north, to 'the grounds of Neulands belonging to the Laird of Braid' on the south; and from the Powburn on the east to the 'Coithouse belonging to the Laird of Wryte's Houses on the West.' Wryte's House, or Castle – from which the neighbouring houses derive their name, now corrupted into Wright's Houses – a building of considerable architectural pretensions, was built in 1379, and stood on the site now occupied by Gillespie's Hospital, to make room for which it was removed at the beginning of the century. It had no separate existence from the rest of the Borough-moor down to about the end of the 17th Century, when we find it mentioned as the lands of 'Brownisfield'.

By which of the kings of Scotland the Borough-moor was first presented to the town is not known, as the city's archives only go back to 28 May 1329, of which date the town possesses a charter of Robert I. The want of records of the early transactions of the city is accounted for by the frequent ravages committed by the English, 'who not only frequently spoiled it of everything of value, but carried off its records and burnt the town.' Maitland, however, presumes that as 'David (David I, 1124–1153) was the first of our kings, when they made royal burghs, to grant to the community of each of the said burghs a large territory or district of ground ... I am of opinion that the large district of land lying on the southern side of Edinburgh, called the Borough-moor, was given to the magistrates, '&c' by the said king David.' At this time it was covered with an oak forest, and is described by Drummond as a 'field spacious, and delightful by the shade of many stately oaks.'

The Borough-moor is rich in historical associations, and if fields of battle constitute what is termed classical ground, it has its full share, as being the scene of many sanguinary battles, the issue involving at times the fate of the kingdom. Here in 1303, during the struggle which Edward III maintained with Scotland for the restoration of the Baliol dynasty as a race of vassal kings, was the scene of a desperate conflict betwixt the troops in the pay of the English monarch, under Count Guy of Namur, and the Scottish patriots under the Earls of Murray and March and Sir William Ramsay; here also Robert II in 1384 summoned his army for the purpose of retaliation against Richard II; indeed from this latter date 'the array of Scotland was generally made on the Borough-moor.' And it was here that in 1513 James IV mustered his forces previous to setting out for Flodden, where he was slain and his army defeated.

In 1508 the Magistrates applied to James IV and obtained a charter, generally called the Golden Charter, empowering them to let the Borough-moor in feu, and the 'stately oaks' mentioned by Drummond were shortly after rooted out as a public nuisance, all the citizens who chose to cut wood being permitted as a premium for their industry to use it in extending their houses several feet into the street. The Borough-moor after this date was gradually feued out till all that now remains is the Meadows and Bruntsfield Links. Among the feus thus granted we may mention one in 1695 to the predecessors of the present proprietors of Bruntsfield Parks, of the lands of 'Brownisfield' – which the late Sir George Warrender enclosed with the present stone wall in 1820, previous to which the parks were surrounded with a low dilapidated wall having the remains of an old hedge, with a stile where the present doorway stands as a means of access to and from the parks, – and another in 1752 to Mr. Brown, tailor in Edinburgh, and Mr. Fairholm of Greenhill, which latter was challenged by Mr. Cochran as an invasion of the rights of the citizens, and the point litigated in the Court of Session. As we get an idea of the state of the green at the period from the papers in the case, we have given some extracts from them. Cochran in his memorial gives the following account of the dispute:-

> In 1752, Robert Brown, a tailor in Edinburgh, a man in spirit and ambition much superior to the most of his profession, formed the resolution of perpetuating his memory, which he thought he could not do more effectively than by a house. Though the fine common belonging to the town of Edinburgh, called Bruntsfield Links had been for ages appropriated to the pleasure of the inhabitants, and preserved inviolate from all encroachments, yet Mr. Brown's enterprising genius prompted him to aspire to some acres of it, which he thought would afford him a delightful situation for his villa. Adam Fairholm of Greenhill, Esq., not disdaining to take the hint from Robert Brown, though but a tailor, petitioned for some acres of the Links. By a variety of ways and means, which it is more easy to imagine than proper to enumerate, the Magistrates of Edinburgh were prevailed on to comply with the request of the several petitions.

The Memorial then goes on to deal with the law of the question, and concludes by accusing Mr. Fairholm of using 'most scurrilous and unprovoked reflections against some of the memorialists, which are expressed in language and enlivened with the wit of Billingsgate,' and asks the Court to make Brown and Fairholm 'smart for such an outrageous insult to the public.' Brown and Fairholm accuse Cochran of having been instigated to commence the litigation because the Magistrates had refused to grant him a feu of another part of the Links, and state, in their Memorial, that:

> ... the Borough-moor belonged in property to the town, but the bulk of it had been feued out, and little more of it now remains but that field which now passes by the name of Bruntsfield Links. The northmost part of these Links next to the Meadows is tolerably open, and neither encumbered with whins nor quarries; and it is there that the inhabitants sometimes amuse themselves at the golf. There is a string of quarry holes beginning near the east end of the links, and running westward, separates the

ground from a narrow strip of arable land between those quarry holes and the parks of Bruntsfield. The upper part of these Links is quite covered with whins and full of quarry holes, insomuch that it is an unfit place for any person to walk in, or indeed for any use but the sheep who can scramble up and down the sides of the quarry holes.'

Mr. Cochran was unsuccessful in his attempt to prevent the Magistrates from feuing the Links.

At what date golf was first played on Bruntsfield Links we cannot say, and we have been unable to find any notice to aid us in this. It could not, however, be much earlier than the middle of last century, the green previous to that time not being in a fit condition for golfing on, as we see from the description given of it by Messrs. Brown and Fairholm in their Memorial to the Court, a description which applied down to the beginning of the present century, when, in consequence of alterations in the vicinity, such as the building of Gillespie's Hospital, Bruntsfield Place, etc., a number of the quarry holes mentioned were filled up with earth taken from the founds, and the appearance of the green generally altered in consequence of the increased amount of traffic on its surface.

Its eligibility for golfing on at the beginning of this century will best appear by describing the golfing course, premising that those portions of the Links not used for golfing on was either cut up with quarries or covered with whins. Starting from the first hole as we do now, the course to the 'east end' was close by the side of the Meadows to avoid a quarry on the right; then up by a narrow strip of clear ground between the quarry holes mentioned in Mr. Fairholm's Memorial and Warrender Parks to the 'mid;' thence up to a hole where the 'sixth' hole is, avoiding the quarry at the corner of Mrs. Haig's wall on the left and whins on the right; thence up by another strip of clear ground to a hole near the present entrance to Greenhill Gardens; thence across – which was a short hole, for the reason to be afterwards noticed – to the hole at the road leading to Morningside, returning to the first hole by the same clear strip by which we ascended. As noticed above, the hole crossing from the 'Priest's to 'Smellie's' was a short one. At that time the wall separating the Links from Greenhill was not so straight as it is now. The Links took in a part of Greenhill, between the road to the Nunnery and the entrance to Greenhill, and the wall made a semi-circular curve and took in the quarry near the present entrance to Greenhill, and which now forms part of the Links. By arrangement between the proprietor of Greenhill and the Magistrates, the former gave the quarry and the latter the piece of ground – at the time covered with whins – at Bishop Gillies' house, and the wall was straightened. When playing between these two holes it was necessary to drive across the two walls forming this curve.

In 1827 the City Improvement Act was passed, which contains the following clause with reference to the Links:-

> That it shall not be competent to or in the power of the Lord Provost, Magistrates, and Council of Edinburgh, or any other person or persons, without the sanction of Parliament, obtained for the express purpose, at any time hereafter to erect buildings of any kind upon any part of the ground called the Meadows and Bruntsfield Links, so far as the same belong in property to the said Lord Provost, Magistrates, and Council.

Little remains to be said about the Links, except to notice the change that has taken place – for the worse, so far as golfing is concerned – in consequence of Greenhill having been feued for villas. The inhabitants of Greenhill have managed to get an opening in the wall, which leads by a footpath across the green and seriously interrupts the play. Not content, however, with getting leave to open this gap in the wall, they memorialised the Town Council in 1860 to get golf abolished from the green altogether; but after sundry procedure the Magistrates, wisely as we think, declined to interfere. It is to be regretted that this gap is allowed to remain, for what is now accepted as a privilege will in a few years hence be claimed as a right.

Bruntsfield Links is far from being the best green for the pursuit of our national pastime, and far too limited in its extent; but it is to be hoped that the day will yet come when our Town Council, reversing their old policy, and recognising the necessity of providing the means of outdoor recreation for the people, will secure for us some other, and it is to be hoped more suitable place, whereon to practice our favourite amusement, for should the ground in the vicinity, such as Bruntsfield Park, ever be feued, it is to be feared that those who now practise golf there will require to vacate and seek some other place.

Appendix 2

Workshop and Family Addresses

WORKSHOP ADDRESSES

5 Gillespie Place, Edinburgh 1874–1924
(Remained in family ownership until 1945)
41 Leven Street, Edinburgh 1893–1894
26A Wright's Houses, Edinburgh 1894–1900
Golfer's Tryst, Braid Hills Golf Course, Edinburgh 1900
(Workshop and clubhouse. Remained in family ownership until 1946)

FAMILY ADDRESSES

Caverton Mill, Roxburghshire, Borders (birthplace of Tom Carruthers in 1840)
Town Yetholm, Roxburghshire, Borders (birthplace of son, Peter, 1860, and daughter, Euphemia, 1865)
Oakfield Court, The Pleasance, Edinburgh (birthplace of daughter, Jane, in 1863)
22 Home Street, Edinburgh (birthplace of daughter, Agnes, in 1868)
26 Home Street, Edinburgh (birthplace of daughter, Jessie, in 1870)
Birmingham, England 1871
8 Tarvit Street, Edinburgh (birthplace of daughter, Lizzie in 1872)
5 Gillespie Place, Edinburgh (birthplace of daughter, Margaret in 1874 – remained in family ownership until 1945)
32 Wright's Houses, Edinburgh 1877
18 Valleyfield Street, Edinburgh (birthplace of son, Thomas, in 1879)
34 Leven Street, Edinburgh (birthplace of son, John, in 1881)
9 Marchmont Street, Edinburgh (birthplace of sons, Robert, in 1885 and George, in 1887)
42 Bruntsfield Place, Edinburgh 1891
37 Gillespie Crescent, Edinburgh 1894
9 Lauriston Park, Edinburgh 1903
21 Gilmore Place, Edinburgh 1910
19 Gilmore Place, Edinburgh 1915
(Tom Carruthers died at this address in 1924)

Appendix 3

Royal Letters Patent Granted By Queen Victoria, 3 December 1890

1890.
No. *19684*

VICTORIA, BY THE GRACE OF GOD,

Of the United Kingdom of Great Britain and Ireland, Queen, Defender of the Faith: To all to whom these presents shall come, Greeting:

WHEREAS *Thomas Carruthers of N85 Gillespie Place Edinburgh Dairyman*

hath represented unto us that he is in possession of an invention for *'A new or improved socket for metal golf playing clubs'*

that he is the true and first inventor thereof, and that the same is not in use by any other person, to the best of his knowledge and belief:

AND WHEREAS the said inventor hath humbly prayed that we would be graciously pleased to grant unto him (hereinafter, together with his executors, administrators, and assigns, or any of them, referred to as the said patentee) our Royal Letters Patent for the sole use and advantage of his said invention:

AND WHEREAS the said inventor hath by and in his complete specification particularly described the nature of his invention:

AND WHEREAS we, being willing to encourage all inventions which may be for the public good, are graciously pleased to condescend to his request:

KNOW YE, THEREFORE, that We, of our especial grace, certain knowledge, and mere motion, do by these presents, for us, our heirs and successors, give and grant unto the said patentee our especial license, full power, sole privilege, and authority that the said patentee, by himself, his agents, or licensees, and no others, may at all times hereafter, during the term of years herein mentioned, make, use, exercise, and vend the said invention within our United Kingdom of Great Britain and Ireland and Isle of Man in such manner as to him or them may seem meet, and that the said patentee shall have and enjoy the whole profit and advantage from time to time accruing by reason of the said invention during the term of fourteen years from the date hereunder written of these presents: AND to the end that the said patentee may have and enjoy the sole use and exercise, and the full benefit of the said invention, We do by these presents, for us, our heirs and successors, strictly command all our subjects whatsoever, within our United Kingdom of Great Britain and Ireland and the Isle of Man, that they do not at any time during the continuance of the said term of fourteen years, either directly or indirectly, make use of, or put in practice, the said invention, or any part of the same, nor in anywise imitate the same, nor make, or cause to be made, any addition thereto or subtraction therefrom, whereby to pretend themselves the inventors thereof, without the consent, license, or agreement of the said patentee in writing under his hand and seal, on pain of incurring such penalties as may be justly inflicted on such offenders for their contempt of this our Royal command, and of being answerable to the patentee according to law for his damages thereby occasioned :

PROVIDED that these our letters patent are on this condition : that if at any time during the said term it be made to appear to us, our heirs or successors, or any six or more of our Privy Council, that this our grant is contrary to law, or prejudicial or inconvenient to our subjects in general, or that the said invention is not a new invention as to the public use and exercise thereof within our United Kingdom of Great Britain and Ireland and Isle of Man, or that the said patentee is not the first and true inventor thereof within this realm as aforesaid, these our letters patent shall forthwith determine, and be void to all intents and purposes, notwithstanding anything hereinbefore contained : PROVIDED ALSO, that if the said patentee shall not pay all fees by law required to be paid in respect of the grant of these letters patent, or in respect of any matter relating thereto, at the time or times and in manner for the time being by law provided ; and also if the said patentee shall not supply, or cause to be supplied, for our service all such articles of the said invention as may be required by the officers or commissioners administering any department of our service, in such manner, at such times, and at and upon such reasonable prices and terms as shall be settled in manner for the time being by law provided, then, and in any of the said cases, these our letters patent, and all privileges and advantages whatever hereby granted, shall determine and become void, notwithstanding anything hereinbefore contained : PROVIDED ALSO, that nothing herein contained shall prevent the granting of licenses in such manner and for such considerations as they may by law be granted : AND lastly, we do by these presents, for us, our heirs and successors, grant unto the said patentee that these our letters patent shall be construed in the most beneficial sense for the advantage of the said patentee.

IN WITNESS whereof we have caused these our letters to be made patent this *third day of December* one thousand eight hundred and *ninety* and to be sealed as of the *third day of December* one thousand eight hundred and *ninety*.

Appendix 4

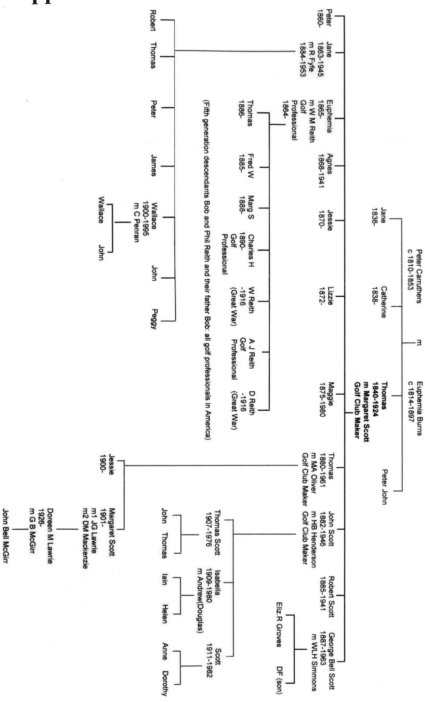

The Carruthers Family (Yetholm & Edinburgh)

Peter Carruthers
c 1810-1853

m

Euphemia Burns
c 1814-1897

Jane
1836-

Catherine
1838-

Thomas
1840-1924
m Margaret Scott
Golf Club Maker

Peter John

Peter
1860-

Jane
1863-1945
m R Fyfe
1884-1953

Euphemia
1865-
m W M Reith
Golf
Professional
1864-

Agnes
1868-1941

Jessie
1870-

Lizzie
1872-

Maggie
1875-1980

Robert

Thomas

Thomas
1886-

Fred W
1885-

Marg S
1888-

Charles H
1890-
Golf
Professional

W Reith
-1916
(Great War)

A J Reith
Golf
Professional

D Reith
-1916
(Great War)

Peter

James

Wallace
1900-1995
m C Penran

Wallace

John

John

Peggy

(Fifth generation descendants Bob and Phil Reith and their father Bob: all golf professionals in America)

Thomas
1880-1961
m MA Oliver
Golf Club Maker

John Scott
1882-1946
m HB Henderson
Golf Club Maker

Robert Scott
1885-1941

George Bell Scott
1887-1963
m WLH Simmons

Jessie
1900-

Margaret Scott
1901-
m1 JG Lawrie
m2 DM Mackenzie

John   Thomas

Thomas Scott
1907-1976

Isabella
1909-1980
m Andrew(Douglas)

Scott
1911-1982

Eliz R Groves   DF (son)

Doreen M Lawrie
1926-
m G B McGirr

John   Thomas

Iain   Helen

Anne   Dorothy

John Bell McGirr

List of Sources

Books

The Badminton Library – Golf, Horace G. Hutchinson, Longmans Green, London, 1898.

Braids United Golf Club – United for 100 Years, Jim Forson, Edinburgh, 1999.

Brief History of Carrickvale and Carricknowe Golf Course, James N. Hastings, Edinburgh, 1999.

Britain in the Twentieth Century, Volume I, Institute of Contemporary British History (1900–1939).

Bruntsfield Links Golfing Society, Stewart Cruden, privately published, 1992.

The Chronicle of the Royal Burgess Golfing Society of Edinburgh 1735–1935, J. Cameron Robbie, Morrison & Gibbs, Edinburgh, 1936.

The Clubmaker's Art, Jeffery B. Ellis, Zephyr Productions Ltd., Washington, 1997.

The Clubmakers' Golf Club, Philip H. Knowles, privately published 1997.

Collecting Antique Golf Clubs, Peter Georgiady, Airlie Hall Press, Greensboro, 1998.

Compendium of British Club Makers, Peter Georgiady, Airlie Hall Press, Greensboro, 1997.

Early United States Golf Clubs by A. G. Spalding & Bros., Wright & Ditson and Bridgeport Gun Implement Co., J. M. Cooper.

Edinburgh and Leith Post Office Directory 1850–1925.

Encyclopaedia Britannica.

The Encyclopaedia of Gambling, Peter Arnold, William Collins Sons & Co.Ltd., 1978.

English Saga (1840–1940), Arthur Bryant, Collins, London, 1944.

Everyman's Encyclopaedia, J. M. Dent & Sons Ltd.

The Game of Golf, W. Park Jun., Longmans Green, London, 1896.

The Golfing Annual, 1887/8–1905/6, Editors Bauchope/Duncan, London.

The Golf Book of East Lothian, John Kerr, T. & A. Constable, Edinburgh, 1896.

Golf Implements and Memorabilia, Kevin McGimpsey & David Neech, Philip Wilson Publishers Ltd, London,1999.

Golf in the Making, Ian T. Henderson & David T. Stirk, Henderson & Stirk Ltd., Winchester, 1982.

Golf My Life's Work, J. H. Taylor, Jonathan Cape Ltd., london, 1904

Great Golfers in the Making, by Thirty-Four Famous Players, Henry Leach, Methuen, London, 1907.

Guide to Edinburgh and its Neighbourhood, Oliver & Boyd, Edinburgh, 1860.

Historical Gossip About Golf and Golfers, George Robb, Edinburgh, 1863.

History of England, Cassell & Co. Ltd., London, Paris and Melbourne.

James Braid, Bernard Darwin, Hodder and Stoughton, London, 1952,

Kay's Edinburgh Portraits, James Paterson, London 1885.

Manual of British Rural Sports, Stonehenge (John Henry Walsh) London, 1875.

My Golfing Life, Harry Vardon, Hutchinson & Co., London, 1933.

North American Club Makers, Peter Georgiady, Airlie Hall Press, Greensboro, 1998.

Old and New Edinburgh, James Grant, Cassells, Golpin & Co., London, Paris and New York, 1882.

The Pedestrian's Record, J. I. & J. M. K. Lupton, W. H. Allen & Co., 13 Waterloo Place, London, 1890.

Powderhall and Pedestrianism, D. A. Jamieson, W & A. K. Johnston Ltd., Edinburgh & London, 1943.

Reminiscences of the old Bruntsfield golf club, 1866–1874, Thomas S. Aitchison & George Lorimer, 1902.

The Rise of Respectable Society, A Social History of Victorian Britain, 1830–1900, F. M. L. Thompson, Fontana, 1988.

Royal Blackheath, Ian T. Henderson & David I. Stirk, privately published by Royal Blackheath Golf Club, 1995.

Running Recollections and How to Train, A. R. Downer, Gale & Polden, London, 1900.

South Edinburgh in Pictures, Charles J. Smith, Whittingehame House Publishing, Haddington, 1998.

Taylor on Golf: Impressions, Comments and Hints, J. H. Taylor, Hutchinson & Co, London, 1903.

Turnpike Road to Tartan Track, F. C. Moffatt, privately published, 1979.

Newspapers and Periodicals

Aberdeen Free Press, 1871.

Aberdeen Journal, 1868–1871.

Bell's Life in London and Sporting Chronicle, 1862–1870.

Birmingham Daily Post, 1871.

Derby and Derbyshire Gazette, 1896

Dumbarton Herald, 1872.

Dunoon Press, 1871.

Edinburgh Evening Dispatch, 1886–1921.

Edinburgh Evening News, 1924.

Glasgow Herald, 1868–1870.

Golf, 1890–1899, London.

Golf Illustrated, 1899–1924, London.

Golfer, The, 1894–1898, Edinburgh.

Golfing, 1899–1910, London.

Golfing and Cycling, October 1898, London.

Hamilton Adviser, 1869.

History of the Chiltern Forest Golf Club (website)

History of the Warrender Golf Club, Edinburgh Evening Dispatch, 1906.

Illustrated Sporting and Theatrical and Musical Review, 1862–1865, London.

Illustrated Sporting and Theatrical News, 1865–1870, London.

Kelso Chronicle, 1858–1867.

Lancaster Guardian, 1862.

North British Daily Mail, 1863

Outing, 1896–1903, Outing Publishing Co., New York.

Professional Pedestrianism in South Wales in the Nineteenth Century, Emma Lile.

Royal Liverpool Golf Club (website).

Scotsman, 1865–1924, Edinburgh.

Scribner's Magazine, 1895, Charles Scribners Sons, New York

Sheffield Daily Telegraph, 1857–1872.

Sheffield Post, 1870–1873.

Sheffield and Rotherham Independent, 1871.

Sheffield Topic, Eric Macintyre, 1979–1980, Sporting Sheffield.

Sites and Landscapes of Horse Racing in Scotland Before 1860, John Burnett, National Museum of Scotland.

Sporting Chronicle, 1898

Sporting Life, 1864–1872.

Sporting Life Companion, 1889.

University of Edinburgh Archives (website).

Index